GENDER AS A VERB

For Keith with love

Gender as a Verb

Gender segregation at work

ANNETTE FITZSIMONS
University of Hull, UK

ASHGATE

Published by
Ashgate Publishing Limited
Gower House
Croft Road
Aldershot
Hampshire GU11 3HR
England

Ashgate Publishing Company
131 Main Street
Burlington, VT 05401-5600 USA

Ashgate website: http://www.ashgate.com

British Library Cataloguing in Publication Data
Fitzsimons, Annette
        Gender as a verb : gender segregation at work
        1. Sex role in the work environment 2. Sexual division of
        labor 3. Women - Employment 4. Men - Employment 5. Occupations
        - Sociological aspects
        I. Title
        305.3

Library of Congress Control Number: 2002100327

ISBN 0 7546 1630 4

Printed in Great Britain by
Antony Rowe Ltd, Chippenham, Wiltshire

Contents

List of Tables

Acknowledgements

Part of chapter seven of this book has been published as 'Gender, Technology, Power' in Lennon, Kathleen and Margaret Whitford (eds.) (1994), *Knowing the Difference: Feminist Perspective in Epistemology and Knowledge* (London, Routledge), pp.122-132.

I am indebted to the following for their support, friendship, food and stimulating debate: Keith Russell, Miriam Fitzsimons, Lucy Vulliamy, Glynis Clemno, Jean Kellie, Les Garry, Caroline Wright, Daniel Vulliamy, Humphrey Forrest, Brian Milsom, Sam Fitzsimons, Maggie Blagdon, David Coates and John Grayson (who helped me to develop a love of teaching). A special thank you to Kathleen Lennon for her time, intellectual rigour and friendship. Of course, any errors, omissions or misunderstandings are all mine.

Chapter 1

Conceptualising Gender: Introductory Remarks

Beginning

In 1984 I completed a MA in Political Sociology at the University of Leeds. There were twelve other students on the course - all men - and the lecturing staff were men. The majority of the students, including myself, were all involved in left wing organisations and the differences between us led to some very lively and stimulating discussions. The fact that I was the only feminist in the group meant that I had to develop a very distinct and articulate defence of my theoretical position, which at this time I defined as Marxist-feminist and I found this extremely difficult to do. I began to realise that I had adopted the position without properly understanding the complexities of either term. This led me to scrutinise feminist theory and the writings of Marxist-feminists. From this study I began to develop a critique, in the first instance of the theory of patriarchy and then the concept of patriarchy, especially in relation to the conceptualisation of gender that flows from the concept. I also began to develop an understanding of the limitations of Marxist analysis of gender, 'race' and class. The work began with the idea that it was possible to construct a materialist explanation of women's oppression that would overcome the theoretical problems I had found in my survey of Marxist-feminism. Much of this literature was centred on issues relating to women's labour, both paid and unpaid, and by the early 1980s the debates had become sterile and unproductive. I wanted to explore the possibility of constructing a new approach to these issues that would help to revitalise the Marxist-feminist perspective. Thus the main aim was to contribute to feminist theorising in the area of women's paid employment by developing a theoretical framework for analysing gender at work. I wanted to overcome both the limits of feminist theorising of the 1980s that relied heavily on a theory of patriarchy, and the inadequacies of Marxist-feminist theorising of the same period. The work that I want this theoretical framework to do is to clarify the relationship between the gender division of labour and the capitalist labour process in order to explain the reproduction of a gender ideology which legitimised women's subordination and oppression both in work and in the home, and which took account of male power and dominance. All of this now seems ridiculously ambitious.

I began by constructing a critique of both patriarchy and Marxist-feminism. Originally, I intended that the work would be purely theoretical, for a number of reasons. It was a constant struggle as an undergraduate to understand 'theory'. Theory was both an intellectual challenge and a way of 'proving' to myself that I could be considered an intellectual and therefore an academic. I also believed that 'theory' was the only way to understand and therefore change the world. The eleventh theses from Feuerbach had long been a slogan I was fond of repeating in my attempts to explain to others my insistence on 'theory', and, of course, it had to be grand theory: a theory which would explain the world. I wanted to construct a totalising explanation of women's oppression, a meta-narrative. It was not that I necessarily thought that I would ever achieve this ambition, rather I believed that this way of approaching an understanding of women's oppression was the correct one - the one true path to obtain the necessary knowledge needed to overcome oppression. The essence of feminism seemed to be just that - a movement that struggled to understand and explain, in order to overcome the subordination of women worldwide. It never struck me that I was being overly ambitious.

The sociological perspective that constituted my theoretical framework was Marxism. Marxism represented both a method and an analysis. The method was dialectical historical materialism and provided me with a way of looking at and understanding the world, not only as it is organised now but also historically: how it had developed and changed. The Marxist analysis of capitalism helped me to understand how the system operates and provided a theory of how it can be overcome. However I was aware of the limitations of this analysis, especially in relation to differences between people. The abstractness of the Marxist analysis of capitalist social relations meant that it tended to objectify human beings in relation to labour as a commodity which neglected their subject position and how these positions are shaped by gender and 'race'. Marxism ignored the role of gender in similar ways to mainstream sociology. Therefore Marxist-feminists had to establish 'women' as a gendered category for Marxism as well as for conventional sociology.

It was suggested that I should conduct empirical research in order to 'test' out some of the theoretical problems. Reluctantly, I dragged myself away from the 'masters', and put together a project that involved interviewing women and men who were involved in computers. I chose the field of computers for a number of reasons. Before my entry into higher education, I had worked as a computer operator. I had always wanted to become a programmer but at the age of twenty-three had been considered 'too old' to learn the 'new' world of computers. I worked for nearly 10 years in a number of organisations as a computer operator and so it was an environment in which I felt very comfortable and secure. If there was one thing I had some confidence in, it was the world of work, especially in the computing industry. I also wanted to ask questions of men as well as women at work. Most of the literature from Marxist-feminists had produced accounts of women's work in order to explain the segregation of work in terms of gender and there is a tendency in these accounts to explain the specificity of women's work as a consequence of male dominance. I wanted to put this type of explanation to one side by exploring an area of work that was to some extent gender-neutral.

Feminist writings on technology and science had begun to appear in the 1980s and a small number of these were concerned with computer programmers. Some of these argued that since computing was a 'new' industry, women had more opportunities for equality at work. There is also a status to the industry that is linked with the idea that people involved with computers were very intelligent and very clever. This association of cleverness and intelligence with computer technology is a legacy of the way science and technology is linked. The feminist literature tended to put the critique of science and technology together, as though there is no distinction. However from my experiences as a worker in the industry I did not remember this association being made and I was curious to discover if this recollection was accurate and if there were any implications to be drawn from the connection of technology with science.

The interviews I conducted with computer programmers turned out to be one of the most challenging experiences of my career. The impact on my research was such that I became interested in the study of masculinity. I realised that despite my critique of patriarchy and the way men were positioned by the theory of patriarchy, I had incorporated the radical feminist critique of men as the enemy into my view of men. Just as my conclusion on feminist theorising was that it was no longer possible to discuss women as a unitary category, I realised that I was still carrying around in my head the view of men as a unitary category, and the view of men as 'the enemy'. Men were constructed in many of the works I had examined as patriarchal - meaning dominant, powerful, dangerous for women to know. However, I was now discovering that the men I interviewed could not be understood with this type of explanatory framework. The operation of gender at the workplace was much more contradictory and complex. I turned then to the literature on organisations, in order to determine the extent to which the structure of organisations shaped the antagonisms and sharpened the gender differences between men and women. If it was no longer possible to 'blame men' as it were, for all the problems facing women at work, then perhaps the solution lay in the way work was structured in capitalist social relations. This was familiar ground. Was I though, in danger of forgetting my feminism and simply reproducing a simple Marxist explanation of the labour process? How could I hold on to the fact that women are oppressed by men?

Two concepts help me to interpret the complexity and contradictions I had discovered as a consequence of the empirical research: namely the concept of gender and the concept of discourse. The discussion of my research data is framed by a very specific theorisation of gender that developed from a number of sources. Through the literature on men and masculinities and the essay by Teresa de Lauretis (1987) on 'The Technology of Gender', I began to adopt an approach to gender which viewed it as being continually reproduced in different sites in society: at work, through the media, the education system, and the political system, including the state and governmental legislation. In this formulation gender is not static and fixed but rather fluid and shifting.

To clarify the theoretical approach which I am taking I need to say some more both about my conceptualisation of gender and of discourse. However before I do this I would like to provide a brief account of the theoretical approach that is adopted in the book. My theoretical approach is dictated by an attempt to understand gender in relation to difference, contradiction and change whilst recognising the fluid and shifting processes and practices of its production. The term that now sums up my thinking is the precariousness of theoretical understandings of the world. So rather than looking for certainty or correct interpretations of women's oppression my approach seeks to interpret the instability of gender, identity, subjectivity, truth and knowledge. I realise now that I had expected theory to provide sure knowledge about the world, and that despite my critique of Marxism and feminism, I still retained a Marxist epistemology in relation to knowledge and truth. In other words, the approach to gender and my use of the concept of discourse shifted my theoretical approach from Marxism to postmodernism. But what kind of postmodernism? I am unable to begin to answer this question now as this would be the subject of another book, however I am aware that I have 'borrowed' concepts from the postmodernism *oeuvre* which fundamentally challenges the whole notion of theory.

Conceptualising Gender

Gender is conceptualised in two distinct ways in the analysis of the labour market. There are those who use gender as simply a sociological variable, like other categories of stratification, and those who view gender as much more than simply another category of analysis. So for example, Siltanen (1994) analyses gender as a sociological category, like class, age, 'race', whereas Cockburn (1991) uses gender as a relational concept. The variation in use is not always clearly visible. Rather the conceptualisation of gender has a tendency to be vague, ill defined and indistinct. This has meant that there is an almost imperceptible shift that has emerged in the analysis of gender in sociological studies of employment. A crucial point here is that whichever way gender is analysed there is a tendency to formulate gender as stable and fixed categories, framed by the concept of patriarchy.

There are a number of explanations for the source of these two theoretical approaches to the study of gender, and for the lack of clarity in relation to way the concept is analysed. Firstly, the change from women's studies to gender studies in the study of women's paid employment produced a blurring of the focus of the analysis of gendered work. Secondly, and relatedly, the way that some aspects of feminist analysis of women's employment have become incorporated into mainstream sociology has reproduced the conceptualisation of gender as a category rather than as a process.

Before the emergence of second wave feminism, sociological studies of work did not use either women or gender as an analytical category and did not view gender and gender relationships as important dimensions of either the structuring of the labour market or the social relations of production and reproduction. From the 1970s feminist sociologists have struggled to establish women as significant in sociology. However, what happened is that gender became instituted as a *category* in mainstream sociological analysis. A clear example of this can be demonstrated by the debates in sociology on class and stratification (see Crompton and Mann 1986). In order for women to be discussed in sociological debates, the point of entry that proved less threatening to mainstream sociologists was that gender, like class, as a concept was rendered apolitical. Treating gender as simply another sociological variable detracts from the political thrust of feminist analysis of male power and women's oppression and subordination. This shift was not very difficult to achieve, given that there is no one 'feminist' position, nor an established feminist position on gender. Rather there are a number of feminist perspectives each of which uses a particular vocabulary and proffers a particular strategy in relation to women's equality and emancipation. The lack of a firm theoretical basis for feminism alongside the theoretical problems produced by the concept of patriarchy in the attempt to analyse gender at the workplace, provide the means by which gender as a sociological variable developed as an approach to the issues. As my theoretical position was formed by Marxist-feminism rather than mainstream sociology, this means that I do not treat either 'class' or 'gender' as sociological variables. The relational approach to the concept of gender that informs my work can be likened to the Marxist concept of class. The analysis of class is a critical aspect of the social relations of production, reproduction and the distribution of power, wealth, authority and status in capitalist societies. So too is gender. The concept of gender that informs my work is that gender is embedded in the organisation of capitalism in just the same way that class is. The distinction between this position and the Marxism of the 1960s and 1970s is that, for me, class is gendered.

Problems within Feminist Sociology

These shifts and challenges are evident in the literature on women and paid employment, and two distinct feminist approaches can be detected. The distinctiveness of a specific feminist contribution to the study of women and work has becomes increasingly blurred because of the success experienced by some feminist sociologists of incorporating feminist analysis into mainstream sociology. However, the way that gender is now an acceptable and respectable area of study in sociology has meant that it is treated as a sociological variable or category in the manner described above. The acceptability of gender studies has meant that the political thrust of analysing gender has become ambiguous. The distinctiveness of feminist work as opposed to sociological work has become obscured. This is, in part, due to the fact that anyone who chooses can call themselves a feminist. Gender when viewed as a sociological variable - an approach more in keeping with mainstream sociology - therefore presents a particular political as well as theoretical approach to the topic.

The alternative approach to the study of women's work is the one influenced by Marxian sociology (see Cockburn and Ormrod 1993; Cockburn 1991; 1985; 1983; Beechey 1983; 1979; 1978; 1977; Barrett 1984; Pollert 1981; Westwood 1984). This position is embedded in the political project of feminism, it is not simply an intellectual or an academic project. The writers in this tradition were and are concerned with constructing theory in order to aid social change and gender equality. It is an approach to the subject area of sociology that is informed by a critique of capitalism and capitalist societies rather than industrialism and post-industrial social formations. This means that the central concern of this approach is not only the liberation of women from gender inequalities and sexual oppression but also for the liberation of all those who are oppressed by the system of production and reproduction which dominates capitalist societies. There are a number of key concepts that signify this theoretical position. These are the concept of ideology; the concept of class consciousness; the concept of capitalist social relations; the concept of power; and, of course, the concept of patriarchy. Therefore these two approaches, although different in relation to the political thrust of the analysis, are linked. They both conceptualise gender as fixed, stable and static and this approach dominates the analysis of gendered work. The notion of patriarchy though political in so far as it engages with differentials of power, reproduces the notion of social roles and sexual categories which make it difficult to explain the persistence and stability of occupational segregation in terms other than male power and control. This approach is unable to account for the contradictions, pleasures and choices women exercise at work. Cynthia Cockburn (1988) divulged the 'embarrassing fact' of feminist explanations of occupational segregation that revealed that women were deliberately choosing their positions in the labour market rather than being coerced or controlled by men.

Sociology of Women and Paid Work

Before the emergence of second wave feminism, sociological studies of work did not use gender as an analytical category and did not see gender and gender relationships as important dimensions of both the way in which employment is structured and the way in which work is experienced (see Brown 1976; Beechey 1983; 1979; 1978; 1977). In comparison with the early 1970s, by the beginning of the 1990s, there is now a vast literature on both women and work and gender at work.

In the 1980s, feminist debates on women's paid employment focused on the inequalities experienced by women in the workplace and demonstrated the type of work women did, both historically and present day. In some senses, for feminist sociologists, this task was made easier than for feminists working in other disciplines by the dramatic increase in the numbers of women, especially married women, who had entered the workplace from the 1960s. The two theoretical frameworks which various feminists drew on in order to comprehend women's place in the labour market is indicative of two dominant strands in sociological analysis:

Marxist sociology and mainstream or bourgeois sociology. However both of these frameworks used the concept of patriarchy and this hindered the attempt to theorise women's position in the labour market in a number of ways. Kate Purcell (1989) explains how the concept of patriarchy has encouraged forms of explanation that focus on 'women's' jobs rather than the process by which jobs get labelled in this way. The conceptual framework that was adopted by early feminist explorations of women's work assumed that women's work identity was already established by their roles within the family. By the late 1980s, it became clear that the problem with 'patriarchy' was that the gendered experience of domesticity and employment relations, and the practices and processes by which these experiences structure women's and men's lives, is both contradictory and conflictual. Neither the theory nor the concept was able to explain what feminists had uncovered by the studies of gender at work in the past ten years.

These accounts of women and work were reporting on the diversity and differences between women, and the complexity of women's experiences and attitudes to their paid employment. By the early 1990s it was clear that a new approach was needed in order to understand the persistence, despite equal opportunities legislation and the expansiveness of women in the labour market, of occupational segregation. A study at the end of the 1980s concluded that,

> The unequivocal evidence of the twelve years following the enactment of equal opportunities legislation is that the provision of formal equality of opportunity in training and employment makes an impact on, but does not radically alter, gender segregation and occupational inequalities. A clearer understanding is required of the links between gender stereotyping, group behaviour and the dynamics of organizations - particularly the significance of sexuality, which can have a major stabilising or destabilising influence on work relationships. (Purcell 1989, p.179)

But Marxist-feminism was not equal to this task. A large number of writers from this tradition had attempted to explain occupational segregation by using concepts drawn from Marxist analysis of capitalism (see Seecombe 1974; Gardiner 1975; Coulson, Magas and Wainwright 1975; Smith 1978; Delphy 1984). The emphasis in these writings was on the contribution of domestic labour and women's position in the labour market to both capitalist accumulation and the reproduction of the system. These debates became paralysed by problems of Marxist economics, and this effectively sidetracked any real progress in the feminist analysis of women's paid employment. It also weakened the popularity of this theoretical and intellectual position. A further weakness with this tradition is that within the Marxist analysis of capitalism labour is only analysed with reference to its use as a commodity. Therefore the subjectivity of labour is not a factor in this account. However, the relationship between human beings as both subject and object in capitalist social relations means that their subjectivity will influence, shape and interact with the social relations of production, and this subjectivity is gendered. Studying the links between subjectivity and paid labour has received a new stimulus through the impact of Foucault's work on the social sciences. His work provides a critique of the unitary and rational subject that dominates sociology. Foucault's analysis of the relationship between power, discursive practices and subjectivity provides a number of conceptual tools from which to re-examine the contradictions of women's experiences of paid work. I have therefore drawn on these theoretical resources in an attempt to develop an explanation of occupational segregation that overcomes some of the problems with previous accounts. This brings me to the second of the key concepts that I used to interpret the research data - the concept of discourse.

The Concept of Discourse

My use of the concept of discourse is based on a number of sources. Chris Weedon's (1987) discussion proved very useful, especially her exegesis of how Foucault employs the term. She discusses how:

> Discourses, in Foucault's work, are ways of constituting knowledge, together with the social practices, forms of subjectivity and power relations which inhere in such knowledges and the relations between them. Discourses are more than ways of thinking and producing meaning. They constitute the 'nature' of the body, unconscious and conscious mind and emotional life of the subjects which they seek to govern. (Weedon 1987, p.108)

In light of Weedon's discussion I use the term discourses to mean practices and narratives through which people live, think and speak. They are the stories or scripts through which people understand and operate in the social world. Another useful discussion of the concept is provided by Purvis and Hunt (1993) which explains that:

> What the concept tries to capture is that people live and experience within discourse in the sense that discourses impose frameworks which limit what can be experienced or the meaning that experience can encompass, and thereby influence what can be said and done. Each discourse allows certain things to be said and impedes or prevents other things from being said.

Discourses thus provide specific and distinguishable mediums through which communicative action takes place. (Purvis and Hunt 1993, p.485)

The notion that 'discourses impose frameworks' led me to attach the concept of hegemony in order to signal tensions in the concept that need to be addressed. There are some discourses that are more powerful than others and therefore have a much more powerful impact on subjectivity. In order to draw attention to this I use the term 'hegemonic discourse'.

The notion of discourses enabled me to interpret the way individual subjectivity operates and represents the practices which structure people's understanding of themselves in relation to the world. However, as Weedon points out, this subjectivity 'is precarious, contradictory and in process, constantly being reconstituted in discourse each time we think or speak' (1987, p.33). She also states that some discourses are more powerful than others, but (and this is a weakness in Foucault's work) there is no way of determining why or how some discourses are more powerful and some marginal. Some aspects of the connections between discourse, knowledge and power are discussed in this book in relation to science and technology, but that does not address the issue of how some discourses are more legitimate than others. Using these concepts I set myself the task of interpreting the discourses which impact on and shape women's experiences at work by exploring the processes and practices that constitute computer programming.

Organisation of the Book

The organisation of this book reflects the theoretical shifts and developments discussed above. The next chapter explores how the sociology of women and paid work has been affected by these theoretical shifts. A key aspect of this discussion is the argument that the conceptualisation of gender that is embedded in the concept of patriarchy, is one that views gender as a category rather than a process. The discussion of this aspect of the problem of patriarchy is a distinctive contribution to the study of gender segregation, and provides the theoretical unpinning for my review of a number of key ethnographic studies of women and work. This review attempts to show how these debates shaped the discussions of gender at work - a central focus for Marxist feminists - and surveys the impact of this approach on the study of occupational segregation. Because of the dominance of Marxism from the late 1960s to the early 1980s, especially in studies that examined the labour process, the examination of women's paid work became skewed in a particular direction. The empirical studies produced in the 1970s and 1980s on women's work which attempted to apply this analytical framework, as will be shown, slanted the analysis of gendered work towards attempting to trace the mechanisms whereby patriarchy intersected with capitalism, and so the significance of gendered work for the gendering of identities and subjectivities was not incorporated into studies of the labour process. In chapter three by re-examining a number of key ethnographic studies on women's work which were framed by the theoretical debates discussed above, I illustrate the tendency towards description rather than analysis when the concept of 'gender' is framed as a *sex-role* rather than as a *process* in order to show the limitations of the 'sex-role' conceptualisation of gender. The theoretical framework adopted in these studies locate men in powerful positions in relation to women, endowing them with technical competencies, skill and strengths, and by definition conceals, or at best, minimises, the extent to which women's technical competencies, skill and strengths are exercised at work. I also explain how the practices and processes around the gendering of work is obscured by the lack of theoretical attention to the constant cycle of negotiation, reproduction and resistance practised by women and men at the workplace. The contradictions confronting women and men as they negotiate, resist and take pleasure from the social constructions of masculinity and femininity were noted and described but not addressed in any depth. These studies reflect the successes and failures of the Marxist feminist perspective that had a considerable influence on the study of gender and work. I argue that the studies of women and work which used this approach constructed a feminist account which obscured women's power, skills and strengths by constantly positioning them as controlled and dominated by a powerful patriarchy of men and that this story continues to have a very strong presence, in feminist theory. Chapter four examines the sexual division of labour amongst computer programmers in a number of computer software houses. The focus in this section is the process of occupational segregation that is developing in this industry. Several considerations made computer work a useful case study. Firstly, computer work is a relatively new field as it emerged during the second World War (Kraft 1977) and therefore did not have a long historical tradition of gender stereotyping. Secondly, there are a number of studies which analyse women's increasing representation in computing, providing some examples of different feminist perspectives on the issues, (see Game and Pringle 1984; Lloyd and Newell 1985; Strober and Arnold 1987) and which point to some of the contradictions for women working as computer programmers. Thirdly for the purposes of this study the occupation had to be one in which women and men had the same job title and worked alongside each other. This was because all of the studies on women's work that were available as I set up the research project were studies of women in segregated employment. In order to highlight interests central to the research, it was important to analyse gender at work rather than women at work. In chapter five, I outline the factors shaping gender segregation in the workplaces visited. The organisational culture of computing is the main focus here. I discuss the culture of the different companies I visited, highlighting the differences between in-house computer installations and software houses by analysing the working conditions and philosophy with reference to the beliefs and rituals that shaped this occupational community. In chapters six, seven and eight I analyse the sexual division of labour amongst the computer programmers I interviewed using the concept of discourse. Beginning with the responses from the men interviewed, I devise a typology of hegemonic masculinity and examine the connections between this discourse and the gendered nature of organisational discourse. The conflicts and contradictions of this discourse for men are explored using both the interview material and the literature on men and masculinities. This section is also an elaboration of how my concept of gender changed from one that implied a social role, to one that signified a social process. Some of the theoretical problems with an analysis of gender relations that relies on simply studying men rather than women and men are also signposted at this stage. Chapter seven examines the debates on gender, technology and power and provides an alternative reading to the account which has dominated much of the literature on women's relationship with technology. Here I begin to construct an alternative theoretical framework of technology and gender by demonstrating how a Foucaultian concept of power can produce a reading that empowers women. A chapter that explores the transcripts for responses from the women computer programmers in order to investigate how they negotiate and resist the culture of computing and organisations follows this. By constructing a typology of hegemonic femininity I analyse how this is negotiated and utilised by the women in the organisations visited and how different aspects of femininity shape women's position at the workplace. The concluding chapter presents an overview of the alternative theoretical framework that I used to interpret the empirical data and outlines some of the problems with the conceptual tools I used in the research. This section also outlines a number of conceptual and theoretical issues that need to be clarified and developed in order to advance the understanding of gender relations in organisations.

Summary of Argument

The question that pervades this book is how workplace segregation between women and men is produced and maintained. By the early 1990s it was clear that a new approach was needed in order to understand the persistence, despite equal opportunities legislation and the expansiveness of women in the labour market, of occupational segregation. Thus the overall aim is to present an alternative approach to the study of gender segregation at work. This book tries to construct a theoretical explanation for the process of segregation using computer programming as the focus of study. In order to overcome some of the theoretical problems of the Marxist/feminist perspective which had framed the empirical research, I use the concept of discourse in order to explain and capture of process of transformation, negotiation, manoeuvring and resistance which characterised the interviews I had conducted in the organisations I visited. This concept enabled me to develop a framework for understanding how the discourses around work, organisations, computing interact with the dominant discourses of masculinity and femininity. By devising a typology of the discourse of hegemonic femininity and hegemonic masculinity, I demonstrate the links between these discourses and the other discourses which gender work in the computing industry and also show the impact of hegemonic femininity on the subjectivity of women workers. The aim of this account is to advance the study of women and work by focusing on discourses that condition the reproduction of gendered subject positions in the workplace. In this account gender is regarded as a process rather than a category. Using this theoretical framework I analyse the empirical data I collected on computer programmers and attempt to construct an alternative explanation to the process of occupational segregation at the workplace. This account demonstrates how an analysis of the discourses which structure the subjectivity of female and male computer programmers upholds practices which have the effect, though not necessarily the intention, of reproducing gender inequality. The key point is that these discourses are interdependent and enable both the structuring of gender at work and the structuring of work by gender to be analysed as interdependent processes. These discourses condition the reproduction of gendered subject positions in the workplace. They also structure the practices that have the effect of reproducing job segregation and gender inequality.

Chapter 2

Gender Segregation at Work

Before the emergence of second wave feminism,[1] sociological studies of work did not use gender as an analytical category and did not see gender and gender relationships as important dimensions of both the way in which employment is structured and the way in which work is experienced (see Brown 1976; Beechey 1983; 1979; 1978; 1977). In comparison with the early 1970s, by the beginning of 2000, there is now a vast literature on both women and work and gender at work.

In the 1980s, feminist debates on women's paid employment focused on the inequalities experienced by women in the workplace and demonstrated the type of work women did, both historically and present day. In some senses, for feminist sociologists, this task was made easier than for feminists working in other disciplines by the dramatic increase in the numbers of women, especially married women, who had entered the workplace from the 1960s. The two theoretical frameworks which various feminists drew on in order to comprehend women's place in the labour market is indicative of two dominant strands in sociological analysis: Marxist sociology and mainstream or bourgeois sociology. The greater part of work in the area was produced by feminists who drew on Marxist concepts developed from analysis of the capitalist labour process. They utilised terms such as reserve army of labour; the ideology of femininity and masculinity; the concept of patriarchy and linked these with the concepts of reproduction and production. Other feminists, again utilising a concept of patriarchy analysed women's position in employment with reference to notions of a segmented labour market and dual labour market theories, using concepts developed by bourgeois economists rather than sociologists. For both types of analysis of women's work the key theoretical problem is the explanation of the persistence of occupational segregation. A key indictor of the theoretical position taken by these different writers is the extent to which they refer to the highly gender *segregated* or *segmented* nature of the labour market.

Regardless of the theoretical framework adopted by the writers in the field there is now a great deal of knowledge of the types of work that women do, the attitudes and aspirations of women and the extent to which gender influences the labour market.   In other words there are a large number of empirical and descriptive accounts of gender and work.   But the reason why employment continues to be characterised by a high level of differentiation between women and men is still slippery.   Feminist debates about women's paid work and occupational segregation make assumptions about men's orientation to paid work, domestic work and childrearing which explain occupational segregation as determined by the sexual division of labour in the household and/or by men organising to keep women out of the labour market, or by men keeping the better paid jobs for themselves.   A number of writers have provided historical analyses of men's opposition to women at work that strengthened these explanations for gender segregation (see, Witz 1992; Walby 1986; Cockburn 1983; Hartmann 1981).   These historical accounts explain the continued persistence of this phenomenon showing that gender segregation whilst not static, still continues to reproduce itself.   What links the different arguments in these accounts is the use of patriarchy as a theoretical tool which problematises the attempt to theorise women's position in the labour market in a number of ways.

The Concept of Patriarchy

The concept of patriarchy has dominated much of feminist theory and practice since its appearance in the work of Kate Millett in what is now considered her feminist classic *Sexual Politics* (1970).   Since then, patriarchy has been used as an analytical tool which explains male dominance and women's subordination and oppression not only present day, in the capitalist mode of production but also historically, across differing epochs and through various social formations.

Throughout the 1970s the usefulness of the concept and the role it has played and continues to play in feminist analysis was keenly discussed, and many important theoretical points and inadequacies exposed.   The criticisms concentrated on the ahistorical and essentialist nature of the concept.   This can be summarised by a quote from Sheila Rowbotham's article for the *New Statesman*:

> 'Patriarchy' implies a structure which is fixed, rather than the kaleidoscope of forms within which women and men have encountered one another.   It does not carry any notion of how women might act to transform their situation as a sex.   Nor does it even convey a sense of how women have resolutely manoeuvred for a better position within the general context of subordination. (Rowbotham 1979, reprinted 1982, p.74)

Unfortunately Rowbotham does not carry through this critique of patriarchy as 'fixed' - to an understanding of how a related error occurs with the concept of gender that is attached to the concept of patriarchy.

The concept of patriarchy sets up a fixity to gender categories that obscures the way gender is both relational and fluid. In order to construct an alternative framework for interpreting gender segregation at the workplace it is essential to grasp gender as a process, and this proposition is a critical argument of the book.

The Unhappy Marriage of Marxism and Feminism

The problem encountered by Marxist-feminists in attempting a synthesis of Marxism and feminism and/or constructing a dual systems theory of patriarchy and capitalism were addressed in a now famous essay, 'The Unhappy Marriage of Marxism and Feminism' by Heidi Hartmann (1981). Hartmann's opening paragraph rails against the fact that within the marriage, feminism was losing out:

> The marriage of Marxism and feminism has been like the marriage of husband and wife depicted in English common law: Marxism and feminism are one, and that one is Marxism. (ibid., p.2)

The main criticism that can be made of this article is that her main argument is directed against the Marxist side of the union. This one-sided approach is further marred by the fact that the Marxism she attacks is, 'a conception of Marxism that is itself inadequate and largely economistic' (Vogel 1981, p.197). In many ways she appears to view the Marxists as men and thus as having a very limited understanding of feminism, and to believe that feminists are women who obviously are equipped theoretically with a faultless concept of patriarchy.[2] By her lack of appreciation of the many schisms and debates within the Marxist paradigm, Hartmann fails to understand how these theoretical difficulties opened a space from which Marxists-feminists could begin to develop a feminist-Marxist synthesis. Despite the limitations of the Hartmann essay, her work is very important because she indirectly revealed the contradictions that have plagued the work of Marxist-feminists. Her article enabled Iris Young (1981) to discuss the inconsistencies in many of the attempts to produce the marriage of Marxism and feminism. For, as Young points out, throughout Hartmann's essay, it is Marxism that is attacked and not feminism. Though Hartmann only questions the limitations of the Marxist analysis of capitalism and not the limitations of the feminist analysis of patriarchy, she is nevertheless obliged in her concluding paragraph to remark:

Patriarchy as we have used it here remains more a descriptive term than an analytic one. If we think Marxism alone inadequate, and radical feminism itself insufficient, then we need to develop new categories. What makes our task a difficult one is that the same features, such as the division of labour, often reinforce both patriarchy and capitalism, and in a thorough patriarchal capitalist society, *it is hard to isolate the mechanisms of patriarchy.* (op.cit., p.29) (my emphasis)

Heidi Hartmann's article enabled the contradictions to surface that had been bubbling away for years in the theoretical project of constructing a Marxist-feminist analysis. Iris Young in her essay, 'Beyond the Unhappy Marriage: A critique of the Dual Systems Theory' (1981), argues not only against Hartmann's version of the wedding but also against most of the analyses which have put forward similar versions of the dual system theory. She does this by expressing severe doubts about the feminist dowry of patriarchy. By logically working through the contradictions present in these dual-system theories, she asks how is it possible to 'separate patriarchy from a system of social relations of production even for analytical purposes' and she correctly concludes:

> it seems reasonable, however, to admit that if patriarchy and capitalism are manifest in identical social and economic structures they belong to one system, not two. (ibid., p.7)

By now the problems encountered by various writers who have attempted to construct a dual-systems theory were becoming commonplace. The inadequacies of the theory of patriarchy, which has placed feminist theory in a blind alley of description and which has failed to produce an analysis of women's oppression, became increasingly exposed. Doubts and dilemmas still surrounded these critiques of patriarchy because the writers were also aware that the theory of patriarchy had enabled feminists to describe and analyse women's role in the family, in the economy, in the domestic sphere, and their role in reproduction. However, where the theory was least successful was in moving beyond women's domestic roles into the sphere of production, without reducing women's role in production to their reproductive role. It was this reductionism in analysing women's productive role that appeared to grant traditional Marxism theoretical hegemony. As Young explains:

> All versions of the dual systems theory start from the premise that patriarchal relations designate a system of relations distinct from and independent of the relations of production described by traditional marxism. (Young 1981, p.45)

In Summary

In summary, despite the problems caused by the concept of patriarchy,[3] a theoretical framework had become established for the study of the sexual division of labour in both the 'public' and the 'private' sphere. The universalising aspects of patriarchy were used to interpret this division. Occupational segregation was said to reflect this division, with men being concentrated in men's occupations which were more prestigious, and culturally more powerful and important than women's occupations which reflected their domestic responsibilities (see Stacey 1981).

Thus the theory of patriarchy ironically duplicated the way traditional sociology had regarded women's paid work, which was to regard it as marginal or peripheral to their work in the home. Mainstream sociology had, in the majority of cases before the 1970s, either ignored women's paid work altogether or discussed it as problematic for their roles as mothers and housewives (see discussion in Beechey 1978, 1983; Brown 1976). The idea of separate models for men's and women's relationship to paid work was re-inforced by the theory of patriarchy which explained sex segregation in terms of male power and in this way male domination and female subordination was taken as a given. Rather than challenging these assumptions the debates shifted to attempting to incorporate women into classical Marxist analysis of the labour process, as gender had hitherto been conspicuously ignored.

Kate Purcell (1989) explains how the concept of patriarchy has encouraged forms of explanation that focus on 'women's' jobs rather than the process by which jobs get labelled in this way. The conceptual framework that was adopted by early feminist explorations of women's work assumed that women's work identity was already established by their roles within the family. By the late 1980s, it became clear that the problem with 'patriarchy' was that the gendered experience of domesticity and employment relations, and the practices and processes by which these experiences structure women's and men's lives, is both contradictory and conflictual. Neither the theory nor the concept was able to explain what feminists had uncovered by the studies of gender at work in the past ten years. These accounts of women and work were reporting on the diversity and differences between women, and the complexity of women's experiences and attitudes to their paid employment.

At the beginning of the 1980s Heidi Hartmann concluded that:

> The present status of women in the labour market and the current arrangement of sex-segregated jobs is the result of a long process of interaction between patriarchy and capitalism. I have emphasised the

actions of male workers throughout this process because I believe this to be correct ... Capitalists have indeed used women as unskilled, underpaid labour to undercut male workers, yet this is only a case of the chickens coming home to roost - a case of men's cooptation by and support for patriarchal society, with its hierarchy among men, being turned back on themselves with a vengeance. Capitalism grew on top of patriarchy: patriarchal capitalism is stratified society par excellence. (Hartmann 1982, pp.468-9)

Gender segregation at the workplace is thus explained by reference to a system of patriarchy whereby men oppress women. Although in Hartmann's article it is recognised that some men have more power than others, she argues that all men benefit from the domestic, reproductive and sexual subordination of women. The formulation contained in the quote had a decisive impact on feminist studies of women's work both paid and unpaid. Despite the fact that the notion of a universal patriarchy has been widely criticised for its failure to explain the mechanisms of gender oppression it is still the case that the conceptualisation of gender which is the corollary to this framework still continues to assert an influence on explanations of gender segregation at work. I am referring here to the way women and men are positioned as oppositional with men having power over women thus producing a particular interpretation of gender relations at the workplace. This conceptualisation came to dominate feminist studies on job segregation which foregrounds women's oppression and subordination in relation to men and marginalised women's power and resistance. What is now very noticeable about these accounts is the level of abstraction of the discussion of gender relations. In effect, gender is never analysed as such, rather the issue becomes the system of patriarchy and the focus is on the relationship between this system and capitalism. This level of abstraction inevitably produced a static conceptualisation of gender with the result that the process by which gender segregation operates is obscured.

Gender Segregation at Work

Paid employment has become an increasingly important activity for women and involves a greater proportion of their lives, although still very few follow the stereotypical male pattern of continuous lifetime employment as full-time workers (Dex 1985).

Despite the development of equal opportunities policies and the growth in employment of a few women in professional, managerial and some traditionally male dominated occupations, most women are employed

in sex-segregated jobs which are not defined as skilled and large numbers
work part-time (Beechey 1987, p.1; Hakim 1979).

> Segregation concerns the tendency for men and women to be employed in
> different occupations from each other across the entire spectrum of
> occupations under analysis. It is a concept that is inherently symmetrical ...
> Concentration is concerned with the sex composition of the workforce in an
> occupation or set of occupations. Whereas segregation refers to the
> separation of the two sexes across occupations, concentration refers to the
> representation of one sex within occupations. (Siltanen et al. 1995, pp.4-5)

These definitions refer to 'horizontal segregation' as opposed to
vertical segregation that is defined as:

> Vertical occupational segregation exists when men and women both work in
> the same job categories, but men commonly do the more skilled,
> responsible or better paid work. For example the majority of school heads
> may be men while the majority of teachers are women, the majority of
> hospital consultants may be men while the majority of nurses may be
> women. (Hakim 1981, p.521)

Attempts to examine occupational segregation have operated with
various foci that Beechey (1987) summarises in the following way. In the
1950s, 1960s and early 1970s, the focus for analyses of women's work and
occupational segregation was policy orientated in that it described women's
'two roles' (i.e. their involvement in paid work outside the home, and
unpaid work inside the home) and identified ways of overcoming the
problems women encountered (see for example Myrdal and Klein 1968).

By the mid-1970s the feminist sociologists who were concerned with
the analysis of women's work adapted mainstream sociological concepts
and theories in order to make women and the concept of gender visible.
For example, they applied neo-Marxist categories to women's position in
the family and focused on the relationship between women's unpaid work
in the home and the wider economy, which later became known as the
'domestic labour debate' (Beechey 1987, pp.6-12).

The Marxist-feminist debates cleared the ground and prepared a path
for a new and alternative approach to the study of women's position in the
labour force, but the conceptual tools with which to begin such a study
were lacking, especially with reference to the concept of gender. The
critique of the concept of patriarchy had not exposed the static nature of
gender which characterised the accounts of women's work, both paid and
unpaid. Men remain untheorised not only in Marxist-feminist analysis but
also in radical-feminist work. The position of men in relation to women,
the nature of their power, their role in reproduction and production and how

they understand their role, needed to be examined, and this is one of the reasons why men are interviewed in this study.

Because of the dominance of Marxism from the late 1960s to the early 1980s, especially in studies that examined the labour process, the examination of women's paid work became skewed in a particular direction. The attempt to relate a sex/gender system to the relations of production was excessively functionalist, economically reductionist and insufficiently historical. The empirical studies produced in the 1970s and 1980s on women and work which attempted to apply this analytical framework, as will be shown, encountered similar problems. The attempts to understand and explain gender segregation at work from within this paradigm, slanted the analysis towards attempting to trace the mechanisms whereby patriarchy intersected with capitalism, towards abstract theorising. It is interesting to reflect that a different Marxist feminist analysis of gender segregation at work could have been available if more attention had been paid to the work of Juliet Mitchell, especially her *Psychoanalysis and Feminism* (1974) which was an early example of work from a perspective which attempted to interpret the psychological dimension of the social: i.e. subjectivity. Unfortunately the perspective was diverted into, as one writer put it,

> the tendency ... to see how much mileage could be got out of existing Marxist categories if they were applied to women. (Phillips 1981, p.92)

and so the meaning of gender and work for the gendering of identities and subjectivities was not incorporated into studies of the labour process. Michèle Barrett's (1980) use of the concept of ideology introduced the relationship between the construction of subjectivities and work identities, but her stress is on the structuring of the labour market not the gendering of the labour process. A thorough discussion of ideology and discourse only becomes available in her later work (1991), and this book is not concerned with the issues of segregation at work. It is, however, of interest to note the way in which the issues of gender construction, identity and subjectivity, despite the lack of theoretical concepts with which to interpret them, keep appearing and re-appearing in the women and work studies that are examined in the next chapter.

To summarise, gender segregation from the Marxist-feminist perspective is explained largely in terms of the benefits of women's labour for capitalism, thus producing a functionalist explanation which failed to explore the process of gendering: a process which involves the study of men as well as women. The concept of patriarchy had set up an orthodoxy of male power over women and this went largely unchallenged. The concentration on Marxist categories in the Marxist-feminist project led to a polemical attack couched in the following trenchant criticism. Christine Delphy wrote that the purpose of a Marxist-feminist analysis is the, 'exemption of men from all responsibility for the oppression of women' (1984, p.179). Delphy accuses Marxist-feminists of being the protectors of the enemy - *men*. This is obviously a crude simplification of these writers' positions, yet it is a fact that this feminist problematic was not theoretically examined in any great depth. Marxist-feminists failed to directly address this important aspect of the radical feminist position: that is, that men benefit from the unequal division of labour both in the home and at the workplace. For example as Anne Phillips points out:

> Radical feminists seemed committed to a theory that men and women were intrinsically antagonistic, and that male power over women was founded in women's role as child-bearers; socialist feminists counter-posed to this the argument that sexual antagonism was based in the social relations of production and could be socially transformed. But increasingly, socialist feminists felt themselves trapped by this into a position which underplayed the extent of sexual division and antagonism - significantly, it was radical feminism which took the lead in the analysis of sexual violence. (Phillips 1981, p.93)

Contribution of Mainstream Sociological Approaches

Alongside these Marxist-feminists debates a rather different approach, based on the 'dual-system' approach was developed in order to examine women's place in the labour market (Barron and Norris 1976). This approach builds on the concept of 'dual labour market' that had been first employed as an attempt to understand the phenomenon of racial discrimination in employment in the United States (Doeringer and Priore 1971). In describing how labour markets seemed to be divided into primary and secondary segments in which the primary sector work was characterised by good stable working conditions and pay levels and the secondary sector was characterised by considerable instability and poorer conditions of employment and pay levels (Doeringer and Priore 1971), analytical analogies were drawn between the position of migrant labour and black people in Western capitalist economies and the position of women (Barron and Norris 1976).

The debate on gender segregation then became one that adopted either a labour market approach or those who supported a Marxist-feminist approach and there were various internal debates within each tradition. By the late 1970s interest began to shift away from the role of employers in constructing the primary and secondary sectors towards examining how the interplay between employers and organised labour, and the strategies adopted by some workers in the primary sector, secured advantages for these groups (Goldthorpe 1980; Rubery 1978; Rubery and Wilkinson 1994).

Studies by the Cambridge Labour Studies Group (Craig et al., 1984) indicate that attention had turned to the collection of detailed empirical data particularly that of case studies in order to examine how different social groups came to occupy a labour market sector. Alongside this, Marxist-feminists such as Beechey (1987, pp.11-12) whilst still rejecting the approach of the dual labour market theorists, began to retreat from abstract theory and engaged in more empirically based research in order to analyse trends in women's employment and to document women's experiences of both paid and unpaid work.

In recent years the task facing the analyst of gender segregation is more complex. The expansion of questions, areas of inquiry and approaches has occurred alongside the emergence of the global economy. Feminist scholars view economic inequalities between men and women not only as the result of economic developments or market forces but also stress that women's work is economically devalued: that women are in less desirable jobs than are men and are treated as marginal, and that as a group, women are likely to be influenced and controlled by men. In some western industrial societies there has been an inflow of women into previously male-dominated occupations posing the issue of re-segregation; and computer programming has been the subject of such research (Wright and Jacobs 1995). Other research on occupational gender segregation by Robert Blackburn and Jennifer Jarman (1997) concentrate on what should be encompassed by the term 'segregation'. The emphasis here is on the indices that attempt to measure the inequalities of wage levels and produce a statistical and mathematical analysis of segregation. The variety in the type of studies of gender segregation has two main objectives; to document the extent and impact of segregation and to proffer explanations as to the persistence of the phenomenon. As discussed above there are two main types of explanations: those that emphasise the role of the market and employment practices and those that emphasise the role of gender ideologies. This book concentrates on the latter and attempts to utilise the concept of gender as a process in order to analyse factors operating in a specific occupation to produce gender segregation.

To summarise, gender segregation has been explained in relation to either the structure of the labour market (Rubery 1978; Hakim 1978; Barron and Norris 1976), or by writers who attempts to link understand the phenomenon by suggesting a dual-system - capitalist/patriarchal approach (Hartmann 1982). Hartmann states that job segregation can be explained by the 'hierarchical domestic division of labour (which) is perpetuated by the labour market, and vice versa' (1982, p.449). This formulation demonstrates the way the focus of research on women's paid work shifted away from descriptive policy oriented data collection, to the attempt to add women to macro theories of labour processes. It then moved to more micro case study analyses. This shift in focus enabled an increase in understanding of the experiences of women and employment that has encouraged closer analysis of the ways in which gender is constructed. However, though many of the studies of the last decade can be seen as contributing to the construction of the whole map of women's employment and the organisation of work, there were a number of differences and similarities in the use of the concept of gender in these accounts.

The Embarrassing Fact of Gender Segregation

Women's participation in the labour market had been increasing steadily since the 1960s despite the economic restructuring of the 1980s, whilst at the same time a heightened interest by some employers in equal opportunities policies tended to conflict with government policies that adversely affected women. Beechey (1987) summaries these developments in the following way:

> ... the Thatcher government policies of deregulating the economy, privatising services and trying to create a low-wage economy have adversely affected women. Moreover, the Government has successfully blocked an array of measures proposed with the European Commission to promote greater sexual equality ... (Yet) A number of companies and public sector employers now have some kind of equal opportunities programme and there has been an upsurge in training opportunities for women. (Beechey 1987, pp.12-13)

This shifted the investigation of gender segregation of work towards organisational practices. The focus for research became the relationship between gender and the organisation of work. Increasingly, Marxist and socialist feminist analyses of work began to examine the processes of social construction and the role of ideology in defining what is skilled work; in questioning why some jobs are predominantly done by women; in questioning why some industries are characterised by part-time work; and in asking what influences men's and women's capacities to participate actively in trade unions? A number of studies, especially the work of Cynthia Cockburn began to demonstrate how certain aspects of masculinity and femininity are constructed and reproduced at work through the labour process as a consequence of the ideological sex typing of jobs. Case studies of organisations highlighted the role of management, trade unions and men in constructing skill definitions and in organising hierarchical systems that favoured men, (Armstrong 1982; Cavendish 1982; Coyle 1984; Pollert 1981). Through these studies it became clear that the concept of a 'job' is a gendered concept, even though organisational logic presents it as gender neutral. A job already contains the gender-based division of labour and the separation between the public and the private sphere. The concept of job assumes a particular gendered organisation of domestic life and social production. It is an example of what Dorothy Smith has called 'the gender subtext of the rational and impersonal' (1988, p.4). The gender neutral status of a 'job' and of the organisational theories of which it is a part depend on the assumption that the worker is abstract, disembodied, although in actuality both the concept of a 'job' and real workers are gendered and 'bodied'.

Sylvia Walby's edited collection of articles on gender segregation (1988) examined the segregation of women's and men's work in a range of different contexts and found that segregation can only in small part be attributed to differences in education and training between men and women, or to the fact that some women have childcare responsibilities. The argument in this book is that gender segregation has more to do with capitalist's desires to maintain low wages and flexibility, and with the behaviour of men. As Cynthia Cockburn suggests in her excellent contribution, men are under considerable social pressure not to be directly comparable with women at work. Men maintain and reproduce their segregated workspace by moving sideways, upwards, or by acting to keep women out. This is not to suggest that differences between women and men are the only form of segregation. As the article by Annie Phizacklea discusses the major division between women is that of 'race', which produces 'ethnic niches' in the gender-segregated labour market. These areas are characterised by high rates of unemployment and job insecurity and low pay. There are also the obstacles suffered by part time women workers in relation to male and female full timers. Despite this, the book shows that the demarcation between women and men's work is being reproduced in all sectors, surviving and re-forming around new technologies, economic restructuring and new work relations. However the book also reveals the 'embarrassing fact' that women are making conscious choices about their positions in the labour market; choices that in several Marxist feminist accounts were considered as 'false consciousness'.

In this chapter I have outlined the problems with this approach. In attempting to overcome the level of abstraction at which the debates were conducted, case study approaches began to shift attention to the process of gendering at the level of social formation. By this I mean, the region, the locality, the organisation, the occupation. These debates cleared the ground and prepared a path for a new and alternative approach to the study of women's position in the labour force, but the conceptual tools with which to begin such a study were lacking, especially with reference to the concept of gender. The critique of the concept of patriarchy had not exposed the static nature of gender which characterised the accounts of women's work, both paid and unpaid. Men remain untheorised not only in Marxist-feminist analysis but also in radical-feminist work.

In Summary

The studies of the last decade can be seen as contributing to an understanding of occupational gender segregation and highlighted a number of problems. The valuable contribution of these studies (e.g. Cavendish 1982; Pollert 1981; Westwood 1984) has been in directing attention to the social processes in the construction of femininity at work. However they have concentrated on the experiences of working class women in manufacturing industries and have stressed that both women's consciousness and women's place in the industries, unlike men's, can be 'read off' from their place in the domestic sphere (Beechey 1987, p.15, p.123, p.190), thus underplaying the evidence they have generated about the role of the workplace in the construction of femininity.

These accounts which will form the focus of the third chapter of this book appear to be radically different, at first glance, from the 'two roles approach' adopted by Myrdal and Klein (1968). However there are similarities in that the analysis of women's paid work is seen as dependent on women's roles in the family. So it appears that ethnographic studies whilst providing detailed accounts of women's employment in specific organisations still look to the family to provide explanations for occupational segregation. In examining these texts there is a conscious attempt made to avoid the assumption that family orientation is primary for women and work orientation is primary for men. This focus follows on from Dex (1985) who in her evaluation of some classic studies from industrial sociology and her analysis of the Women and Employment Survey Data (Dex 1985) suggests that there is a similarity between women's and men's attitude to work. She argues that women and men's orientations to work are influenced by their own employment histories, their position in their life course and the characteristics of the local labour market. She found that there is a 'remarkable degree of convergence' between women and men's employment. She identifies a need for research which utilises a framework which fits the assertion that, 'men's work cannot be understood with reference to women, just as women's work cannot be understood without reference to men' (Dex 1985, p.44).

Notes

[1]   The concept of the second wave is used by scholars to distinguish between the early history of feminism that is usually associated with the Suffragette movement and the women's movement that emerged in the 1960s.

[2]   This impression is given by the fact that when she is talking about feminist theory she uses the term 'we' and 'our' and she put this as oppositional to Marxists. For example: 'It is logical for us to turn to marxism for help in that reassessment because it is a developed theory of social change. Marxist theory is well developed compared to feminist theory, and in our attempt to use it, we have sometimes been side-tracked from feminist objectives. The left has always been ambivalent about the women's movement, often viewing it as dangerous to the cause of socialist evolution. When left women espouse feminism, it may be personally threatening to left men' (1981, p.31).

[3]   See further discussion in A. Fitzsimons (1999) Conflicting Discourses: Gender at Work in Computer Programming. PhD thesis with Open University.

Chapter 3

Women and Work

This chapter examines the ways in which the theoretical difficulties and issues discussed in the previous chapters shaped the feminist writings on gender and work from the early 1980s. Because of the analytical framework adopted in feminist accounts of women and work, this gave rise to largely descriptive studies of women's role in the workplace, and as many of these early studies were more concerned to demonstrate 'patriarchy' in action rather than attend to the process of gender operation and construction, the emphasis is on women's subordination rather than independence. The legacy of this type of theorising is that men are always represented as dominant and powerful in these accounts, in opposition to women who are positioned as inferior, subordinate and powerless. This formulation of gender relations established an explanatory framework for gender segregation that still continues to influence discussions of women's paid work and feminist strategies for change. It became established through a number of influential studies and can be illustrated by a passage from a book which presents a cross cultural and historical analysis of gender-based job segregation.

> Women and men have always had a different relation to technology. Men are seen as technically competent, creative; women are seen as incompetent, suited only for the minding of machines which have been constructed, maintained and set up by men. Notions of skill, too, are founded on gender distinctions. Men capture skilled jobs (that is those involving training, expertise, knowledge) for themselves; moreover all jobs done by men, simply by virtue of that fact, are seen as more skilled than those done by women. Similarly women are pushed into unskilled jobs, and the skills that they do have are seen as 'natural' (cooking, caring for people, sewing) and therefore devalued ... in factories segregated workgroups of women and men develop their own highly specific and mutually excluding cultures. (Bradley 1989, pp.68-69)

In this chapter I want to show how this formulation became established through the concept of gender that is embedded in the concept of patriarchy.[1] I re-examine key texts which investigate gender segregation and the labour process by inspecting the processes performed by women, using a concept of gender as fluid and relational, in order to construct an alternative account of gender and work which can shape an alternative theoretical framework. The concept of patriarchy appears unable to capture the process of women's transforming, negotiating, manoeuvring and resistance in relation to the inequality they encounter in their daily lives. Though the arguments I elaborated on the concept of patriarchy are now generally accepted, it still continues to frame an explanation of gender segregation at work that contains the notion of gender as relating to sexual difference rather than a notion of gender as process. The former conceptualisation of gender positions women and men as oppositional and thus obscures the process of gendering that occurs at the workplace. To continue to state the question of gender in these terms conceals rather than illuminates the practices and discourses which en-gendered women and men, and thus the process by which women are relegated to subordinate positions at work. The notion of patriarchy locates men in powerful positions in relation to women, endowing them with technical competencies, skill and strengths, and by definition conceals or at best minimises the extent to which women's technical competencies, skill and strengths are exercised at work. Using patriarchy as an explanatory device means that the constant and continual negotiation that operates around the gendering at work is hidden. The concept obscures an interpretation of the contradictions confronting men and women as they negotiate, resist and take pleasure from the social constructions of masculinity and femininity and the operation and performativity of gendering (see Butler 1989).

Rather than simply assert this argument, I intend to review some key ethnographic studies of women's work in order to demonstrate how the use of gender as a category helped to establish a feminist approach on gender segregation at work. This view of gender has now become an obstacle to the development of a theoretical framework for interpreting gender relations at work. Ironically these early studies of women and work constructed a feminist approach which obscured women's power, skills and strengths by constantly positioning them as controlled and dominated by a powerful patriarchy of men. I am not arguing here that gender inequalities do not exist; they do. Rather, my argument is that if these inequalities are to be overcome, it is necessary to understand the process by which they are produced and reproduced. I begin by demonstrating the tendency towards description rather than analysis when 'patriarchy' is used as an explanatory device. Next I present a re-reading of these studies in order to draw out a representation of the differences among women and the contradictions of their experiences of work both paid and unpaid. By exploring the actual processes performed by women I want to construct an alternative account of gender and work which can begin to shape an alternative theoretical framework for the study of job segregation.

Women on the Line

The study *Women on the Line* by Ruth Cavendish (1982)[2] is a text that typifies a descriptive rather than a theoretical study and is a classic example, from the beginning of second wave feminism, of an early account of women's work. Cavendish identifies herself as a member of the socialist wing of the Women's Liberation Movement. She became a factory worker, not with the expressed interest of writing a book (this came later), but as part of her political commitment to working class politics. She does not make any great claims for her account: as she explains the notes she made during her seven months stint at the factory were part of a personal diary rather than research notes. It was only as a result of the persuasion of friends that she decided to produce and publish the work. She is chiefly concerned with the lack of participation of working class women in the women's movement and she used the study to demonstrate the double oppression of women as wives and workers. The book is a good example of the inadequacies of Marxist analysis of gender and class divisions within the working class. According to classical Marxist theory the men and women on the factory floor all share a similar class position because of their relationship to the means of production. Cavendish exposes the inadequacy of this formulation in her description of the crucial gender divisions between them in terms of power, authority and status. She also notes that differences of power and authority also exist between the men on the factory floor and the men in management. There are differences too between the women in relation to 'race' and ethnicity. Ruth Cavendish does not share the cultural background of the women 'on the line', not simply because of her period in higher education but because she, unlike the majority of the women in the factory, was born and brought up in England. Over 70% of the women on the line in her study are Irish, with another 20% West Indian and 10% from Gujerat in the west of India.

The book provides an ethnographic account of women's working lives on an assembly line. The line processed components for motorcar manufactures, and the study concentrates on the final assembly stage. All the assembly line workers are women. The pressure of the work, in terms of the physical and mental stress produced by both the discipline of the line and by the male hierarchy, is sharply portrayed. The speed and pace of the work, the operation of the line, the interaction between the women, and sometimes between the women and the men are very clearly presented. The working conditions are described as noisy, hot, and stuffy; the physical space occupied by the women is narrow and restricted. They don't wander around the factory at will: they are confined, continually hunched over their benches, unable to leave their station unless they obtain permission from their supervisor and/or the availability of a relief operator to take their place. In the study the men who work on the factory floor act as charge hands, supervisors, quality controllers, and progress chasers. They are described as having more freedom of physical movement compared to the women as they are at liberty to walk around and stand about without constant supervision. The differences of space according to gender is a constantly recurring theme through accounts of women's work and is related to the fact that women are supervised and controlled much more than men at work. A recent study makes a similar observation,

> Women occupied relatively less space, and less prominent space in the factory than men. This too reflected women's own reticence: we found the majority of women eating their meal at their work station, leaving the dining room to men. (Gomez 1994, p.145)

In *Women on the Line,* the work lives of these women is portrayed as hard, boring, dirty and stressful, with low wages and poor conditions. The rate for the job was so low that a number of the women also needed part-time jobs in order to supplement the wages. The work lives of the women are described as arduous and demanding both in time and energy. Cavendish tells how the work at the factory affected her social and intellectual life; that she had no time for friends, for reading or going to the cinema. She went home, sat in front of the television and went to bed. She explains that from these experiences she began to realise why family and home become the most important activities and relationships for these workers, and offers this as part of the explanation for the lack of participation of working class women in the women's movement and in trade unions. It is clear from this account that women working in these conditions did not have the required time or energy, but chiefly *time*, for political activity or involvement (see Campbell and Charlton 1978, 1980). She argues that it is family responsibilities rather than a man or romance as such, which dominated the lives of the women. Though sexuality is not an issue that is discussed at any length in the book, there is an implicit assumption that the women are heterosexual, as gay and lesbian relationships are never mentioned.

Description rather than Analysis

The study concentrates on describing the labour process of the 'line' in great detail, and the ways by which the women both accommodate and resist the monotony of the job. There are regular descriptions of the sexual division of labour on the shopfloor as well as in the home that stress women's family responsibilities.   Though gender relations are not discussed in any theoretical way, what is clearly argued is differences and inequality of work both paid and unpaid between women and men. These differences are framed around a discussion of women's domestic responsibilities and it is implied that this accounts for the gender segregation of jobs in the factory.   The representation of the work performed by these women is depicted in extremely gloomy and negative terms, and is generally depressing.

However the descriptions of the actual work done by the women revealed the technical nature of the process. Yet this is not commented on, despite the technical skills involved, despite the dirt and the noise, the work was represented unproblematically by the author, as women's work. The women assembled components by hand, using power driven screwdrivers and some simple machines - no problem with screwdrivers here. The flavour of the technical aspects of the work can be demonstrated by the following descriptions:

> the basic mechanism was covered with modules, sprockets and diactors, and some versions also had three transistors and a filter, each with a cover. (Cavendish 1982, p.16)

> Above the benches hung the airguns, power-driven screwdrivers which we had to pull down to operate. On the bench we had a wooden stand to rest the UMO on, or a mechanical jig to fix it in. (ibid., p.17)

> you had to paint two small holes in the basic mechanism with blue silicone, then place a saucer-shaped disc on the basic mechanism, followed by a dial which went on the centre of the disc, aligning pin-head-sized holes in all three. Then you used a magnetized screwhead to pick up pin-sized screws, and screwed them through all three sets of holes to secure the three components together. The silicone was dark and made the holes hard to align. (ibid., p.24)

The work was also very dirty:

> the nuts, screws and basic mechanisms were black and greasy and the bench was covered in dust; so you had to spend most of the breaks cleaning your hands so as to avoid smearing black grease on your food. (ibid., p.24)

The description of the labour process in *Women on the Line* which demonstrates the technical nature of the job - the fact that the components were for motor cars; the noisy and dirty conditions of work - ironically presents a complete contrast to the 'traditional' picture of women's work and, leads to the question: why did the women and the author take it for granted that this was women's work? Is it deemed to be 'women's work' simply because women are doing it? Why were the technical aspects of the work ignored?

I want to argue that one of the reasons why the technical aspect of the work performed by the women is ignored in the account is that technical work is associated with men's labour, the work was designated as unskilled by the management and by the women workers and this characterisation was accepted by Cavendish. Thus the question - how were these women able to reconcile their work with notion of femininity? - is never asked?

The fact that the women did not view the work they were doing as technical, and the fact that they associated technical work with men can be demonstrated by the following classic example of women's claims to technical incompetence. As Ruth Cavendish states:

> I had a set-to with Doreen one morning about wiring plugs. Her hair dryer had broken and she thought the plug had gone, and wanted a man to fix on a new one. I said she should learn how to do it herself; it was much easier than a lot of the jobs we did on the line. But she said no, she wasn't going to learn, because there'd always be a 'fella' around who could do it ... In a way, Doreen was protecting her own sphere - life was hard enough without wiring plugs and putting up shelves as well. (Cavendish 1982, p.75)

An insight into the contradictions and complexities of gendering at work is revealed by this quote. The woman was aware that she had the capability to wire a plug but by asking a man to help her, she was not only making sure he does some work, but she was also affirming her femininity and his masculinity around technical expertise. This woman was manipulating aspects of the discourse of femininity in order to negotiate a division of labour in her favour by pretending incompetence and dependence. A similar observation is made in the study of women and video recorders by Ann Gray (1987). She found that some women adopted an attitude of 'calculated ignorance' in relation to this technology in order to avoid the additional household chore of organising the recordings of television programmes. If women 'pretended' that the technology was too complex, men then had the task of buying the video cassettes, storing them, marking them and recording programmes. The point here is that women's attitudes to technology are complicated, and their 'ignorance' and lack of interest should not be so easily read off as incompetence.

As there is no discussion of the contradictions of gender and work in the study there is no way of knowing why the noisy, dirty, technical work performed by the women does not contradict their identity as female subjects either in their eyes or others. By others I mean here, the men on the shopfloor, the men in management, and the husbands, brothers, fathers, friends and partners and other women. The technical aspect of their work is not constructed as either problematic or contradictory for their femininity. This is so in spite of the fact that the women had 'very definite views about what sort of work was fitting for a man: building work and hard physical labour was much more 'manly' than working in a factory' Cavendish 1982, p.74). Yet Cavendish reports that some of the women would mention, almost *en passant* the fact that their fathers, husbands and partners had prepared dinner and did the housework. She writes: 'It was clear that most husbands did the shopping and cooking if they were at home' (1982, p.30) and 'father cooked the breakfast and did all the weekend shopping' (1982, p.54). It would seem from this that only certain types of work are deemed 'unmanly', by both men and women, and only in some contexts. Yet the contradictions expressed by the women in relation to gendered work is not discussed in the text. The implied explanation for gender segregation given in this account is that women are unable to compete on equal terms with men in the workplace because of their unpaid labour in the household. Rather than problematising the practices by which gender is enacted at the workplace, this account assumes a model of male dominance and female subordination as an explanation for the existence of 'men's jobs' and 'women's jobs'.

Girls, Wives, Factory Lives

Anna Pollert's *Girls, Wives, Factory Lives* (1981) is another study of working class women's work, this time in a tobacco factory in the south of England. This account follows much more closely the work of male sociologists such as Huw Benyon and Theo Nichols (1977), (who writes an introduction to the book) in that it is based on informal interviews and participant observation on the shopfloor. Though she declares a feminist approach (Pollert 1981, p.8), this is not explained or elaborated. It is made clear however that the theoretical framework which is used in the book is shaped much more by Marxism than feminism. As I explained in the previous chapter, one of the problems in constructing a Marxist-feminism perspective was that attention was paid much more to Marxist concepts than feminist ones and this hindered the analysis of gender segregation at work. The theoretical framework adopted in the study can be illustrated by the following statement:

> Class, based on the ownership or non-ownership of the means of production, and not sex, is the basic social antagonism. Woman's inferior position springs from the manner in which reproduction - birth and child-

rearing - are organised in class society. It is neither inevitable, nor biologically determined, nor a product of 'patriarchy'. (Pollert 1981, p.2)

There is no discussion of the literature on dual-systems theory, or of the debates on the 'unhappy marriage' of Marxism and feminism. The only mention of the theoretical problems of using Marxism to investigate gender is a reference to the 'domestic labour debate' (ibid., 1981, p.3). So Pollert adopts a similar formulation to Cavendish, which is that women's oppression begins in the home and in the isolation of their domestic life. Women then carry this oppression into paid labour where they are altered and changed by their exploitation as workers. In explaining segregation at work in this way Pollert is positing a concept of gender that conceptualises gender as something (a category) women bring with them to the workplace. Though she is trying to understand how waged work shapes the sexual division of labour in the home, she is only examining this in respect of women. This means that the interrelationship between the gendering of work and gendering in the home is not explored. Despite this, the richness of the ethnographic material gathered by Pollert indicates the discourses that shape the process of gendering at work, and consequently gender segregation.

Technical Aspects of Women's Work

The structure of the text is very similar in form to the Cavendish study, but it is less descriptive and more analytical because of its' focus. The analytical focus is the extent to which work is experienced, (she uses the term 'felt') in a different way according to gender (Pollert 1981, p.5), rather than a focus on the process by which work becomes gendered. The first section of the book describes the labour process and provides an account of women's, manual work - work that is deemed to be unskilled by the management and the women. Here again, work is deemed as women's work because women are doing it. With only a few exceptions, women and men did not work alongside each other on the same job and there is further evidence here of the freedom men have at work compared to women. As one woman commented: 'They're just standing around. And there's us, we nits, sat down working' (Pollert 1981, p.88). The women earn less than the men and their work was segregated by grades into the four lowest job scales. Part two of the book concentrates on the specificity of women's labour and assesses the importance of women's domestic labour to their waged labour, and the final section assesses the way women resist, negotiate and struggle against the contradictions of their roles. These last two sections are the most important sections of the book, demonstrating both the creativity and power of women's culture and the demands made on their lives by family and home responsibilities.

There is a striking resemblance in the description of the work the women perform in this factory to the portrait of women's work supplied by Cavendish. Once more the work is very labour intensive, controlled and closely disciplined. Women weigh, pack, strip and spin the tobacco, the atmosphere and working conditions are noisy and dusty, 'cluttered with machines, heavy with the clinging smell and dust of the 'rag' (tobacco)' (Pollert 1981, p.30). Despite the fact that the work demands precision, speed and dexterity, the work was classed as unskilled. Here again, it is interesting to note the extent to which women were involved in highly technical processes. In this account women are represented as unskilled workers doing boring, repetitive work - but the work was both skilled and technical.

Women and Skill

The social construction of skill has been an important issue in feminist writing on women's work, as Phillips and Taylor had noted:

> far from being an objective economic fact, skill is often an ideological category imposed on certain types of work by virtue of the sex and power of the workers who perform it ... skill definitions are saturated with sexual bias. (Phillips and Taylor 1980, p.79)

There is now widespread recognition that the division between men's and women's work has very little to do with 'objective' skills (see Cockburn 1985; Crompton and Jones 1984; Collinson and Knights 1986). However the feminist debate on skill by arguing (correctly) that 'the worker's sex, not the content of work, leads to identification as skilled or unskilled' (Phillips and Taylor 1980, p.85), ignored how the technical aspects of jobs are associated with discourses of masculinity rather than discourses of femininity. In other words, simply saying women's work is as skilled as men's misses the impact of these discourses on gendered subjects. It also means that attention is not paid to the technical aspects of women's work and this fails to explore the extent to which performing 'technical' work under 'dirty' and 'noisy' conditions - a description which more usually describes men's manual work - has any impact on the construction and reinforcement of gender subjectivities on the shopfloor. But this never formed part of the discussion of either women's work or gender segregation in Pollert's book. I would argue that this is because of the concept of gender that is used to interpret the ethnographic material.

Pollert analyses the occupational segregation she observed in the factory in terms of the interplay of market and ideological factors. The following illustrate her thinking on these issues. As she explains:

> Qualities such as close concentration, accuracy and manual dexterity which require obvious skill and training in craft or technician's jobs are relegated to 'natural' and untrained 'aptitudes' in women doing women's occupations. And women's 'natural' functions, being family- and home-based, areas which are traditionally patronised as 'mere' women's territory, are hardly regarded as 'real work'. (Pollert 1981, p.65)

The problem with this is that it locates the causes of segregation in terms of their actual or assumed role in the family. That is, women are socialised into gender roles through various ideologies: for example, femininity, domesticity, motherhood and this ensures male dominance and is functional for capitalism. But Pollert's study clearly demonstrates the extent to which gender is a factor at work. This is evidenced by the way the women 'feminise' their working conditions. Pollert argues that the cult of femininity and domesticity which dominate the shopfloor is at one and the same time a point of resistance and a snare as the ideology of femininity ensures that women conceive themselves as primarily housewives and mothers, not as waged workers. As she states:

> dreams of escape were cushioned in a feminine culture as the girls tried to 'feminise' the ruthless atmosphere of the production line. Romance permeated the factory. The glowingly lipsticked magazine covers, the love stories, the male pop heroes, the pictures of boyfriends, the circulation of wedding photographs, all were a bizarre contrast to the racket of the dark oily machines. (Pollert 1981, p.101)

The suggestion in Pollert's work is that romance is an ideological trap that lures women into marriage and thus subordination. But why is romance a snare? It can only be a snare if you believe that women's emancipation and liberation will come through waged work, and if you believe that femininity equals subordination and powerlessness. The concept of gender that she uses is one that conceived gender as a category which one takes to work, and it is this 'gender' that impacts on work and in so doing 'feminises' the workplace. However the gendering process is a dynamic process not a static one, so the discourses of gender are being produced by the practices and strategies adopted by both women and men on the shopfloor. For example, around the notion of 'feminisation' lie a host of contradictory and complex strategies, negotiation and resistance on the part of women and on the part of men. There is a fluidity to the process of the social construction of femininity and masculinity that needs to be grasped. Part of this gendering process is the way women and men interact at work.

Pollert, by her concentration on one aspect of gender - the ideology of femininity - interprets the contradictions of gender operating only in relation to women and the culture of femininity. This one sided view of the operation of gender marginalises the extent to which men and masculinity also occupy contradictory positions, and the process by which masculinity and femininity are constituted through interacting at work.

Gender and Men

The neglect of men and masculinity in this account is one of the weaknesses of the book and is related to the concept of gender that is used. Of men, Pollert writes:

> As breadwinners, men become cut off from the families they support; as oppressors who hold the purse strings over women, they are also oppressed, deprived of children, of domestic enjoyments and skills. Women's oppression is the other side of this coin: the privatised family becomes their cage, the men their overlords. (Pollert 1981, pp.110-11)

The assumption of male dominance and female subordination in the family is evident by this quote. Yet, this view is contradicted by the remarks made by the women when they discuss their attitude towards the family. These women did not experience the family in the manner described above all the time. It is indicated from the interview material presented in the book that the women did not perceive family and domestic life as mundane or empty, and that despite women's ambivalence around marriage (1981, p.98) for both women and men, it is waged labour which is an 'iron cage' which limits their freedom and activities. Work is described as the prison and the family is viewed as an escape route from the alienation experienced at the workplace. As Pollert states:

> But while the immediate experience of the work inevitably 'rubbed off' on to them, ... part of this experience was also aversion to being 'factors of production'. This meant they looked not just to the daily escape from work, but again to a 'career' in marriage, as a total alternative. (Pollert 1981, p.99)

The contradictions and complexity of both women and men's relationship to paid work and the family is continually revealed by the research material, but these contradictions are not attended to. So while it is mentioned that:

> Men too, are centred on their families and discuss them at work. But (according to Pollert) they relate to them differently: their family is part of their concern as father and breadwinner. With women it is the immediate,

intimate and daily concern with actual processes of family care which penetrates and alters their consciousness of work. Work is overshadowed by the family. (Pollert 1981, p.113)

It is not made clear why she thinks the men hold different views of work and the family to women. Unfortunately, there is no discussion of the way men experience work or their relationships with women both inside the factory and inside the family. The assumption made is that men's lives are structured only by their wage labour and their exploitation as workers and that their experience of work is known, and therefore does not need to be examined. She writes:

Their responses would be a subject in itself; but my main preoccupation was not with men or masculine identity for themselves but only in the ways they were woven into the women's experience. (Pollert 1981, p.8)

The lack of analysis of men can be related to her use of a 'gender' model in her analysis of women and a 'job' model in her evaluation of men (see Feldberg and Glenn 1984).[3] These models assume that men's social relationships are determined by the type of work they do and that women's relationships are determined by the family. It is clear that this explanatory framework is shaping Pollert's interpretation of women's work and men's work. Yet her reference to male power in the text demonstrates that her gender model is connected to the concept of patriarchy that represents men as dominant and women are subordinate. This theoretical approach, especially when linked with Marxism, pushes a structural explanation for both women's and men's position in the labour force rather than promoting an examination of the construction and process of gendering at the workplace. So Pollert's account, despite its analytical strengths never answers the question she set herself, which is:

What, in short, is distinctive about wage labour for a woman, because of her socialisation as a woman and her oppression as a woman? (Pollert 1981, pp.5-6)

The problem still remains unanswered. How do the women in Pollert's study 'make sense' of the jobs they do given the discourse of femininity which socialises women - a discourse which positions women as unskilled, technically incompetent, used and abused by technology and science, subordinate and dominated by men and whose major preoccupations are marriage, children and family? For Pollert the answer is that these women are not 'bound' to their work, rather they are tied to family and domestic life:

'Women's work' has a lower status, to both men and women, than unskilled men's work. It is effeminate, to men, without being 'feminine' to women.

> While heavy manual work can be culturally appropriated by working-class men to celebrate maleness and machismo, the so-called 'light' manual work of women cannot be subjectively understood as in any way complimentary to their sexual or class self-image. All it does is confirm further the deprecatory self-perception of women as patient, passive and inferior creatures, fit for the mundane tasks of assembly work and housework. There is no way girls can use the cultural system of inverting the status of mental and manual labour to confirm in their own terms the value of their future in unskilled work. (Pollert 1981, p.97)

In this account masculinity is realised through work, whereas femininity is acquired through marriage, motherhood and family. Pollert's study strives to capture the lived experience of women's working lives and the interplay between women's oppression and their exploitation as waged labour. The originality of this study lies in this analytical focus, that is, the impact on the organisation of work of *women* workers and the impact of paid *work* on women. However by ignoring gender relations at work and the process of interaction between women and men, she is unable to account for the contradictions and complexity of women and men's (gender) responses to work, both paid and unpaid.

All Day Every Day

Sallie Westwood's book *All Day Every Day* (1984) is very similar in content to the one described above. The research for this book was conducted from March 1980 through to May 1981 and it is a good example of someone trying to struggle with the theoretical problems experienced by feminists analysing the workplace at this time. The introductory chapter directly engages with the debates on patriarchy and capitalism and the problem posed to both these analyses by the question of 'race'. From her discussion of the different approaches she provides a rationale for the dual-systems approach. She states:

> My analysis takes seriously the claim that the economic level is also affected by the ideological and the political and that because of this patriarchy has a material base not only in the way in which men control and exploit women's labour power, but in the way in which patriarchal ideologies intervene at the economic level. Ideologies are both outside and within individual subjectivities, and they play a vital part in calling forth a sense of self linked to class and gender as well as race. Thus, a patriarchal ideology intervenes on the shopfloor and subverts the creative potential of shopfloor culture to make anew the conditions of work under capitalism. (Westwood 1984, p.6)

Dual-system theory takes two forms: one stresses the patriarchy side of the intersection with capitalism; the other takes the form of a stress on capitalist interaction with patriarchy. In Pollert's study the stress is on *capitalism* shaping patriarchy whereas in this study the emphasis is on *patriarchy* shaping capitalism. She explains her understanding of the concept of patriarchy with the following quote from Heidi Hartmann:

> The material base upon which patriarchy rests lies most fundamentally in men's control over women's labour power. Men maintain this control by excluding women from access to some essential productive resources (in capitalist societies, for example, jobs that pay living wages) and by restricting women's sexuality. Monogamous heterosexual marriage is one relatively recent and efficient form that seems to allow men to control both these areas. (Hartmann cited in Westwood 1984, p.5)

Male power is assumed in this model and there is also the assumption that capitalism and patriarchy are compatible and sustaining for men. By contrast, women are viewed as subordinate, powerless and negligible in the same operating system. Paradoxically, however, the descriptions of women's lives, as in the texts discussed above, demonstrate the contradictions of this approach. Sallie Westwood writes that her study shows:

> the interaction of patriarchy and capitalism in the factory and the home, and the response the women make to this by generating and sustaining a shopfloor culture which structures the way that becoming a worker, through a woman's role in production, and becoming a woman, through her role in reproduction, are brought together and reinforced. It is an oppositional culture, providing a focus for resistance to managerial authority and demands, while forging solidarity and sisterhood. It is also an ambiguous resistance because it so clearly colludes in promoting a specific version of womanhood. (Westwood 1984, p.230)

This, however, is precisely what needs to be explained. What or where is the source or the origin of the resistance in patriarchal capitalism? Which elements of patriarchal capitalism produce the resistance? What is the process whereby women both resist and collude with their subordination?

Like Cavendish's and Pollert's accounts, Westwood's *All Day Every Day* represents another case study of low-paid, segregated work; this time in a hosiery factory. Both books have a similar structure in that they examine the labour process, the ethnic differences between the women, discuss women's resistance to changes in the wages and bonus scheme, the problem of trade unions and relations with a male hierarchy. In this factory, 43% of the women were from the Asian sub-continent and 5% were Black women of Caribbean origin. There was no mention of Irish

women, though she does say that there is a large Irish community in the
area. It is unclear if the white women workers are Irish or English.

Westwood's account however develops and expands the description
and analysis of women's working lives by introducing a discussion of
distinctions between women on the factory floor.   In this study the
differences between the women are observed, and though this is not
discussed in any theoretical way, the issues of power differentials between
women is mentioned.   So, for example, the personnel manager was a
woman.   Some women occupied supervisory positions as production
managers and time and motion officers.   For the first time in studies of
working women's lives, women workers are shown to have power and
control of both women and men on the shopfloor.   Consequently the issue
of power relations between women other than those of 'race' and class are
added to the combination of gender relations on the shopfloor.   Unlike the
women in Cavendish's study, the women were aware of their skill even
though they were classed as semi-skilled.   The issues around gender and
skill are not a feature of the book.   Rather the distinctive thrust, and main
theme of Westwood's account lies in her analysis and description of the
practices around the 'women's culture' which dominates the shopfloor.
She describes this as 'domesticating production' (1984, p.22) but her study
is more concerned with analysing how this culture colludes with and re-
enforces domesticity.   Both Cavendish and Pollert present women's
workers attachment to marriage and the family as a form of 'false
consciousness' and whilst these women may view marriage as an escape
from dull, noisy work, the view that emerges from these accounts is that
marriage is a location for the reproduction of gender inequalities and thus
traps women into a position of dependence on men.   In contrast,
Westwood's account points to the importance of marriage and family for
women's subject position as women.   The women workers she interviews
refer to marriage as part of the transition to womanhood.   It is about
becoming a woman, becoming an adult and a mother, and thus marriage
represents a celebration of motherhood and femininity and is a crucial
aspect of women's subjectivity and identity.   These aspects of women's
lives are represented in a much more positive light than in the previous
accounts and demonstrate an awareness and consciousness of the problems
of femininity, but also their power in relation to the discourse.   What is
striking in Westwood's account is the detailed description of the elaborate
and joyous shopfloor culture organised by the women around marriage and
motherhood. This emphasis on the 'culture' of the shopfloor is, in part, due
to the discipline that informs the writer.   Westwood is an anthropologist.
So one of the central themes of the book is an analysis of the ideological

components of women's culture in relation to domesticity, love and romance. The focus of the work is the extent to which these elements both constitute 'women's culture' and allow women to both dominate and control the environment of the factory. In this account, the strength of the culture is demonstrated by the ways women are able, at times, to resist managerial control and discipline in the factory.

Discourses of Femininity as Resistance

The key points of resistance were around the celebration of births, marriages, engagements and leave-taking. Much of the book is taken up with detailed discussions of the way celebrations around these events consume so much of the women's energy and time on the shopfloor that they interfere with the production targets at the factory. Westwood tells how the women 'use' material in order to make costumes for the prospective brides. She describes how engagements, birthdays and retirement parties are celebrated inside working hours by long lunches either in the canteen or in the pub. As she says:

> The women of StitchCo ... saw in the informal organisation of the shopfloor the major resistance to management controls, given that the union was not playing the part that many of the women felt that it should. It was also the case ... that the elaborate rituals surrounding weddings and brides meant that company time and resources were used not for profit, but for the women on the shopfloor. Their rights to this time and these resources were acknowledged by management who knew from experience that if they attacked these spaces they would have a walk-off to deal with. . . Women on the shopfloor attacked life with great energy and verve; there was nothing to suggest defeat or submission or that they were cyphers or puppets. (Westwood 1984, p.90)

Hard, Tough, Technical Work

What is evident from the description of the labour process is that the work was hard, tough and hazardous. It was also environmentally stressful due to the amount of dust that came from the material. There are some references in the text to the fact that women are interested in the 'technical side' (1984, p.23) of their work but this is never explored. It is reported that women had to wait for their machines to be serviced and repaired by male mechanics, which also set the machine for tension etc., while women were expected to clean the machines and change the needles. There is a big difference in wages between the women who use the sewing machines and the men who are the knitters (1984, p.41). It is also the case that men are able to secure higher remuneration for their labour in part due to the fact that only male knitters are able to work shifts (1984, p.60). These gender differences are explained, as in the Cavendish and the Pollert studies, by reference to male power and patriarchy as originating in the family. However Westwood's analysis is much more alert to the contradictions and complexities of this explanation. She states:

> The preceding chapters have shown the interaction of patriarchy and capitalism in the factory and the home, and the response the women make to this by generating and sustaining a shopfloor culture which structures the way that becoming a worker, through a women's role in production, and becoming a woman, through their role in reproduction, are brought together and reinforced. It is an oppositional culture, providing a focus for resistance to managerial authority and demands, while forging solidarity and sisterhood. It is also an ambiguous resistance because it so clearly colludes in promoting a specific version of womanhood. ... Women ... have a relationship to the means of production which, on the whole, gives them non-living wages and makes them an impoverished section of the working class; it is because of this that they look to marriage as a means to higher wages and access to resources controlled by men. This means that women have a second relationship to class through their relationship to the male wage which reinforces their dependence and subordination in relation to men. (Westwood 1984, pp.230-1)

On Men and Patriarchy

Westwood analyses men's power and privilege by focusing on male control of women through domestic labour and on the way men maintain this power either by committing and/or threatening physical violence (see ibid., pp.182-6). Thus her focus for the analysis of gender segregation and gender shopfloor relations shifts from the workplace to the family. However she only discusses these relationships from the point of view of women. For Westwood the strong sense of a shared women's culture is constructed through women's commitment to the family, motherhood and children. She writes:

> There was no doubt ... that the family was important to all the women on the shopfloor: it provided them with an area of life that they believed was beyond production and the marketplace and the arm of the state. Neither, of course, is strictly true, but that was how the women understood family life. It was valuable and important and must by protected and nurtured by women who alone had the abilities to create an emotionally supportive environment for others. The family the women spent their time and energy creating and sustaining was a patriarchal family in which men had a

privileged position, just as they do in the workplace. (Westwood 1984, p.187)

Sallie Westwood concludes her study by arguing that her account demonstrates women's deep commitment to their families, especially their children. There is an underlying assumption in the book that men do not share this commitment and, in this way, the traditional separate spheres of women and men are re-presented in a manner which echoes traditional mainstream sociology's assumptions that women and men occupy separate and distinct spheres. This is so despite the fact that she stresses that "the world of work and the world of the home are not two separate spheres" (1984, p.158) but she only discusses this in relation to women. As men are never interviewed around a discussion of their views of the family, there is an underlying assumption that for men family and work are separate worlds.

As Feldberg and Glenn (1984) argue, sociologists and feminists studying women at work tend to bring with them cultural perceptions which shape the way they concentrate on some aspects of women's lives and neglect others. These authors looked at the assumptions that shape the research and suggest that different models operate in relation to studies of women and men at work - namely a job model or a work model for men and a gender model for women. The assumptions of the gender model are that the central life interest and basic social relations are, in the case of women, determined by the family. Men, on the other hand, are seen to be determined by their work and the fact that this is their central life interest. Feldberg and Glenn argue that the role of the family needs to be considered more when evaluating men and work and the opposite needs to apply in relation to research on women and work. Though Sallie Westwood's study, and the other studies examined in this chapter are clear attempts to change these assumptions in respect of women's relationships to their paid work, a similar framework is not adopted in examining the contradictions and complexities of men's relationship with paid work and the family. The result is that the complexities of gender at work are obscured by the emphasis on the family model for women and the work model for men. So, for example, though the women are emphatic about their commitment to waged work (Westwood 1984, p.71), this commitment is constructed as simply a component of women's family responsibilities and is subsumed by the overwhelming concentration in the book on romance, marriage reproduction and domesticity.

Establishing an Orthodoxy

In these accounts, the theoretical framework that is used to study women's paid work represents a model of gender relations that is reminiscent of the static conceptions of sex role categories that dominated functionalist sociology. The contradictory lived experiences of women's lives are discussed as though femininity is a structure that is placed on women by virtue of being born a woman and the way women are socialised. Though the studies demonstrate the contradictions of the ideology of femininity for women's work, they fail to consider the contradictions for men of the ideology of masculinity, work and the family. As Westwood writes: 'For many women (and this is true of men as well) home and family appear as the only area of freedom in a routinised life' (1984, p.157), but there is no evidence presented in the text which report on men's thoughts on the family. Though the study makes numerous references to the ideology of the family which structures the culture of factory life for women, and the contradictions this produces for women, there are no references to the contradictions of masculinity for men. What becomes established by these accounts is an explanation of gender segregation at work which argues that women's position at work is determined by her reproductive role and the role of domestic labourer; and that these roles are structured by the ideology of femininity.

Patriarchy at Work

Sylvia Walby's *Patriarchy at Work* (1986) goes some way to contradict this thesis. Her analysis challenged the view that patriarchy and capitalism interacted as mutually functional systems, and presents an explicitly theoretical defence of the concept of patriarchy to explain gender segregation at work. One of the most interesting changes Walby proposes to the framework that is used in the previous studies is that she characterises the relationship between patriarchy and capitalism as one of *tension and conflict*. Using this formulation she sets out to establish a theory of patriarchy that overcomes some of the commonly acknowledged problems of the concept. She criticises other writers for adopting a functionalist correspondence between these two systems and claims that conceptualising the systems in *tension* enables the problems with patriarchy to be overcome, especially the criticism that many of the accounts using this type of analysis tend to be descriptive rather than analytical. Walby, in an early chapter in the book, critically evaluates some of the criticisms and reservations about the concept of patriarchy established by Beechey (1979), Barrett (1980), and Rowbotham (1982). On the basis of this critique she dismisses any suggestion that patriarchy is unable to produce a theory of women's oppression. She writes:

> The problems of reductionism, bioligism, universalism, and inconsistent definition should be seen as problems in specific texts which need to be overcome in an adequate analysis of gender inequality, not problems with the concept of patriarchy itself. (Walby 1986, p.28)

Using the framework that patriarchy is a system at variance with capitalism she stresses the contradictions of patriarchal structures in wage labour. Her view is that women's position in the family has been largely historically determined by their position in paid work rather than the reverse, and that, when women were denied equality of paid employment either through the strategy of exclusion from areas of work or through the strategy of occupational segregation, they then turn to unpaid employment within the home. She states:

> Against the traditional view that the position of women in the labour market is determined by their position in the family, I will argue for the importance of labour market structures in confining women to a subordinate position in the household. (Walby 1986, p.1)

It is important to note here the shift from a discussion of gender segregation and the labour process (which is the focus for the texts examined above) to the study of gender segregation and the labour market, which is the term that Walby uses.[4]

Historical Analysis of Gender Segregation

Walby demonstrates the significance of patriarchal relations in securing women's occupational segregation through an historical and comparative examination of this process considering three distinct areas of employment, the cotton industry, engineering and clerical work. Through three historical periods: 1800-1914, 1914-45 and post-1945, Walby investigates the conflicts between the desire of capitalists for cheap labour in these industries which produces tensions for male power and desires in relation to their position in the family and their position in employment. By exploring the shifts and movements between the system of patriarchy and capitalism, she analyses the strategies of job segregation used by men to secure their positions in employment. These strategies involve organising to safeguard their jobs by allowing women's jobs to be constructed as unskilled or semi-skilled and actively excluding women from jobs designated as skilled. A particularly good section of the book is the discussion of these strategies around the Factory Acts (1844, 1847, 1867,

1874, 1878, 1891, 1895, 1901), particularly in the engineering and cotton
industries. This section contains a very thorough historical account of the
impact these Acts had on women's access to work and to skilled (or jobs
classified as skilled) jobs. Without the support of similar historical
evidence and data that lays such a good foundation for the theoretical
model, the accounts of the other two periods she studies tend (again) to fall
into purely descriptive accounts of job segregation. If, however, the
richness of the historical evidence was available for the later periods would
her theoretical model hold as a framework for an explanation of gender
segregation?

Critical Review of Patriarchy at Work

Sylvia Walby's analysis of the articulation of the patriarchal mode of
production with the capitalist mode of production, wherein it is the
capitalist mode which is the dominant mode and important in respect of the
dynamic and changing nature of patriarchy relations and strategies is
problematic. This notion of dominance becomes strained when applied to
the analysis of job segregation in the different historical periods. For
example, in her discussion of the cotton industry in the period 1800-1914,
what she fails to explain is why women were encouraged to enter this
industry and by whom? If the answer is by capitalism why was capitalism
stronger than patriarchy at this time and if patriarchy succeeded in
restricting women's employment why was patriarchy stronger/dominant?
In her analysis of the role of the state she does not explain what determined
the position of the state in relation to the Factory Acts. Why was it the case
that the state chose to act on behalf of patriarchal relations and not capitalist
relations on these issues? If I do appear to have many criticisms of
Walby's work, this should not detract from some of its strengths. I found
the study particularly interesting especially her discussion of the period
1800-1914 and the historical research around the Factory Acts, (though
even this period is discussed without any reference to the ideology of
femininity which was gaining such a stronghold from the 1830s). Walby
does usefully point to the notion of conflict and tension in relation to
gender inequality and capitalism; but it proves difficult for her to maintain
this analytical mode throughout the book

In Walby's study of later historical periods, these positions are
reversed. For example, the placing on the statute books of equal
opportunities, equal pay and sex discrimination legislation (however
inadequate) are still examples of state intervention in the arena of women's
employment. What needed to be explained here is the key determinants
underlying these shifts and how women's positions and women's struggles

were pertinent to these shifts. For although women's struggles are referred to throughout the book there is little examination of them. Though it is claimed that:

> Neither did women docilely withdraw from paid work when men wanted them to, on marriage, or at the end of wars, or during depressions. They were pushed vigorously, and vigorously resisted. (Walby 1986, p.247)

What is left unexplained is how and why women resisted these attempts to exclude them from the workplace and why they were not successful? Why were women able to resist men and assert their independence as workers? If these questions are not addressed the historical picture which emerges is a history of the failure of women which repeats the representation that men are stronger and more powerful.

This quiescent image of women appears again in Walby's discussion of part-time work (Walby 1986, p.207) where she writes: 'part-time work thus represented the new form of the compromise between patriarchal and capitalist interests'. Even if this were the case, what of women's own consciousness of part-time work? Part-time work could be conceived by women workers in a positive manner. Recent feminist discussion of the question of 'time' and its importance for women can be linked to a demand that part-time work with proper rates and conditions could well provide a useful model of paid employment and that this alternative can be incorporated into a feminist economic strategy (Phillips 1981).

Thus whilst I can agree with Walby's statement that 'gender inequality cannot be understood without the concept of patriarchy' (1986, p.243), this is only the first rung on the ladder of understanding gender inequality. The understanding produced at this level is that the inequalities between men and women can be demonstrated and described and it is clear that men are a problem - by this I mean the practices which are constituted in discourse which shape men's activities and subjectivity. The different areas that Walby uses in her outline of patriarchy are useful here. She point to 'sets of patriarchal relations in the workplace, the state, sexuality and other practices in civil society' (1986, p.247). Men tend to have more power, authority and status than women. But the nature of that power and the impact on women differs and is dependent on a wide set of variables of class, ethnicity, sexuality, status, geographical location, etc. These same variables also shape differences and diversity amongst men. Patriarchy does not produce an understanding of difference and diversity or an analysis of changes in relation to gender inequality. In order to understand how gender inequality changes, and is both produced, reproduced and resisted, it is necessary to have a more fluid and dynamic notion of gender than that produced by the notion of gender contained in the concept of patriarchy.   Before I examine that question I would like to point to one important theoretical shift Walby makes by her attempt to defend the concept of patriarchy from the charge of biological reductionism.   A key element of the historical analysis she presents is her notion of a patriarchal culture constituted around a set of practices - for example - the practices of exclusion described above.   She then links these practices to the discourses of masculinities and femininities that she argues are important for women and men experiences of work and the shaping of gendered subjectivity (see Walby 1989).   She analyses patriarchal cultural practices as a 'set of discourses which are institutionally-rooted, rather than as ideology which is either free-floating or economically-determined' (ibid. 227).[5]   Though her analysis   concentrates   exclusively   on   social   structure   (1986, p.71) nevertheless this construction of the discourses of patriarchal practices shaping men's and women's experiences of work shifts the emphasis away from positioning men (real) men as having power over women to the analysis of the discourses which shape the gendering of work.   It is this insight that I wish to develop.

Without reference to discourse, the concept of patriarchy is unable to account for differences amongst men and amongst women.   Thus men and women are represented as opposites, as separate, homogeneous groups. Male power and male domination are deemed 'natural' in this account, the origins or sources or reasons behind patriarchy are not explored and one is forced from this analysis to consider the possibility that there is some kind of biological mechanism in men which pushes or forces them to dominate women.   The thinking about gender that informs the use of the notion of patriarchy is still being employed in the texts discussed in this chapter. However there is a very important caveat that needs to be made here.   I have been arguing that patriarchy sets up a particular concept of gender, one that slants the analysis towards gender as a category that is *fixed*.   My argument is that in order to understand gender segregation at work then a concept of gender as *fluid* is necessary in order to capture the process of gendering work which produces segregation.   But there are two different levels of investigating the phenomenon of segregation.   Occupational segregation can be examined either at the level of the labour market or at the level of the labour process.

Studies of the *labour process* need to utilise a concept of gender that is fluid and relational in order to capture the process of gendering at the workplace.   Given the different focus of *labour market* studies it may well be useful for this type of analysis of use gender as a category.   The focus in studies of the labour market is on outcomes rather than processes.   Shifting between these different levels without paying attention to the concept of gender that is most applicable has lead to considerable confusion in the study of gender relations at work.

Constructing an Orthodoxy

In conclusion, in this chapter I have set out how an orthodoxy on gender segregation came to be established through a number of key texts written towards the end of the 1970s and into the 1980s. This orthodoxy relies on a concept of patriarchy that positions women in relation to men as oppositional. In these accounts, men are dominant and women are subordinate. But gender differences and gender ideologies/discourses are not static or rigid. By foregrounding the notion of gender differences and by stressing the implacability of patriarchy, the dynamics of the interplay between women and men, women and women, men and men in the workplace is missing. Women and men do not enter the workplace 'totally' gendered, as unified gendered subjects. Gender is a relational concept not a static one: this means that gender is reproduced in the day-to-day interactions of the workplace and the home. These two spheres, as Joan Kelly (1979) says, interact. These different areas of social reality operate together, not separately. Thus the private intrudes on the public and this includes: sexuality, pleasure, desire - and the public interacts with the private and this includes working at home, having friends at work visit you at home, having friendships at work (perhaps both women and men) as the mainstay of your private life. Kelly argues that it is necessary to understand that:

> in any of the historical forms that patriarchal society takes (feudal, capitalist, socialist, etc.), a sex-gender system and a system of productive relations operate simultaneously ... to reproduce the socio-economic and male-dominant structures of that particular social order. (Kelly 1979, p.61)

Thus, rather than use a notion of gender difference (which patriarchy as a concept more than facilitates) it is necessary to understand and analyse gender as a process, constantly reproducing and (re)presenting, negotiating, resisting the social construction of gender. It is also important to note that process is not only about power, dominance, and subordination but also about pleasure and desire. The problems surrounding the static notion of gender created by the concept of patriarchy has also affected the research on gender and technology, as I will demonstrate in a later chapter. It is important to note that these problems are present even though people do not explicitly use the term 'patriarchy'; gender theorising is still informed by this notion. This is largely because 'patriarchy' was for so long the centrepiece of feminist analysis, and marked feminism off from other sociological theories of segregation.

These theoretical problems were not as obvious to me when I began my empirical research. Though my research project had been developed with some critical reservations around the concept of patriarchy initially this meant that I felt it was important to investigate gender as relational and so I was determined to interview men as well as women. It also meant that I was sensitive to the notion that men and women were not homogeneous groups. Consequently at the stage when I began to conduct the empirical research, the only way my critique of patriarchy informed my approach to the research I undertook on computer programmers was that I wanted to produce a study of gender relations that included men. However I still retained a static conceptualisation of gender that meant that I was not as alert as I needed to be to the notion of gender as a *process*.

The other theoretical problem that affected my research was the feminist orthodoxy on gender segregation that was very firmly established by the time I began to interpret my material. Flowing from this orthodoxy are a number of strategies primarily around equal opportunities policies which were geared towards attempting to change labour market conditions for women as a way of challenging segregation. This approach to gender inequalities at work shifted attention away from the actual processes and practices of gendering at work. The organisation of this book reflects these theoretical shifts and dilemmas. So, for example, in the chapters that examine the labour process of computer programming my discussion is framed by factors affecting the gendering of the labour market rather than the labour process. It is only in the subsequent chapters that I begin to interpret the discourses that shape the practices and thus the process that constitute the work of the programmers I interviewed.

In summary there is obviously a relationship between the two levels of analysis and this is evident by my discussion. Any shifts which occur in relation to destabilising stereotypical notions of what constitutes 'women's work' or 'men's work' will depend on a complex set of factors. Some of these factors include: the culture and traditions of the industry, occupation or organisation; the status of the occupation; the numbers of women in the workplace in relation to men; the extent to which the work is regarded as unskilled; the strength and power of the union organisation and the extent to which the union and management are influenced by equal opportunities perspectives. Another crucial factor is sexuality, especially women's sexuality. In the ideology of femininity women are sex objects, they are marked by their bodies and so bring sexuality into the workplace. There is very little attention paid to this aspect of gender and work in these early studies as the aim was to demonstrate the extent to which gender is a factor in the organisation of work. The texts reviewed in this chapter sought to theorise the reproduction of gender segregation of jobs by drawing attention to the capitalist and patriarchal structures of power. Though the studies also identified the strategies of resistance by women to gender inequalities of power they fail to focus on the process of reproduction of gendered job segregation. Rather they established a feminist orthodoxy which though it enabled the production of a valuable literature, both historical and contemporary of women's work, it failed to theorise: (i) women as an active subject at work; (ii) the contradictions for women's and men's of the discourses which shape the organisation of work and; (iii) the impact of these discourses on gender identity and subjectivies.

Notes

[1]   It is important to note that I am not denying the existence of male power and gender inequalities - and that I use the concept of patriarchy to refer to this system, in other words as a descriptive concept. I am using the term 'system' to signify a complex order whose 'principles of organization shift over time' (Hennessy 1993, p.18). Though I am not entirely happy with this formulation a discussion of the differences between a Marxist notion of systems versus Foucault's use of the term networks is beyond the scope of this book.

[2]   This is a pseudonym taken by the sociologist Miriam Glucksmann, see her discussion in *Women Assemble* (1990).

[3]   A fuller discussion on these models is provided below.

[4]   This is a critical point for studies of gender segregation.

[5]   The distinction between discourse and ideology is discussed in the concluding chapter to this book.

Chapter 4

Programming Sexism

The argument thus far is that the feminist orthodoxy that emerged during the 1980s explained gender segregation in terms of the interaction of patriarchy and capitalism and contained a number of difficulties. (i) It explained segregation as functional for capitalism. (ii) It describes the strategies of male workers but is unable to explain them. (iii) This tended to stress men's power and women's lack of power. (iv) That consequently it is unable to offer an explanation for the contradictions of women and men's positions on the shop floor; (v) and hence to provide an explanation for women's resistance, organisation and feminisation of the shop floor. As Beechey and Perkins concluded this explanatory framework presents

> a gloomy depiction of women, who appear as passive victims of a series of interconnected institutions - the family, the state and the labour market. (Beechey and Perkins 1987, p.123)

One of the explanations I offer for the failure of this model to explain segregation is that the static nature of the concept of gender that is embedded in the concept of patriarchy produced an analysis that emphasised male power and female subordination. This formulation neglects the process of gendering at work and the negotiated and contradictory aspects of gendered social relations. Consequently an explanation of the continual process of the construction of gender identities and subjectivities and the implications of this for the interpretation of workplace practices is lacking.

The research presented in the following chapters attempts to offer a more qualitative approach using the concept of discourse that was outlined in the previous chapter. However before this is discussed a profile of computer programming if offered.

Segregation in the Computer Industry

As a recent overview of occupational segregation in a number of specific occupations in the European Community that included computer professionals, Rubery and Fagan (1993) noted that in theory, 'tradition' a concept that has been used to explain the persistence of segregation couldn't be used as an explanation in this industry. However in practice, they found that 'women are seriously underrepresented among computer professionals in all member states' (ibid. p.70). They also point out that statistics of this occupation are very difficult to compile as different countries and organisations use different titles for staff in computing. Given this proviso, they found that women represent fewer than 30% of the workers in this industry across the European Community.

Table 4.1: Share of women among computer professionals and related occupations

	All	Analysts	Analyst/ programmer	Programmer
Belgium	13 (1981)	-	-	-
Denmark	29 (1991)	-	-	-
Germany	21 (1989)	-	-	-
Greece	-	11 (1980)	19 (1980)	-
Spain	-	25 (1992)	-	45 (1992)
France	22 (1990)	-	-	-
Ireland	28 (1986)	-	-	-
Luxembourg	-	-	-	-
Netherlands	-	8 (1991)	-	13 (1991)
Portugal	-	-	-	-
UK	20 (1989)	29 (1992)	-	23 (1992)

Source: Rubery and Fagan 1993, p.71.

As Rubery and Fagan point out from this table 'women appear to occupy a particularly high share of the lower level programming jobs' (ibid., p.70). Yet, they also found that in some countries women were increasing their share of jobs as computer professionals whilst in others their numbers were declining, see table 4.2. below.

This report makes an appeal for a more qualitative approach to the study of occupational segregation in order to understand why the labour market statistics show that gender segregation is at a high level in every European labour market. This book is an attempt to assist in this approach by studying the process of segregation among computer professionals.

The study of computer programmers presented below examines the process of vertical segregation in this occupation. The focus in this chapter is on the practices that constructed and reproduce gender divisions.

Subsequent chapters examine the research material by exploring the discourses that underpin these practices.

Table 4.2: Trends in female share of computer professional occupations

Countries with increasing shares	1979-85 %	1989-90 %
Spain *	17 (1980)	29 (1990)
France	19 (1984)	22 (1990)
Netherlands		
systems analysts	5 (1979)	10 (1989)
programmers	8 (1979)	15 (1989)
Germany	19 (1980)	21 (1989)
East Germany		15 (1989)
Countries with stable/decreasing shares		
Denmark		
private sector	25 (1985)	24 (1991)
public sector	42 (1985)	38 (1991)
UK	21 (1984)	19.5 (1989)

Note: * refers to mathematicians, statisticians and related occupations.

Source: Rubery and Fagan 1993, p.72.

By 1984, in the literature on women and computing a contradiction had emerged between those studies which suggest that because computing is a relatively new industry, women who have entered the field are employed on equal terms with men, or at least on more equal terms than in other branches of industry or commerce (Deakin 1984). This argument is based on the view that computing as an occupation emerged at a time when there was a greater awareness of the legitimacy of equal opportunities, so that the institutionalised barriers which exist in other industries, which had their basis in traditional attitudes, practices and prejudice were absent due to the 'newness' of the industry.

The opposite view however is suggested by other researchers (Lloyd and Newell 1985; Morris 1989) who claim that whilst historically women in computing experienced similar job chances to men, this has now changed. It is estimated that in the 1950s and 1960s the share of women in programming and analyst jobs was around 50% but by the mid 1980s this share had dropped to around 20% (Newton 1991, cited in Rubery et al. 1992, p.80). The argument is that today women in this industry experience discrimination in computing, and that this discrimination is both widespread and deep-seated. Furthermore the traditional pattern of job segregation, which is a familiar feature of women's position in the labour market, is repeated in this industry (see Kraft 1979; Lloyd and Newell 1985; Strober and Arnold 1987). This means that as in other industries women are horizontally and vertically segregated into certain occupations and into positions which are routine, uninteresting, least skilled, have low status and are on the lower end of the pay scale (Hakim 1979; Walby 1986, Crompton and Sanderson 1990; Rubery and Fagan 1993). Men, on the other hand, do the high status jobs, which involve intellectual activity and 'skilled' technological competence. Men in these positions tend to receive above average rates of pay and have good career prospects. A traditional sexual division of labour has therefore emerged in the computing industry. This is particularly ironic given the fact that women were the first computer programmers. Moreover, in what is both a history and an analysis of the process of de-skilling within this occupation, Kraft points to the fact that,

> one of the ironies of programming is that women pioneered the occupation, largely by accident, only to make it attractive to men once the work was redefined as creative and important. The further irony, however is that the men who followed the women pioneers - and effectively eased them out of the industry - eventually had their work reduced into something that was genuinely like clerical labour. It was at this point that women were allowed to re-enter the occupation they had created. (Kraft 1979, p.5)

The Companies

In order to examine the process of segregation and de-skilling within computer programming, I conducted a series of interviews, from October 1987 to March 1988, in a number of organisations located in the North of England. I gained access to seven companies, five of which are computer software houses of varying sizes, and two in-house computer installations: one a multinational organisation dealing with pharmaceuticals and the other an internationally famous manufacturing company involved with defence.

Software houses are involved with the production of commercial computer applications whereas in-house computing departments develop their own programming systems and support staff. The staff base is usually extremely small, there is a rapid staff turnover and many of these companies do not become established concerns. Two of the houses in my sample are still established, the others have ceased business. *Radola plc* is one of the exceptions to this pattern as it is a nationally established computing business with the head office in Hull and divisions in Middlesex, Cardiff, and Sheffield. The staff base is correspondingly high: the head office employs 470 workers, Cardiff has 42, Sheffield 46 and Middlesex 147 employees and the total sales figures were in excess of £13,071.[1] The other software houses in my sample had a staff base of between 7 and 22 employees. All of these companies supply computer systems including systems design and programming services, packaged software. None of these organisations had an equal opportunities policy. *Ratigan and Co* is one of Britain's largest companies and is owned and managed in this country. The company manufactures products under six main categories: household, toiletry, food, wine, pharmaceuticals, and leisure. The household, toiletry and pharmaceutical division is located in Hull. The group's turnover is in excess of £900 million with 80% of sales coming from overseas.[2] The computer-programming department however was very small, consisting of eight members of staff, and a month after the research began, this section was closed as the company had decided to contract out their programming needs. This was part of a general rationalisation programme in the Hull division. There was no company policy on equal opportunities for women in the company. The annual reports from 1988 contain references to equal opportunities for disabled people, but there are no details available of the distribution of women throughout the companies.[3] The bulk of the interviews were conducted in an in-house installation that was part of an internationally renowned company who manufactured military aircraft. The computer division of this company produced programming packages covering all aspects of aircraft production, though the majority of the programmers worked in the business systems division. The military aircraft division is housed on a large site on the outskirts of the city of Hull. Nationally the company consists of seven divisions that produce, military and civil aircraft, army, air and navy weapons, electronic systems and space and communications systems. The company is one of the largest such companies in the world, has a national and international reputation for engineering and had begun to develop into new areas such as spacecraft and guided weapons systems. In 1985 the total workforce comprised about 75,000 people and in 1985 total sales figures were £2,648 million with 36% of sales to the British Ministry of Defence. The division near Hull employed a workforce of 4,500 people who design, manufacture and assemble components for aircraft such as the Hawk, Harrier and Airbus, and report aircraft in service with the R.A.F.

In March 1984 the corporate personnel department had produced an equal opportunity policy and each division in the company was asked to prepare a discussion paper on the subject. The company had been approached by the Baroness Platt of Writtel, the then chairperson of the Equal Opportunities Commission about the possibility of giving more consideration to the needs of women throughout the organisation. As part of the process of re-appraisal of the operation of this policy it was agreed that I would be able to conduct interviews on the project - gender and computing - and provide a report which assessed equal opportunities for computer programmers in the company.[4] The interview schedule covered a variety of issues centring on the areas of the nature of the work involved with computer programming as a labour process, the training and educational qualifications of these workers, and their family and home responsibilities. An analysis of the job descriptions given by both female and male computer programmers provides an insight into the gender differences in relation to two aspects of programming work. So for example, programming can consist of support for standard applications and project work which is usually a specialised programme for an individual client or a new production. Project work is more challenging, dynamic and complex and has more status and prestige in the occupation.

The Job: Computer Programming

In order to understand the job of a computer programmer it is necessary to outline some of the related occupations in the computer industry. I constructed the table (4.3) in order to outline the range of occupations in the industry.

The best way of explaining these positions, which range from computer engineers through to data-entry operators, is to consider the different jobs involved in the two related areas of computer hardware and computer software. These areas are related to the two disciplines at the heart of these occupations: engineering and mathematics. Hardware consists of those occupations that have to do with either the construction of the actual computer and the workings of the mechanical parts of the machine whereas; software is concerned with the operations of the machine.

Table 4.3: Range of occupations in the computing industry

Hardware	Software
Computer Scientists and Engineers	Computer Aided Design
Computer Design and Manufacturing	Software Engineers and Scientists
Computer Engineers	Data Applications
Computer Communications and Operations	Systems Analysts
	Programmers
Computer Aided Engineering	Support Staff Operators
	Data Entry Operators

The only governmental report on the industry was produced by the Institute of Manpower Studies on behalf of the Manpower Sub-Committee of the National Economic Development Office published in 1985 that reports on the supply and demand for computer related manpower (sic) (Anderson and Hersleb 1980). They list the number of people employed in the industry as 180,000 (ibid. vii) and mention the very high labour turnover rates in the industry. The survey indicates that these rates approach 20% for all computer staff, with applications programmers far exceeding this rate. They list the applications programmers as the entry point for the professional grades in the industry and identify staff shortfalls in this area as a serious problem for the industry. The serious shortages of programmers and analysts reported in this survey resulted in the recruitment of programming staff with varying educational qualifications, ranging from programmers whose qualifications consisted of '0' and 'A' level passes in computer studies, to those with vocational qualifications organised with the National Computer Centre, Training Opportunities Schemes (TOPS) to those with ordinary degrees and post-graduate qualifications in computer science. This wide variation is reflected in the educational qualifications of the respondents in my sample. The developments in computer hardware from the 1960s have been extraordinary and computers are now used in every manufacturing and service industry. As this report states, computers have,

> improved rapidly in terms of programmability, speed, power consumption, flexibility and range of applications, reliability, durability, and above all miniaturisation and cheapness. (ibid., p.3)

In the 1950s and 1960s, computers referred to as mainframes, were large and extremely complicated, occupied a wide area, and were used only by big corporations and the state, usually the military. Computer users (mainly men)[5] at this time would be able to build, program and operate the machine. A division of labour then begins to emerge when the job of programming is given to women, the ENIAC 'girls' (see below). By the 1970s computers were getting smaller, though still filling a small room, and were increasingly being used by a range of organisations, but the operating systems were still complicated and require specialised knowledge. These computers were usually referred to as terminals, though usually this type of machine still needed to be networked into a mainframe. By the 1980s personal computers (pc) became widely available, and more importantly, notably cheaper. No expert knowledge is needed to operate these machines as the applications are programmed for easy use (Fisher 1994). These machines are now commonplace both in the home and in the workplace, and through the growth of the Internet has revolutionised information and communications systems. These developments increased the demand for programmers, and while the cost of computer hardware plummeted, the opposite happened in software manufacture. The ratio of software, relative to hardware, is almost 90%. This, combined with labour shortage of programmers, has resulted in manufacturers of computer hardware moving over into software production, making it more difficult for small software houses to survive. These costs also resulted in much of the software being encoded into the machines, and the development of more and more assessable programme packages in an effort to reduce the rise in the cost of programming skills, especially programme maintenance costs which can take up as much as 60% of a programmer's time (Fisher 1994, p.10). The international division of labour allied with telecommunications is making it increasingly cost effective and efficient for companies to move software production to India, China and South East Asia. (Heeks 1993 quoted in Webster 1994; Shapiro 1994). As mentioned above (Rubery and Fagan 1993) one of the difficulties in researching this area is that similar occupations are given different titles in different areas of industry, in commercial and manufacturing industries and between different companies. So for example, the Manpower Report (see Anderson and Hersleb 1985) attempts to provide statistics for staff employed in the industry by classifying programmers under three different headings: analyst-programmers, software programmers, and applications programmers; which taken together comprise 22.2% of computing staff. These divisions can be roughly understood as reflecting a hierarchy in programming which can be related to seniority, from chief (or head) systems programmer to a junior, or trainee programmer. The term systems analyst has been commonly used from the 1960s for the person who designs and implements a new programme, so effectively they tend to be project leaders. Different types of programmers - depending on the complexity of the programme -

would work with the systems analyst and together they would write specified sections of programme. It is extremely rare for only one person to write a computer programme. Computer programmes consist of different elements, and each programme needs an operating system and an applications programme to name the more obvious requirements. Operating systems programming is more complex and has more status than programming applications. Computer operators direct the computer by either imputing data or simply imputing and cataloguing tapes. Data preparation is where the information is keyed into the machine onto magnetic tape and for which no technical knowledge is required. I constructed the following diagram of the hierarchy of positions inside computing as a guide to the hierarchies in the industry.

Table 4.4: Hierarchy of computing occupations

Computer Scientists
Computer Design and Manufacturing/Production
CAD/CAM Software Engineers and Scientists
Computer Engineers/Data Applications Managers
Systems Analysts in the area of
Computer Communication and Operations
Computer Aided Engineering
Computer Aided Design
Systems Analysts in the areas of
Data Processing Applications
Computer Engineers (Technicians)
Systems Analysts/Programmers
Programmers
Computer Support Staff
Computer Operators
Data Entry Operators

This hierarchy, to some degree, disguises the importance of the software end of the computer, in that in the end, the hardware depends on successful software. This places the work of the systems analyst/programmer at the centre of the industry. In theory systems analysts do not write programmes. Rather their role is to break down the job or application required into a series of instructions that take the form of a flow chart of sequenced tasks. Technically then the systems analyst need have no knowledge of programming. However this is hardly ever the case. Indeed the position of the systems analyst is viewed as part of a career progression for programmers. As Kraft states,

> if the analyst/programmer distinction was, and to a large extent remains, crude, tentative, and porous, it proved that programming could be divided into two main categories of more-thoughtful and less-thoughtful work. "Creative" software specialists - for example, those whose work involved relatively little mechanical detail - could then have much of their work routinized, and the fragments thus created parcelled out to less skilled workers. (Kraft 1979, p.7)

It is the case that there is a division in programming which is similar to the process described by Kraft. However the less 'creative' work tends to be done by women and the 'more thoughtful' work tends to be done by men. The fragmentation of programming was much more noticeable when the software was for mainframes or terminal computers. As one woman explained to me, this has changed considerably given the introduction of smaller and more powerful microcomputers. She said that with bigger and more cumbersome machines the systems analyst would design a system, split it into programmes

> You would have a systems analyst who would design a system, split it into programmes really and then say to all the programmers "right, you write this programme, you write that programme", whereas now the roles have become a bit more mixed really. (Extract from transcripts)

Every programmer today would have access to their own machine that means that they can sort out programming problems on their personal computers rather than waiting to access a mainframe. Because of the flexibility now available with the widespread use of smaller and very powerful machines, the jobs have become more interchangeable, though this only tends to occur in small organisations, the more rigid hierarchy described above, still tends to operate in the larger companies. The division described above by Kraft (1979) is organised through this hierarchy rather than through the fragmentation of the work.

Most of the people I interviewed described their job as analyst/programmer, and all had aspirations to become fully-fledged systems analysts. One company, *Radola,* did not use these titles and the workers who perform programming functions were referred to as systems designers. In another company, *CCola*, there was no such thing as a systems analyst - everyone was a programmer. These job titles have implications for pay rates for programmers. In my sample and nationally throughout the industry there are wide variations of pay. These can be related to the size of the organisation, the professional qualifications of the programmer, and local and regional factors on job rates.

The type of programming undertaken, and the hierarchical divisions outlined above depends very much on the particular industry with which workers are involved, and the size of the company. As one woman said:

> Because it was such a small company, we used to sell micros and things, just small computers and I was literally doing everything, designing systems, programming, acting as customer support. (Extract from transcripts)

In software houses specific programmes are either tailor-made: 'bespoke' to specific customer requirements, or are 'standard' software packages which programmers adapt to suit their customers needs. A 'bespoke' is an original programme designed to a customer's requirement and specifications. Programmers as creative and challenging view 'Bespoke' programming. Joy, one of the women computer programmers interviewed, who worked very hard, putting in extremely long hours, and was ambitious to work mainly with 'bespoke', expressed her preference for this type of programming:

> Bespoke stuff, it's a challenge, it's creativity, it's something from nothing. It's yours when you've done it, you get a feeling of achievement. (Extract from transcripts)

This type of original work is increasingly exceptional as more commonly standard software packages tend to be used as a base for specific applications for customers. Usually the software originates alongside the particular hardware recommended and marketed by software houses. The other option is that the same company, the best example of which is *IBM* and *Apple*, produces, markets, designs and supports its own software and hardware. In the case of one of the companies included in the research, *MB Alando*, the firm had at one stage both these sections under one roof and under one company title. This changed as the business grew and developed. Bob, who had worked for this company during both of these phases, explained what happened when the software company emerged in its own right:

> There's been a change in the working atmosphere because the new company has become stricter and more rigid. The old company used to have engineers, programme people, salesmen ... - the programme people didn't make money, which they never did for years, then the engineers made plenty of money to cover it, but the engineers only had the work to do because we wrote the programmes, so everybody carried each other. But now we're just programme people. We've got to make our own money, we've got to keep to time schedules and you've got to make sure people are in line to keep them in check a lot more now. Before it was quite easy going really. (Extract from transcripts)

Programming Sexism: Occupational Segregation and Programming

There is a marked contrast between the organisational culture of software houses and the organisations that have their own 'in house' computer department. Inside 'in-house' computer divisions the programmer's work is chiefly concerned with changing the software packages provided by the company that supplied the hardware, and which has been 'tailored' to suit the needs of the individual workplace. These departments may also devise programmes in order to adapt the computer to a variety of users' needs in the workplace. Differences also exist amongst programmers who work at different levels of abstraction and complexity. The major distinction here is the use of a range of programming languages, from machine code to higher-level languages. Machine code is the original programming language, it is therefore the most difficult and the most old fashioned way of producing software and I have no evidence that it is still in use. It is helpful to bear in mind that the higher-level the language the programmer uses, e.g. BASIC, COBOL, PASCAL, FORTRAN, the more basic and less complex the operation. The other point to note is that as women were the first computer programmers, during the 1940s and 1950s, they were using a programming language that requires a high level of abstraction and complexity. The designers who engineered ENIAC, the operational computer built for the United States Defence Department in the early 1940s, assumed that the job of programming the machine would be a simple clerical operation. So it was given to women. It transpired that in order to programme the machine these women, the ENIAC 'girls', had to devise a 'machine code' which, as Kraft says,

> means being comfortable with abstract logic, mathematics, electrical circuits, and machines, as well as some substantive field, such as aerodynamics or cost accounting. (Kraft 1979, p.4)

In the course of my research I discovered that the same process appears to have occurred in this country. I interviewed a woman, Sandra, who had worked at GCHQ in the 1960s who told the same story about the early history of computer programming. The computer section employed mostly women, and hardly any men, and they originally programmed using machine codes. She said:

> We were Ministry of Defence and were quite distinctly the lower grade, which annoyed us because mostly the girls had Higher Nationals, and had passed degrees. The lads, the people of the Foreign Office, didn't have to have any qualifications at all, and they got more money and special payment for being programmers. (Extract from transcripts)

In the sample of fifty-two programmers interviewed for this research, I met only three women who had worked during the 1950s and into the 1960s, at the level of programming using machine code. At the more basic programming levels described above there are still divisions into essentially complex and simple programming tasks. What determines the distinction is the amount of work a programmer has to do, the amount of areas on the disc and whether the programme has to access different files and databases. As one man explained:

> I mean if you want to produce several reports or change lots of data on the system, I mean the whole programme - you can have a programme that you have split to five or six places because it just won't run the system. You have to chop it and run piece after piece and it just does so much work like accounting when you get to the month end. You've got to print out all the details off the system and then clear everything down ready for the new month. I mean with something like that, that's pretty well complex and it's not just the complexity of it, everything got to go right. If it goes wrong you've had it mate. There's no going back to it. (Extract from transcripts)

The Process of Segregation

On a number of levels the differences between in-house computer installations and software houses are quite marked. One such contrast is the stress and pressure of work. In the software houses the stress was palpable and the situations described below were a common occurrence:

> A customer had an old machine collapsing, they wanted a new system working alongside and they did a fortnightly run and it took 28 hours and it stopped after about 22 hours - just dropped out and the three of us were here till half past ten one night finding out what happened, where it stopped and we actually sent programmes on the telephone lines to start it off. (Extract from transcripts)

Computer software companies tend to be more dynamic and highly pressured as compared to the pace of work of the 'in-house' computer departments. The time scales the programmers' work to are very tight and people are expected to work at a very high level of pressure all the time. The programmers worked very long hours, including Saturdays and Sundays. One woman who was divorced and whose husband had custody of her two children, told me about the demands of the job,

> Well I just wouldn't come in on a Saturday, but I often came in on a Sunday after I've dropped the children off just because I want to get my head down to do something. Then obviously Fridays and Wednesdays, if I had to work

late, then I'd have to get a friend to take them: it's best to keep them in a routine. (Extract from transcripts)

The smaller the software house, the more furious the pace and the greater the problem. One man explained his working hours as follows:

Well the official hours are 9.00 in the morning to 5.30 at night, 5 days a week, with an hour for lunch. We very rarely have lunch. We work right through and there are Saturdays and Sundays involved as well and it's very rarely that I get away before six, half past six, seven o'clock. The work is always there. (Extract from transcripts)

When I asked how often he had to work at the weekends, he replied:

Well what we're trying to do at the moment is cut it down because that doesn't allow us any refresh time as it were and it has been in the past every three Sundays out of four. Because in a small company you see, if you've got the work, you've got deadlines to meet, those deadlines are paramount you've got to meet them. The customer isn't really interested in your problems. You've undertaken to deliver the goods to him, therefore you must do it. (Extract from transcripts)

Another man made a similar point:

Whatever happens, the pressure is on for you to get the customer back up and running and that's your job. And you get in there and you've got to go into the programmes, find what's doing and if you can get back and start it up again and come back to the customer. (Extract from transcripts)

The demands of the job, on the simple basis of flexibility and availability around *time* means that a number of women would not be able to participate in the same way as men, given the amount of time spent by women on housework and childcare, (see Church and Summerfield 1995; Charles 1993; Kidder 1981). Yet, the women I interviewed, though they found this pressure difficult to manage at times, did work into the early morning and weekends if there was a job to be finished.

In the last few weeks I've been sort of getting dragged in. It was half past one in the morning one day, so it's a bit stressful when you've got to get up the next day for work but obviously it's not like that all the time. It's just as well really. (Extract from transcripts)

Another women commented,

I suppose excitement is the wrong word but yet, it's kind of stimulating. I mean, you know, it can fail for all sorts of different reasons and we just get among it and say this job's failed and just sort of track back and find out, find the error, and try and analyse why it has happened. I mean we had a cracker somewhere last year and it took us a whole week until we solved it. (Extract from transcripts)

Despite the fact that many of the women in practice did work under the same pressure as men, they tended to minimise this rather than boast or brag. The work of Fergus Murray (1993), which is discussed below, supports this observation. In exploring the relationship between masculinity and technology he examined the culture of software development and details both the pressure of the job, and the satisfaction and status acquired by men working under these conditions. He tells of the culture and tempo of project-based work that 'sets it apart from much routinized work'. Quoting a male project manager, he writes:

> It is a different mentality. The mentality in admin. is very much nine to five. Here, I mean my God, I come in at eight in the morning, I leave at seven in the evening, and there's still people here. It's a different mentality. If you ask people for a little bit of extra effort you get it. (Murray 1993, p.73)

Murray similarly discusses the dilemmas for women workers trying to operate within an occupation dominated by the 'project mentality'. There is an immediate problem for women in that this mentality is shaped by the discourse of masculinity rather than femininity - and the difficulties are exacerbated in the case of women who have the responsibility for childcare. As Murray says, 'for anyone with even minimal childcare responsibilities there are major problems' (1993, p.74). When I discussed this dilemma with men, one response was that it was an organisational issue as it would be a problem for women to be working unsupervised outside 'normal' working hours. A more common response is illustrated by the following extract.

> Men are more likely to be available for odd hours than women are, because I think most people are conscious of the much more tight families commitments than the men. Yes, I think people anyway would still consider somebody's got to look after the family, probably the wife more than the husband. I suspect it's being in other people's minds that it wouldn't be fair to put pressure on a women to volunteer her for a job if you could avoid it. (Extract from transcripts)

The Emergence of a Sexual Division of Labour

The presumed lack of a 'project mentality' and the implied assumption that you do not have the concomitant 'organisational commitment' militates both against women who welcome and enjoy working in a pressured environment and against women who are unable to work in this way because of child care responsibilities. As Murray states:

> High status work tends to be associated with high profile new software development. It is prized for the inherent challenge it offers and the promotion prospects that follow the successful completion of major projects. (Murray 1993, p.73)

The exclusion of the majority of women in my sample from this 'high status work' is one of the factors involved in the sexual division of labour in programming, and demonstrates the means by which women are segregated into lower status positions. The process which shapes job segregation in this occupation is the distinction between the 'bespoke' and the standard package produced by software houses. The female programmers I interviewed tended to be either concentrated in or slowly being moved into the area of standard packages. Working with standard programming packages does not have the prestige, status and creativity associated with the work of 'bespoke'.

> Bespoke means it's been tailored to suit that customer. You've heard of a bespoke tailor who'll make your suit. We design to the customer's requirement a particular system and obviously my function then is to programme to that specification. That's bespoke. (Extract from transcripts)

With 'bespoke' the programmer has a high level of customer contact at the beginning of a project. They would be involved in putting together a proposal that involves the software and hardware requirements of the customer and they would also take responsibility for the staff team delivering a presentation to the customer. As these projects involve substantial sums of money, not only are project teams gaining valuable experience about budgetary systems and marketing skills but they are also involved in high status, exciting and innovatory projects. They will also be associating with people outside the normal scope of their work, and if they control the project, selecting programmers to test the computer system and have overall responsibility for the implementation of the software. Some projects can take up to two years to implement. In this way not only do project leaders acquire some managerial skills, but they also have the opportunity to make new contacts and build networks that can lead to other projects. This type of experience makes the person more marketable, more experienced and more likely to gain promotion. In the companies I visited, with two exceptions, project managers were men. The following quote is from one women, Jean, - a twenty-six year old whose job title at *Radola* was Applications Development Manager, which meant that she was in charge of the software programming staff and the systems analyst staff based at the Hull Office. She describes the importance of the project leader's job as follows:

> How it actually works is that, starting right from the beginning we get an invitation to tender, probably from a consultancy company. We would put together a proposal of the type of software and hardware that would fulfil their requirements. Then we arrange a presentation, where we would demonstrate the software. ... if we're lucky enough to get that contract and actually sign up, then that project leader would control how that project was run, how the development was run and who would control the hardware implementation. It actually would be done by the engineers but it would be the project leader who would control it, who would arrange all the training and support for that company. Again, this would be done by the training team but the project leader is still responsible as the single source of contact for that customer. ... They would also arrange for any specialist consultancy they might need, and financial or manufacturing systems. So they arrange everything ... (and) while they're working on that project the project leader is effectively the boss. But then, there's actually the software development and the installation of software that would be done by that project leader's own programmers and he's (sic) got to make sure that he (sic) specifies it to the minute detail. The programmers do the programming and testing the documentation that's actually installed and everything goes in line with the implementation plan. So that's how it would normally work, and now a lot of that work would be done on site with the customer, particularly the specification and it would be very interactive and we don't just go out and find out what the requirements are, we then come back and develop it. It's a two-way thing all the time because otherwise you'd find it would go wrong and so at Radola we put a high stress on people being able to communicate reasonably well. (Extract from transcripts)

Where are the Women?

They are working on the standard packages where simple maintenance programming is generally the only requirement. The work involves supporting customers who may want to make changes or are having problems on a routine application, such as a payroll package that would require low level programming skills. The role of a programmer here would be to alter the programme in line with government changes in legislation. They may also be asked to refine or readjust the standard package in line with the customer's requirements. The packages tend to be used as a base and it is very rare that an actual system would get written from scratch, as in the 'bespoke' process described above.

Applications Support: 'Women's Work'?

Women were also largely confined to the area of computer support. In one company in the sample, *Radola*, this area was dominated by women whose job involved training the customer's staff to use the computer and to understand the software packages. These women were not involved with specialist programming. In another software house the women who were involved with programming standard packages also provided customer support. This type of work was not regarded as prestigious: rather it was described as a large headache. As one man explained:

> Support. That's where you get all the earache on the telephone when the customers ring up. I was doing support for over two years and it's enough to drive anyone round the bend. (Extract from transcripts)

The management view was that women were much more suited to the position of customer support than men, as it was said that they were better at defusing customers' and users' anger and impatience over problems with the applications. One woman described how she was 'ear-marked' for support, and how this area was considered to be the 'dregs'.

> They've been trying to push me onto packages since last January and as yet, because of my present workload I've avoided it. I did some of it last January and hated every minute of it. (Extract from transcripts)

When I asked her why she did not want to work in this area she said:

> Everybody wants to be an analyst in the bespoke department because that's where the interest is. That's the really interesting system. You go in, you're meeting people, you design new systems and you're not getting the flack all the time. Because on support all they're doing is ringing in because there's a problem. (Extract from transcripts)

The majority of the women were very aware of the problem with support work and tried to resist being moved into this area.

> It always seemed to be that if a client had a problem it was me that went and sorted it out. Whether that was just a coincidence or not I don't know. I mean I complained to the director about this at one time. It was a bloke called Ray J, because I felt that Mike was sitting in the office doing nothing all the time and I was running round the country sorting people out you know and I didn't think it was right and Ray agreed with me and that again just seemed to be the way it sort of evolved. Even after Ray had talked to Mike it always used to be that if a client rang up it was "Oh I think you'll be better off talking to Christine" and he'd hand the phone to me which meant that if anybody had to go out it was me because it was me they had spoken to and Ray talked to Mike and told him not to do it as much as he was doing

it and to deal with clients himself if he could, but he still did it and I still went out and sorted the clients out. I don't know I think it's just the sort of society that we live in, the way that men are expected to do the work with the screwdriver in their hand and women are expected to talk to people. (Extract from transcripts)

Even women who disliked 'support' and were aware of the practical costs of being ghettoised in this area felt that women were better suited to it than men. Another woman said:

You have to deal with some shirty people, even at top management level. On the telephone sometimes they can be, you know, nasty, the way they speak to you and you've got to hold your tongue a lot of the time. If somebody spoke to me outside of work like that then I wouldn't think twice about retaliating but in work in the job you're doing you've got to have a lot of patience and understanding and not a quick temper.

A.F. Do you know of any man who works around the department who could do what you do?

Not offhand, no. A lot of them haven't got the patience. (Extract from transcripts)

And some women liked support.

You get more involved sort of with the users and you are looking into systems rather than just writing the programmes. (Extract from transcripts)

There is an interesting contradiction here in that the qualities which are needed to be a good support worker is one that requires a good deal of expertise and knowledge of the programmes and very good communication skills yet this qualities were not particularly highly regarded in the software houses.

Well you've got two parts to your software. You've got the operating system which is machine work in itself and the software we're written, and if it's for anything at all to do with machines, then you've got to know how the hardware works, you know if the wrong lights go on you've got to know what's happening, when to call an engineer, if a disc is going wrong you've got to know what the noises are and things like that. Really your support people should be the most experienced people. (Extract from transcripts)

This is in contrast to the 'in house' computing departments where people who had these qualities were promoted much quicker and were more highly regarded than staff who were simply 'technical'.

Gender Differences in Pay and Status

It is difficult to compare the ratio of women programmers to men in software houses and in-house installations because the organisations are so different. There was also some variation between the software houses that is discussed above. The one common feature is that that all the secretarial and administrative support staff are women.

Radola one of the five software houses included in the research is twelve years old (in 1988) and in comparison with similar companies is considered an 'old', well established company, employed no female programmers. However Jean, the Software Applications Manager is in charge of all the software programming staff and is also responsible for recruitment. She was recruiting programming staff at the time of the interview and despite having eighty applicants for the two positions available, no woman had applied. In the previous five years they had employed only one female programmer. During her interview, Jean made it clear that her attitude to employing women programmers was influenced by the fact that they 'would get married and leave because their husband has moved jobs'. In her discussion of the lack of female computer programmers in the company, she said:

> Well up until about a month ago I did have one female programmer. Now, as an individual case, and I certainly wouldn't make this a generalisation, she felt that she wasn't suited to full-scale programme development, she just didn't have the knack for it, it wasn't her forte. She actually transferred to a customer support role that suited her own abilities much better. Now before that I had a female member of staff who had a very high capability which is very unusual I must admit. I've found in my experience here that women like this have been very few and far between and those that I have had have not necessarily been of a high level. Now she actually left to have children. On average throughout the company nationally there's probably 9 male programmers to 1 female. (Extract from transcripts)

A survey of computer staff conducted by APEX (1979) indicates the representation of women on the lower end of the hierarchy of computer occupations by the beginning of the 1980s.

Table 4.5: APEX (1979) survey of computer staff

5-15% of computer programmers are women
10-25% of computer operators are women
75%-100% of data preparation and data control staff are women

A similar pattern appears again in a 1986 survey conducted by Computer Economics (cited in the Guardian 25.2.1988) that showed that:

Table 4.6: Computer Economics (1986) survey of computer staff

2% of data processing managers are women
18% of computer programmers are women
95% of data preparation staff are women

A similar pattern of segregation is revealed by American research (Strober and Arnold 1987), though here there are more women in each of the different computer occupations.

From the 1991 Census[6] the following sex ratios within computing occupations are listed and show a very similar pattern of segregation, though unfortunately the figures for computer operators and data processing staff are listed together. Excluding the company *Radola*[7] the other three software houses[8] in the sample showed some variation to this pattern in respect of computer programmers because of the small staff base.

Table 4.7: Strober and Arnold (1987) survey of computer staff

5% of computer engineers were women
22% of computer scientists/systems analysts were women
31% of computer programmers were women
17% of computer engineering technicians were women
59% of computer operators were women
92% of data preparations staff were women

Shields employees totalled 7 and this was one of the companies in the sample which had no women employed as either programmers or systems analysts. *CCola* employed ten programmers of which five were women. The programmers are divided into three grades; trainee, junior and senior, and women were equally represented in each category. *MB Alando* employed fifteen programmers, of which two were systems analysts, one of whom was a woman; one other woman was a programmer. None of the women in this company were available for interview.

Table 4.8: Extract from 1991 census - computer staff

Occupation Title	Total	Men	Women	Female %
Computer engineers, installation and maintenance	2090	1968	122	6%
Software Engineers	5857	5083	774	13%
Computer systems/data processing managers	6628	5397	1231	19%
Computer analyst/programmers	14530	11489	3041	21%
Computer operators, data processors etc.	16055	4793	11261	70%

Software Houses

It is difficult to compare these companies with the national picture as the figures are based on small staff numbers. Within the 'in-house' installations, *Ratigan and Co* were dismantling the department and I was able to interview the remaining three programmers. At the manufacturing company much larger numbers of staff were involved.

The Business System Division consists of 155 systems analysts, software engineers and computer programmers, 39 of which were women. I interviewed 37 people from this section, 15 men and 22 women. The category of system designers/ programmers in this company would appear to represent quite a fair distribution of women within this computing division, though women are in the lower grades, however on closer inspection it was found that the women were programming in the more traditional female areas such as clerical, payroll and administrative sections rather than in the areas of production, engineering and communications.

The category of system designers/ programmers in this company appear to represent quite a fair distribution of women within this computing division, though women are in the lower grades, however on closer inspection it was found that the women were programming in the more traditional female areas such as clerical, payroll and administrative sections rather than in the areas of production, engineering and communications.

Table 4.9: Business systems department

Occupation Title	Total	Men	Women	Female %
Group Leader	12	11	1	8%
Computer systems manager (Senior system leaders)	8	8	0	0%
Computer systems manager (Junior system leaders)	4	3	1	25%
Systems Designers Senior	36	31	5	14%
System Design Junior	19	3	16	84%
Trainee system design	76	60	16	21%
TOTALS	155	116	39	25%
Computer operators	*			1%
Computer data processors	*			100%

Note: * indicates no real figures available for these groups.

Salary Differences

The women are earning less than the men. The gender divisions on the different salary scales from all the companies involved in the research are as follows:

Table 4.10: Salary scales in the department

Salary Bands	Female	Male
Below £5,000	1	1
£5,000 - £7,000	1	0
£7,000 - £10,000	11	1
£10,000 - £13,000	9	9
£13,000 - £15,000	5	2
£15,000 - £20,000	2	5
£20,000+	0	5
TOTALS	29	23

(In the case of the one male worker who was earning below £5000, he was a student doing a one-year placement as part of his degree. The woman however was a highly experienced programmer who on the birth of her child had opted to work on a 16 hours a week part-time basis). From these figures it seems because women are polarised into relatively routine and junior positions in the department this accounts for the earning gap between women and men. Overall, Humberside is a low wage economy in comparison to the rest of the country, although males' manual earnings are higher than nationally. Figures from the 1991 census indicate that males on average earn £20,370 per year compared with the national average of £18,720 and women earn £12,662 compared to £13,653 nationally. As the following figures from 1987 and 1986 indicate the salary scales for the respondents listed above were in line with the local average.

Table 4.11: Earnings in full time occupations 1987

	Humberside	Great Britain
Men		
Manual Occupations	190.90 (175.60)	185.50 (174.40)
Non-Manual Occupations	243.20 (220.40)	265.90 (244.90)
All Occupations	210.50 (192.60)	224.00 (207.50)
Women		
Manual Occupations	112.90 (105.30)	115.30 (107.50)
Non-Manual Occupations	140.40 (131.30)	157.20 (145.70)
All Occupations	133.00 (123.60)	148.10 (137.20)

Note: Figures relation to average gross weekly earnings and include overtime and shift payments. Figures in brackets relate to 1986.

Source: New Earnings Survey April 1987.

In the analyses by occupation from the New Earnings Survey the gross weekly earnings for systems analysts and computer programmers that are classified as social class two are as follows:

Table 4.12: Gross weekly earnings for systems analysts/computer programmers

	Gross weekly earnings 1987	**Gross weekly earnings 1991**
Full time Male	Lowest decile 174.4	Lowest decile 226.9
Full time Female	*	232.2

Note *: There is no listing for female full time systems analysts, computer programmers before 1991.

Source: New Earnings Survey 1987 and 1991.

As explained above it is difficult to interpret statistics for computer professionals as different companies used different job titles, so the comparison between male and female computer professional's pay can be misleading, though the indications are that 'computer programmer/analyst is a relatively higher paid job for women that for men' (Rubery et al. 1992, p.86).

Local Labour Market

There is a very small ethnic component to the labour market compared to the national average as is indicated by the following table. The gender composition of the labour market in Hull varies from the national picture. Whilst employment and unemployment in the city of Hull and the local region of Humberside have tended to follow the overall national trend, there is some variation between the Hull economy and the national picture that affects the gender composition of the labour market. In terms of the share of total employment, the main differences between the UK and Humberside is that the region has proportionately fewer full-time employees than nationally (58.3% and 62.1% respectively) but proportionately more part-time (27.7% and 25.1% respectively). Female full time employment is proportionately lower than nationally while female part-time employment is far more important. Female full time employment accounts for 41.1% of total female employment compared to 50.0% nationally, while female part-time employment accounts for 50.7% of all female employment compared to 43.7% nationally. The most striking feature of the local situation is the variation with the national rates for self-employment. Between 1994 and 1997, it is estimated to have increased by over 13% compared to a national growth figure of 1%. Over the last ten years, the structure of employment nationally and locally has shifted away from the primary, manufacture and construction industries to the service sector. However, in Hull and Humberside this process is happening more slowly than nationally. Employment in manufacturing fell at the rate of 1.1% per year compares to a national rate of 1.9%. In broad terms, the employment structure in the region is not entirely different to that of the national picture but with two major exceptions, Humberside has around 6% more of its employees engaged in manufacturing and around 6% fewer in banking, finance and insurance.

Table 4.13: Ethnic composition of Kingston upon Hull

Ethnic origin	Local Population	% of Local Population
White	250,934	98.7%
Total Non-White	3,183	1.3%
Black Caribbean	137	1.0%
Black African	356	1.0%
Black Other	369	1.0%
Indian	318	1.0%
Pakistani	237	1.0%
Bangladeshi	235	1.0%
Chinese	537	2.0%
Other Asian	317	1.0%
Other	677	3.00%

Source: OPCS 1991.[9]

In Summary

It is obvious then that women are not only under represented in relation to their numbers in the labour force in the computing industry but they also suffer inequalities in relation to pay. Job segregation is evident by the emergence of a division of labour around 'bespoke' programming, standard packages and the area of customer support. A number of elements were found to be operating in the different companies that can help to account for this process. In organising these factors I have to some extent followed the list provided by Reskin and Hartmann's study of *Women's Work, Men's Work: Sex Segregation on the Job* (1985) which catalogues research from a range of American companies. This book represents the findings of the Committee on Women's Employment and Related Social Issues that documents the extent of job segregation in the USA. The factors which where found to be crucial to this process were: cultural beliefs about gender and work; sex stereotypes and occupational segregation; discriminatory acts and behaviour; institutionalised barriers, informal barriers in the workplace and childcare and occupation segregation. The next chapter examines these factors.

Notes

[1] Source: Business Ratio Plus 1988.

[2] Source: Company Report 1988.

[3] There was a sharp reduction in employee numbers in 1987-1988 mainly from the disposal in 1987 of the group's cleaning business. This directly affected employment in the Hull business. The numbers dropped from 1987: 12,500 to 1988: 5,400. Source: Annual Report 1988.

[4] This caused problems for the research project as it tended to associate me with the management. See my discussion in chapter four and for a discussion of the problems with being perceived as a 'bosses man' (sic) - see Willis 1977 and Ramazanoglu 1989.

[5] There is, at the moment, no historical evidence of the involvement of women in building the machines. There is evidence of women's very early involvement in programming. (See Kraft 1977; Lloyd and Newell 1985)

[6] Source: 1991 Census 10% Sample Data on Occupational Structure and Sex Ratios.

[7] The total staff base at Radola was 470 workers but the breakdown was not made available to me.

[8] The fourth company Hobsons was part of a firm of business consultants rather than a separate software house - so I have not included figures for this group.

[9] Two of the people interviewed for the study were from ethnic minorities: a British born Asian woman and a British born African.

Chapter 5

Factors Shaping Segregation

This chapter examines the extent to which embedded traditions of discrimination have shaped the process of vertical segregation in computer programming despite the fact that both women and men had an estimated 50% share in programming and analyst jobs in the 1950s and 1960s. Not only have the figures for women programmers fallen to approximately half of this figure but organisational practices have lead to a sexual division of labour in computer programming which has resulted in a new category of worker emerging in the industry - the 'help desk analyst', who are predominantly women. The following table demonstrates this trend, and the fall in the share of women in the industry.

Table 5.1: Female share of computer professional occupations 1991

	Females as % of occupation		Average age (change since May)		Female earnings as % of male	
	May	Nov.	Male	Female	May	Nov.
Data Processing Manager	3	3	44	41(+1)	95	99
Project Manager	14	14	39	36	97	98
Systems analyst	28	29	34	32	96	99
Analyst Programmer	26	25	30	31	99	98
Programmer 1	25	23	28(-1)	30	99	99
Systems Programmer	13	13	30(-1)	30	94	93
Operator	15	16	26	28	98	102
Network Operator	39	35	28		91	95
Help Desk Analyst	64	63	30	30(+1)	93	91

Source: Computer Economics, May and November 1991, cited in Rubery, Fagan and Humphries 1992, p.90.

In their interpretation of these figures Rubery et al. (1992) point out that this survey suggests that

> the share of women is still falling in the profession: the overall share of women is falling and the average age is rising suggesting that women are accounting for smaller shares of young recruits. This computer pay survey data provides the best estimate of women's position within the various occupational categories that come under the heading computer professionals. The only occupation where women predominate is "Help desk analyst", an occupational area where women's social skills have presumably been considered an asset. Women are particularly poorly represented in management posts, in operating jobs and in systems programmers' posts. (ibid., p.81)

Traditional ideas and practices did contribute to the process of vertical segregation in the companies studied and the next section reviews these factors.

Institutionalised Barriers

Institutionalised barriers existed in all of the companies regardless of the type of computing concern. In the software houses, the most established of which had only been a going concern for twelve years, the near total male management had incorporated an organisational structure that was based on largely traditional forms of organising. The only exception in these firms was the apparently 'fluid' nature of the promotion ladder. It was stated by a member of the management team of one of these companies (*Radola*) that:

> There is a loose structure but it's kept very fluid and its kept that way deliberately because it makes us more flexible because we are working in a very dynamic environment and we have to react very quickly. Now if we had a predetermined structure we couldn't do that. In an in-house computer department it's maybe more structured and conventional and you have to take steps up a ladder at pre-determined times. Now, in this company that doesn't happen. You're judged purely on ability and opportunities that you make for yourself and I think it's true that there are less women who are relatively able or willing, I would say willing, rather than able, to make that sort of commitment to a career and to forcefully promote themselves. (Extract from transcripts)

Despite the advantages of the flexible system of promotions which was found in software companies, over more traditional practices, this is not in itself sufficient to overcome the other factors which discriminate against women and which structure job segregation. Within 'in-house' establishments the institutionalised barriers have their origins in traditional practices and prejudices, which are consequently more enduring and entrenched. For example, in one company the personnel practices made it extremely difficult for women programmers to return to work on a part-time basis. A woman who had been with the organisation for a number of years, took time out to have a child. After the birth of her child, she hoped to work from home, which technically should be a very easy option for a programmer, given that all they need is a personal computer. Despite the fact that her immediate manager was in favour of this arrangement, the administrative practices of the company could not sanction these 'new' working conditions and proved to be very inflexible on the issue. The compromise solution reached by the manager of the computer department with personnel was to allow the woman to work in the evenings, which was obviously not very satisfactory from her point of view. At the time of interviewing she said that if this arrangement did not change, and they were unable to allow her to work part-time at home, that she would have to leave the job.

Another woman experienced problems when she applied for maternity leave. She was only the second person to take what she termed 'proper maternity leave' at the company.

A.F. 'proper maternity leave'?

Come back. I was only the second person to do it and as far as I know I'm only the first to do it for the second child, out of choice you know, other than the people that have had to come back to work through, you know, loss of a husband or something like that and I resent the fact that they aren't a bit more helpful in terms of you know, they just pay the minimum. They also, when I told them that I'd be working up to Christmas, they also at one time refused to sign my form because they thought they may be liable in some way. They wanted to check up. So I mean, and that really annoyed me. I was quite cross about that ... they had no set procedures for maternity. They don't know the rules properly. (Extract from transcripts)

This woman not only challenged the administrative procedures of the organisation but also resisted assumptions from some women and some men that she should not return to work.

Well they said how much they disagreed with it, (returning to work after giving birth) you know people that had been my colleagues and to a certain extent friends, made me feel slightly awkward in that they did put forward their opinions on why they thought, you know, that is was not a good idea and why I shouldn't do it. Some just didn't believe that I would, you know, there was one chap that you know believes that maternal instincts are so strong that there's no way, you know, that any women could possibly come back to work, he was a complete idiot mind. So there was a bit of that. I think there was a certain amount of resentment to me having to have a couple of months off again. (Extract from transcripts)

Networking a Promotion

In terms of mobility ladders and promotion opportunities, whilst 75% of the women interviewed and 90% of the men stated that they were seeking promotion and advancement, the opportunities are limited by the rigidity of the hierarchical structure. There were a number of marked differences between men and women in the discussions on promotion. The men were quite clear on the question of their promotion chances and possibilities. They could also virtually recite the hierarchy in each company in their immediate areas and also in related areas. They had a fund of stories about promotion and how various people had achieved or acquired their positions. In a discussion of his progress through the company one of the men interviewed mentioned that he had 'lost an empire' when he was outmanoeuvred by men from other departments. Their main complaint concerned the rigidity of the structures, though they were aware that movements in different directions and different areas were possible if not always feasible. Many of them had also considered 'freelance' programming and discussed the 'huge amounts' of money that could be made in this area. One woman had considered this option and rejected it, and only one other considered it as a serious career move.

The women did not express the same determination or have the same company knowledge with regards to promotion opportunities and the following quotation illustrates a common response.

I'm quite happy with what I'm doing with the amount I've got. I mean, I wouldn't mind taking more responsibility, but as far as work is concerned I'm not particularly bothered about being in charge of people. (Extract from transcripts)

The women were much more concerned with doing their present job with a high degree of conscientiousness, in the expressed belief that 'virtue has it's own rewards'. This conscientious attention to detail and consistent hard work was self-acknowledged: i.e. the women were aware they worked hard and held a firm belief that they worked harder than many of their male associates. The men also stated that women worked harder than many men and women were more patient and methodical in their work. Indeed, the woman from *Radola* who claimed to have problems recruiting women programmers said:

From the women that I have employed they tend to be more methodical than men. I think the women I have had, have been excellent and have been better that the men. (Extract from transcripts)

Both women and men viewed promotion in terms of increased status. However women also tended to view promotion in terms of more responsibility whereas men tended to concentrate on promotion in terms of a growth in prestige and power. Very little staff development beyond the practical aspects of the job was available to either men or women, and this made the informal and formal network systems crucial for progress and promotion in an occupation. Many of those interviewed made reference to the number of courses available to them that were directly related to the practical aspects of their jobs as programmers. These courses were largely information courses about new software packages and programming languages. There did not appear to be discrimination in terms of access to these courses for women. In the case of one large company whose data preparation staff was totally female, (see figures above for Business Systems Department), little or no staff development or career development opportunities were available. Although on request, an aptitude test to become a programmer could be taken, this depended on the initiative of the individual woman. The 'received knowledge' in this department, based on the previous experiences of women taking this test, is that it was extremely difficult and beyond the capabilities of the data preparation 'girls'. A number of the women reported to me that,

> the aptitude test is very difficult, and in fact, going back to when I first started here there was a girl in our department who did actually do the aptitude test and I mean I can't remember this happening at the time but I've been told that the girl came out of the aptitude test in tears and made a total fool of herself. Now whether that's true or not, I don't know, but that's just going on what I've actually been told. (Extract from transcripts)

One woman who made the transition from secretary to the business systems department said:

> They very meanly put me through a test. There's a rotten old test, I don't know whether you've seen it. I thought it was horrendous, I cried nearly half way through with frustration because I couldn't do it and I though "Oh God", you know they're going to find me out, I'm not clever enough and anyway you get a new breath half way through and I managed to do three quarters of the paper. The last two questions I made a mess of, well, I just couldn't attempt to do them but when they got the report back I don't quite know how many percent I got so it was quite bad but if you don't get like in the upper 80s they're not interested in you anyway and you can't do the job as a systems designer. I think the report came back with something like,

you know, "not a systems designer but consider her for the job of information technology consultant". But they were a bit mean putting me through it. Ever since I've been here I've always had to prove myself. (Extract from transcripts)

Jenny, a woman who had made the transition from data entry to programming explained how, despite getting the required mark on the aptitude test, she was not moved out of the data control room for a further two and a half years. She hung on however and when she was finally moved there was still no hurry to set her off down the path to programming, so she had to wait a further nine months before she actually became a trainee programmer. Hence women have to be tenacious and highly motivated in order to challenge traditional practices and unspoken assumptions about women's desires and capabilities.

What can be another 'natural' progression - the move from data entry operator to computer operator - was also closed to these women as they assumed (incorrectly) that women were not allowed to work the twenty four hour shift system operated in the computer section. The policy of the company that women can't work shifts, though not in existence officially, is acted upon, and this has serious repercussions for women who wish to move to gain promotion as it is not possible to be promoted to shift leader if you can't work shifts.

In a discussion, on this issue with Mark, a group leader, with reference to one of the women he said that he did not think she 'would have wanted to work shifts'. When questioned further on this he spoke about his assumption that:

I think people were just a bit worried about being able to look after them at night.

A.F: Why do women need to be looked after?

Because they've been such a minority I think. I think it's different in a smaller office rather than a big factory.

A.F. Women work shifts in hospitals and factories.

Well, other places have all got a definite structure of supervisors and there's always somebody at the top to deal with a department. We haven't got that structure. There's a bit of structure in the works but anything in between would perhaps come back to the security people. (Extract from transcripts)

Cultural Beliefs about Gender

Cultural beliefs about gender refers to the socially produced distinctions between men and women that constitute gendered processes and practices in work organisations, and sexuality is part of this ongoing process. As Burrell (1992) explains, sexuality and women's bodies are used as grounds for exclusion or objectification. Sexual harassment is an example of how the discourses of gender, sexuality and organisations conflict and can block a women's progress through a company. The point I would make here, is that this is an important aspect of the way women's opportunities at work and women's paid work can be traumatic and constraining. Only one case of ongoing sexual harassment was disclosed to me during the research and the woman asked me to keep the information confidential. Another woman had reported her section manager for harassment, however she had to do this on a number of occasions before he stopped. She explained how:

> He wouldn't take me seriously. He used to pat me on the bum now and again. You know, nothing excessive really, just annoying stuff and he used to make sexist jokes in meetings and to a certain extent belittle me in meetings which I took offence to. (Extract from transcripts)

Less overtly sexist mechanisms exist which act in informal ways to restrict women's opportunities at work. Reskin and Hartmann (1985) explain how it is

> More problematic because it is a daily affair in women's exclusion from informal networks ... in which information is shared and alliances develop (and this) has implications for their learning and performing their job and their chances for advancement. (Reskin and Hartmann 1985, pp.54-5)

A significant number of the men and women interviewed mentioned the importance of such alliances in the progress of their careers. In the areas of computer programming/systems analysts, as in other occupations (see Reskin and Hartmann 1985) these alliances play an important part in career development. There are frequent shifts of personnel around the different software houses, and staff are constantly being poached, much of which is done through personal contact. Another important factor in the informal culture of organisations is the role of sponsors or mentors. These are people who take others 'under their wing'. Sometimes these relationships are based on friendships or on a shared interest in some kind of sporting activity. More usually they take the form of father and son, or older and younger brothers relationships, and are mostly male. Because men hold a disproportionate number of positions of importance and so few women hold positions with high status so as to be as effective in this way, most available potential sponsors are men. There are also a number of barriers to men being effective sponsors of women. It is not as socially acceptable or comfortable for men to have such relationships with women. Men do not see women as people with that you can have this type of relationship, in large part because of the sexual connotations that are suggested in relationships between women and men. As Harry said to Sally in the film *When Harry Met Sally* (1992) 'men and women can't be friends because the sex part always gets in the way'. There is also the problem of the cultural beliefs and stereotypes that follow women in work. The irony here is that these beliefs about women's 'innate' capabilities, interests and aspirations which can be characterised as the three Cs, caring, clerical and cleaning, (see Rubery et al. 1992; Beechey and Whitelegge 1986) are reinforced and strengthened by job segregation. These cultural beliefs about gender and work were expressed by a small percentage of the men I interviewed.

They expounded the view that married women with children should not be out at work, but ought to be at home. As mentioned above one woman who had a child and was on maternity leave with the birth of her second child referred to the fact that some men tried to talk her out of returning to work.

I put a question to each interviewee, asking if they thought that both men and women were equally capable of doing their job. The vast majority of men qualified their initial affirmative response, by saying that the woman who could do 'their' job would have to be 'special', that she would 'need to project herself', and would need 'good technical ability'. Women on the other hand responded by saying that a man would have no difficulty doing their job except in those areas of work dominated by women: e.g. data preparation. It was said that men would not have the patience for this job and would be unable to handle the tedium. A large number of men and women interviewed also expressed the belief that men are more committed to their jobs than women as men have greater responsibility because of family commitments and have different orientations to work.

Manju: Men have to work. Women go to work for the companionship.

Nick: Men are more ambitious, they respond to power struggles.

Lewis: Female characteristics are innate.

Christine: At work there is less commitment from women. The overall impression I have is that women are not as interested as men. Women are less interested in the technical side of things.

Robin: Most women don't want a career though. The majority of them don't. They'll probably get married and have kids and probably come back to it. But all the women in our department have either been married and not had kids or are not married. Like Rose is married and she hasn't got any kids so obviously they want careers rather than a family. (Extracts from transcripts)

Yet, when men were questioned about specific women colleagues they work with, they did not regard them with the perspective on women indicated by their own comments (see above). They referred to their women colleagues as 'incredible', 'very knowledgeable', 'technically very competent', 'able', 'ambitious', 'exceptionally good workers'. They did not appear to notice the contradictory nature of these statements that challenges their more general cultural beliefs about women. Similar contradictions were also apparent when the issue of women's aspirations was discussed. For example the stereotype of what constituted good management material tended to be cast in masculine terms in that phrases such as 'dynamic', 'competitive', 'ambitious', 'strong', 'ruthless' were used. There was general acceptance amongst the majority of the men that some women were exceptional, and when asked why these 'exceptional' women were not well represented in terms of the management structure, Mike, commented:

The females that we have are more oriented to doing their job and probably enjoying it than they are to getting up the next rung in the ladder. The females that we have are not as willing to engage in the politics and the organisational hassle outside their own environment. (Extract from transcripts)

A different series of obstacles face women who attempt to combine a career with childcare and home care. Evidence from other studies suggests that women are limited to jobs that can accommodate these responsibilities (see Martin and Roberts 1984). Only two women in the sample had small babies and were attempting to combine childcare with a career. In the 'in-house' installations this was made easier as the hours of work were routine and the pressure of work was not as great in comparison with the software establishments. In these companies, 29% of the women lived on their own; 15% lived with partners and had no children; 14% were divorced and had no responsibilities for children, as was the case with the 42% who were separated. Given the pressure and long hours of work demanded by these companies it would be extremely difficult for any woman bringing up children on her own, and as demonstrated by the figures, women with these types of responsibilities did not work in this environment. A small number of the men interviewed disclosed their desire to be more involved in their children's upbringing and they recognised that this was having the effect of limiting their aspirations for career development in the short term. Ian told me of the affect on his life of the birth of his child.

> My son has changed me. (His child was 15 months old.) My wife and I, our relationship has altered since he came along, as you would expect. I find I'm not willing to put the hours in as much because I do realise that I really want to get home and not only see the boy but see her as well, and relieve her of some of the stress. I will go one of two ways, I'll either draw away from the family life and then throw myself even heavier into work or I will do the opposite. (Extract from transcripts)

All the women interviewed were conscious of the dilemma they face in combining a career and child rearing. None of the companies in which the interviews were conducted had any specific paternity agreements or domestic leave agreements. Neither did they have any specific maternity policies beyond the legal minimum requirements. In the 'in-house' installations, flexitime was mentioned as a partial solution to their difficulties with childcare responsibilities by many members of staff, and thought to be highly desirable. The women programmers in the company *Business Systems Department*, told me that there were insurmountable problems around the introduction of flexitime and job sharing given the structure of the organisation and, as demonstrated by the example of Alison who wanted to work from home, some of these problems can be solved by a more adaptable approach to terms and conditions of work and the needs of people with responsibilities for others. None of the companies had an equal opportunities policy. Jenny said to me:

> If you are career minded, *don't have any children*. The only reason I had them was because my husband said that he wanted them more than I did, otherwise I wasn't going to have any. Not that I was career minded, not in teaching. I just didn't know what I wanted to do until I came here. I hadn't got a purpose in life and so I got pregnant and this friend said, "You know he's expecting you to change your mind about going back to work". I felt like somebody had put me in jail for twenty years. (Extract from transcripts)

Gender Processes in Gendered Organisations

The empirical material I collected as a result of my interviews with computer programmers suggested the process of gender segregation in this occupation. I have detailed a range of factors that are gradually concentrating female programmers in positions of low status with positions of low status with poor promotion prospects. The classic pattern of gender segregation that is documented in a wide variety of feminist sociological and historical studies (see Bradley 1989) would appear to be clearly evident. These findings would also support studies that document gender segregation in computing (see Rubery et al. 1992; Lloyd and Newell 1985; Davidson and Cooper 1987; Turkle 1984; Morris 1989; Webster 1994; Shapiro 1994; Green, et.al. 1993). However the explanation and interpretation of this evidence of gender segregation is framed by the feminist orthodoxy that was outlined in chapter three. A good example of this is the following excerpt from an article by Juliet Webster (1994) that describes the nature of gendered relations and technology with reference to the historical development of men's power and patriarchal social relations. She writes:

> Feminist analysis has begun to point to the ways in which the gendered nature of society influences technological development, and by implication, the impact of technologies. It has shown that technological artefacts have gender relations actually embedded within them, and also that the institutions of technology, the acquisition of technological know-how, and indeed the very culture of technology itself, have come to be dominated by men at the expense of women. An identification of the processes whereby technology has become 'masculine' provides some explanation as to why the introduction of technologies has had differential impacts on women's and men's jobs, and why it has been experienced differently by men and women. ... For there are broader issues which shape women's experience of technology in the workplace, and their relationship to paid work in general. The role of women's unpaid labour operates in conjunction with factors within workplaces, including the process of occupational sex typing and the exclusion of women from technology. Moreover, women's subordination in the workplace and in the wider society is rooted in a host of broader social institutions, including the family, the education system, and the state. The dynamics of gender and technological change in the workplace form just one component in this complex array of factors shaping women's subordination. (Webster 1992, p.321)

The problem with this formulation is that it is difficult to apply it to women who are involved with technology. The historical evidence of women's involvement with technology and their contradictory relations with men at work, some of which is documented in chapter three (see, Pollert 1981; Westwood 1984; Walby 1986; Bradley 1989) is difficult to explain using this model. Why and how do some women resist? Why only some? What explains these differences between women? Rather than explaining the *exclusion* of women from technology and the computing industry, how can their *presence* be explained?   And what are the consequences of their presence?

A number of women in my sample were combining their paid work with childcare - why? If women are subordinated by men through domestic labour, how can women's lack of subordination, independence and power in organisations be explained, and what are the implications of the presence of these women for gender processes at work? And what of the men? The men I interviewed during this project were also resisting some elements of gender stereotyping.   They were attempting to combine their paid work with domestic responsibilities and were very complimentary about the abilities of their women colleagues.   How can this image of men's relationship to work, to the family and to their women colleagues be accounted for in the rigidity of the story about gender segregation that is given by the feminist explanation outlined above?

As I explained in the previous section, the static nature of this account can be traced to the concept of gender that is embedded in the concept of patriarchy.   This account correctly points to the problem of gender segregation; unequal gender relations at work; differentials of pay, status, and unequal gender power relations, but if gender is 'not something that people are in', but is in a constant process of production, and something that,

> occurs in the course of participation in work organisations as well as in many other locations and relations', then it is necessary to interpret the practices of gender which give rise to contradictions and complications for this process. (see Acker 1992, p.250)

The emphasis in the orthodox approach is on control of women's labour by men. I want to suggest that by attending to the practices within various labour process which are being negotiated, renegotiated and transformed and which suggests contradictions and reversals, the concept of gender as process can help to capture the changes, ambiguities and flux of the process of gender segregation.

There is another problem with the orthodox account that strengthens the case for attending to the process of gendering - this is the question of agency. This means that

> research must look for an understanding of the social construction of gender relations in specific historical contexts. It is therefore necessary to focus not only empirically, but also theoretically, upon human agency, which the concept of practice necessarily presupposes. This, in turn, requires an exploration of how human beings both think and act. (Collinson, Knights and Collinson 1990, p.50)

As well as the tendency to see gender as static there is also a tendency to view technology in the same way. Flis Henwood makes an appeal for a transformation of the dominant theoretical frameworks that are used to examine these issues, and argues for the necessity to view,

> both technology and gender not as fixed and 'given', but as cultural processes which (like other cultural processes) are subject to negotiation, contestation and, ultimately, transformation. As such, they might be thought of as 'discourses'. (Henwood 1993, p.44)

In the following chapters I explore these discourses in order to suggest how these shape the practices of computer programming, and consequently present another interpretation of the process of gender segregation that is suggested by my research material.

In Summary

The empirical research outlined in this chapter suggests that segregation does exist in the computing industry and amongst computer programmers. The process of gender segregation in the occupation is related to the sexual division of labour that has emerged around different aspects of the organisation of software production. There are a number of issues which influence this process: hierarchical divisions in the industry and the association of women with areas of programming - such as application support - which is rationalised by the notion of 'natural' sex differences - which suggests that women are better suited to, or have abilities for some types of work rather than others. Consequently cultural attitudes towards gender stereotyping suggest the appropriateness of women's labour for some kinds of programming rather than others - like project management. These attitudes influence recruitment and promotion opportunities for women. These practices are reinforced by the differences between women and between women and men in relation to domestic responsibilities. The 'job' model for men and the 'gender' model for women (discussed in a previous chapter) is not simply a problem of sociological or feminist research. These models also operate at the workplace and are constituted by the discourses of organisations, masculinity and femininity. Sexuality discourses also affect the practices of gendering in the workplace. In this chapter I make reference to two examples of the impact of sexuality in organisations: the problem of men mentoring women, and the issue of sexual harassment. I have suggested that organisational practices need to be examined for their potential discriminatory impact on women, especially those that do not acknowledge the effect of family responsibilities on workers. Sexist cultural beliefs held by men in regard to women's abilities and interest in paid work further encourage the process of segregation.

In the computing industry a number of discourses are operating - discourses on masculinities, on organisations, on femininity, on sexuality, on technology: all help to shape the process of gender segregation in computer programming. Specific organisational practices such as the lack of staff development for women or inflexible administrative procedures (as in the examples given above), will make changes to job segregation more difficult. Common sense discourses of the 'natural' association of sex roles and gender roles (and thus men's jobs and women's jobs) also help to establish gender segregation. Gender hierarchies in organisations, and the associated networks and alliances between groups at different levels in the organisations, encourage and maintain the notion of the 'naturalness' of men's work and women's work. As Joan Acker (1991) points out,

> the gender segregation of work, including divisions between paid and unpaid work, is partly created through organizational practices. Second, and related to gender segregation, income and status inequality between women and men is also partly created in organizational processes; understanding these processes is necessary for understanding gender inequality. Third, organizations are one arena in which widely disseminated cultural images of gender are invented and reproduced. Knowledge of cultural production is important for understanding gender construction (Hearn and Parkin 1987). Fourth, some aspects of individual gender identity, perhaps particularly masculinity, are also products of organizational processes and pressures. Fifth, an important feminist project is to make large-scale organisations more democratic and more supportive of humane goals. (Acker 1991, pp.162-3)

The dimensions of the process of gender segregation that I concentrate on in the subsequent chapters are the discourses that shape the organisation's gendered structure of work and the demands for gender-appropriate behaviours. The study of gender segregation cannot however simply be restricted to women. In order to interpret the positions that men occupy in the informal structures and networks of organisations and their practices in maintaining their positions in programming, it is necessary to explore the discourses that constitute male practices in organisations. What needs to be explored as a result of the argument presented in this chapter are the practices that shape the processes of gender segregation in the companies I visited for this research in order to explore the extent to which gender segregation is related to: (i) the culture of organisations and organisational discourses; (ii) discourses of masculinity and the culture of masculinity; (iii) the discourses of femininity and (iv) the discourses of science and technology.

Chapter 6

Masculinity at Work

In seeking to construct an analysis of gender segregation that will avoid a static conceptualisation of gender in this and subsequent chapters I explore the discourses that constitute computer programming. In order to explain how asymmetrical power relations are reproduced, rationalised and resisted at the workplace it is necessary to produce an analysis of gender relations that captures the process of gendering at work. This requires a study of men as well as women and the consequences and contradictions produced by the discourses of masculinity and femininity that shape their social practices. Masculinity and femininity are viewed:

> as 'products' of, or themes in, different discourses. [And though both are] vague concepts can be defined as values, experiences and meanings that are culturally interpreted as masculine and typically feel 'natural' to or are ascribed to men more than women in the particular cultural context. (Alvesson and Billing 1997, p.83)

The feminist orthodoxy referred to in the previous chapters produces a view of men as dominant that made it impossible to interpret how the discourses of masculinity and femininity are negotiated, understood and resisted by women. As Wendy Hollway has commented:

> One of the puzzling things about feminists' analyses is that they stress men's power and women's lack of power as if they were immutable principles. (Hollway 1984, p.124)

The concept of patriarchy that produced this type of analysis also had an impact on the study of men and masculinity. The first part of this chapter examines this literature and uses it as a base from that to explore the interview material from male computer programmers.

The Concept of Patriarchy in Critical Men's Studies

The masculinity debates began in earnest in the late 1980s coinciding with the time I carried out the empirical research for this study. At this stage the study of men and masculinity from a feminist perspective was in its infancy. There are still only a small number of texts that analyse masculinity from this perspective (Cockburn 1983, 1985; Segal 1990). However the past fifteen years has witnessed a phenomenal growth of studies whose central anxiety is the way men are defined in the dominant discourse on men and masculinity. Only a small section of this literature is based on the recognition that women are subordinated and oppressed by men, with the result that masculinity is recast as a problem for men rather than as a problem for women. There are only a handful of writers in the genre of masculinity studies that acknowledge that men inhabit a structure of power that oppresses women. This was not always the case. Ironically, the early texts in 'critical men's studies' were concerned to display an awareness of feminist politics, so, for example, an early review of the literature states,

> The political meaning of writing about masculinity turns mainly on its treatment of power. Our touchstone is the essential feminist insight that the overall relationship between men and women is one involving domination or oppression. This is a fact about the social world that must have profound consequences for the character of men. (Carrigan, Connell and Lee 1985, p.552)

By making a reference to patriarchy and feminism the writers of 'critical men's studies', as opposed to 'new men's studies', acknowledge male power and women's oppression. In these writings patriarchy functions as a political concept rather than as a theoretical one and it is used, partly, in order to separate 'radical' and pro-feminist writing on men and masculinity from other writings in the genre. As Carrigan, Connell and Lee remark, one way of distinguishing between different writers on masculinity is that some writers,

> insist on the importance of the concept of patriarchy; and tries to relate men's oppression of women to the oppression of workers, blacks, and - almost uniquely among Books About Men - gay men. (Carrigan, Connell and Lee 1985, p.575)

References to patriarchy is an indicator of a literature that is attempting to be part of the movement towards the creation of radical social change, (Rutherford 1992) as opposed to those texts that reproduce reactionary and conservative accounts of masculinity. As stated:

> At the risk of oversimplification, there are thus two conflicting styles of men writing about masculinity: One celebrates male bonding and tells men they are OK, and the other focuses on issues of power using academic feminist interpretative frameworks. The former approach sells many books and receives much media attention. The latter approach, of that this volume is an example, focuses on the contradictory meanings and experiences of

manhood and aligns itself with the women's movement.   (Brod and Kaufman 1994, p.42)

But these critical studies of masculinities rarely discuss the concept of patriarchy in relation to the conceptualisation of gender that pervades feminist critiques of men and masculinity.   Rather than making a link between the concept of masculinity contained in feminist analysis of patriarchy they explore the construction of specific forms of masculinity and fail to analyse the impact on women of gendered power relations. Though the reference to 'patriarchy' indicates an acknowledgement of women and power relations, there is no attempt made to theorise how masculinities are constructed in relation to discourses of femininity - in order to devise a theoretical framework for the study of gender relations rather than simply masculinities.   The point I want to make here is that the idea that there are a multiplicity of masculinities supports my argument that the conceptualisation of masculinity that flows from the concept of patriarchy owes more to an ideological version of masculinity than to the actual lived experiences of men.   It is *crucial* to emphasise here that I am not suggesting that there is no relationship between feminist patriarchal analysis of men and masculinity and the behaviour of men.   In other words, there are gross inequalities surrounding gender power relations.   Rather my argument is that the notion of masculinity that flows from the concept of patriarchy is 'hegemonic masculinity'.   The view of men and masculinity that appears in the feminist orthodoxy on gender segregation is *this* discourse on masculinity.   This is a discourse that positions men as strong, virile, powerful, dominant, and technical.   Yet men are not homogeneous - that is why the notion of masculinities is more useful than masculinity as the differences between men that give rise to different types of masculinity also produces contradictory and complex practices at the workplace and elsewhere that will differentially affect the process of gendering at work. However these masculinities are constituted by a dominant discourse on masculinity and it is to this that I now turn.   In order to examine this 'hegemonic' discourse, it is necessary to review the emergence of the literature on men's studies.

Theorising Masculinity

In an important article that provides the basis for a theoretical rather than a descriptive account of masculinities, Carrigan, Connell and Lee (1985) elaborate the concept of hegemonic masculinity.   Their starting point for a discussion of masculinity is not patriarchy but rather the conceptualisation of gender, namely 'sex-role' theory that still continues to dominate the debates on sex and gender in sociology. Through a critique of role theory this seminal article began to lay the foundation for a theory of gender that is dynamic rather than static, and set the framework for the study of gender as a *process* rather than as a *structure*. This analysis of the sociology of gender that predates the emergence of second wave feminism establishes the theoretical connections between traditional sociological writings on men and masculinity, the 'new men's studies and feminist analysis of patriarchy.

The paper begins by evaluating the growth of 'new men's studies' from 1971 to 1985 and provides a useful outline and discussion of the themes that dominated the literature between those dates. The article discusses the focus on the social construction of masculinity in the texts and presents a summary of the conflict men experience with traditional masculinity. Some of this conflict is expressed in terms that echo feminist writings on the experiences of women. Some writers refer to the way they are oppressed and alienated from mainstream masculinity and the strategies they follow in order to gain 'liberation'. Carrigan, Connell and Lee (1985) make the point that very little of this literature is radical in the sense of being politically directed in relation to the concerns of feminism, rather:

> The central theoretical proposition of the 1970s masculinity literature, even if it sometimes remained implicit, was that men are oppressed in a fashion comparable to women. But the oppressor was not taken to be women (except in the view of the right wing of the men's movement ...). Rather, it was taken to be the *male role*. (Carrigan, Connell and Lee 1985, p.567)

This emphasis on the 'male role' Carrigan, Connell and Lee attribute to the dominance of Parsonian functionalism in the sociological analysis of sex and gender. Functionalism states that there is a shared societal consensus on values and norms of social behaviour without that society could not function. According to this perspective socialisation is the process by that men and women learn rules (*social roles*) that enable them to behave in socially acceptable ways within a society. The concept of 'role' is used to conceptualise the relationship of individuals to society. It is not only functionalism that stresses the importance of roles and socialisation. For example, the symbolic interactionists, Berger and Luckmann, state,

> Roles appear as soon as a common stock of knowledge containing reciprocal typifications of conduct is in process of formation, a process that ... is endemic to social interaction. (Berger and Luckmann 1966, p.92)

Sociological perspectives will differ as to the prescriptive or normative stress on structure and agency in the analysis of social roles. In functionalist analysis sex-role theory has a tendency to view masculinity and femininity as scripts that are learnt in order to enable individual men and women to carry out their respective gender roles.[1] The content of masculinity is learnt through the various agencies of socialisation, the family - for functionalists the primary site of socialisation - and via the education system, religion, work, and the state. The concept of sex roles and socialisation dominates textbook sociology and is used to explain gender divisions and gender relations. Gender inequalities are explained through an analysis of the social construction of gender differentiation through socialisation. An example of this type of analysis can be illustrated by the following quote from a well-known introductory sociology textbook,

> Parents may sometimes be unaware that they treat their sons differently from their daughters; at other times they may find themselves doing so against their own intentions. A set of interviews with feminist mothers revealed that - despite their avowed intentions to allow children to develop with minimal regard to conventional gender roles - boys (though less so girls) were often raised in sex-stereotyped ways. (Van Gelder and Carmichael, 1975 quoted in Bilton, et al. 1987, p.187) (see also Giddens 1995, Haralambos and Holborn 1990)

Sex-role theory skews conceptualisations of gender, and the attributes associated with masculinity and femininity, towards the notion that these are *fixed roles* that are learnt, either well or badly, depending on the quality of the socialisation. Any abnormality in the performance of role, for example, homosexuality rather than heterosexuality is 'abnormal', 'dysfunctional' and deviant. Boys and men learn a script called masculinity and they either learn it well, or not; whatever the case may be; women also learn a script called femininity - again either well or not. As Carrigan, Connell and Lee (1985) point out, 'conflicts' in masculinity are analysed by some writers as incorrect socialisation and/or the lack of male role models.[2]

In the history of sociology functionalist analysis has been widely criticised for its inability to theorise social change and social conflict and for the claim of consensus in relation to shared values and norms. Sex role theory is also unable to explain either role conflict or social change in relation to gender roles and the social relations of gender. As Carrigan, Connell and Lee point out, 'Sex role theory cannot grasp change as a dialectic arising within gender relations themselves' (1985, p.580).

The Concept of Gender in Feminist Sociology

This discussion of the problems of conceptualising gender in terms of sex-role theory helped me to understand the conceptualisation of gender that is embedded in the concept of patriarchy. It is the notion of sex-differentiated gender roles that pervades this concept that is the basis for the theoretical problems outlined in the first three chapters of the book. These theoretical problems can be traced to the conceptualisation of gendered sex roles that is embodied in patriarchal analysis that produced these theoretical and analytical dilemmas. I began to realise that sex role theory has dominated not only 'mainstream' sociology but also feminist sociology (see Abbott and Wallace 1990). From its inception, feminist analysis took the hegemonic discourse on masculinity and referred to it as *the* male role. In contrast to functionalism, feminist analysis emphasised the dysfunctional character of the role and argued that the 'sex-role' assigned to women (traditional discourse on femininity) that is said to complement the male role, is also dysfunctional and oppressive. Functional and dysfunctional are not terms that are used in feminist sociology; rather the emphasis is on the *conflict* women experience with the male role. All feminist perspectives, whether liberal feminism, socialist feminism or radical feminism (see Tong 1989) analyses and challenge the content of the roles/scripts that women are expected to both internalise and reproduce. Rather than constructing a critique of the conceptualisation of gender in terms of sex roles, feminist sociology criticises the conflicting and oppressive elements of the sex-roles into that women are socialised. Feminist analysis describes the ways by that women are subordinated, oppressed and conflicted by the prescriptive and normative scripts of masculinity and femininity. However this theoretical model reassembles a static conceptualisation of gender and makes it difficult to analyse not only social change in relation to gender relations but also the way women resist, negotiate and challenge the dominant discourses of femininity. Moreover, this way of theorising gender reproduces a discourse on men and masculinity and a discourse on women and femininity that contains aspects of a traditional, (hegemonic) and reactionary discourse on gender. Even when writers such as Cockburn (1991) attempts to use gender as a relational concept not a static one - the framework established by patriarchy skews the analysis towards viewing gender relations in terms of gender difference, as oppositional rather than as contradictory and inter-related discourses. Her book *In the Way of Women: men's resistance to sex equality in organizations* (1991) by its very title positions women and men as oppositional. Though she problematises gender relations at work much more usefully and successfully than any other writer in the field an analysis of the fluidity of gendering at the workplace is missing from her analysis. Despite the subtlety of her analysis part of her concluding chapter reaffirms the feminist orthodoxy of male power and women's subordination described in chapter three. She writes:

> Men reward women for sexual difference when they are in their proper place; penalise them for it once they step into men's place. These are the means whereby men control women. They exert a masculine cultural hegemony that makes it unlikely that women will willingly forfeit men's approval, will identify with each other or with feminism. (Cockburn 1991, p.218)[3]

As Beechey explains in her discussion of Cockburn's work, that although her work is 'wonderfully insightful' she still retains the dualism of a patriarchal system interacting with capitalism as the basis of her theory of gender so that her categories 'are rather all-embracing' (1988, p.57). The problem with dual system theory has been discussed in more detail in an earlier chapter. It is the problematic use of patriarchy setting up the category of gender as static that is the issue here. The consequence of using the sex role framework is that it elaborates a static and abstract interpretation of gender differences and gender relations which make it difficult to interpret and analyse the actual activities and power of women in different social contexts. As Carrigan, Connell and Lee point out:

> The result of using the role framework is an abstract view of the differences between the sexes and their situations not a concrete one of the relations between them. (Carrigan, Connell and Lee 1985, p.580)

It is important to conceptualise gender not as something that pertains to sexed bodies but rather to conceive of gender as 'the set of effects produced in bodies, behaviours, and social relations' (Foucault 1990, p.127).

The Concept of Hegemonic Masculinity

Carrigan et al. (1985) developed the concept of 'hegemonic masculinity' as an attempt to introduce a more fluid and dynamic approach to the study of masculinity. In light of their critique of sex role theory they argue that,

> What emerges from this line of argument is the very important concept of hegemonic masculinity, not as "the male role", but as a particular variety of masculinity so that others - among them young and effeminate as well as homosexual men - are subordinated. It is particular groups of men, not men in general, who are oppressed within patriarchal sexual relations, and whose

situations are related in different ways to the overall logic of the subordination of women to men. (Carrigan, Connell and Lee 1985, p.587)

Throughout the article the importance of male homosexuality is cited as providing a route into understanding masculinity and gender relations. The sexuality of gay men challenges the discourse on heterosexuality that is a strong element of hegemonic masculinity in that men - 'real' men - that is, are only interested in heterosexual sex. Historically, of course, this has not always been the case. As the authors state:

> A passion for beautiful boys was compatible with hegemonic masculinity in renaissance Europe, emphatically not so at the end of the nineteenth century. In this historical shift, men's sexual desire was to be focused more closely on women - a fact with complex consequences for them - while groups of men who were visibly not following the hegemonic pattern were more specifically labelled and attacked. (ibid., 1985, p.593)

Why this desire, heterosexual desire that is, takes the form of male dominance and women's subordination is not examined or discussed anywhere in the article despite the authors insistence that 'hegemonic masculinity is centrally connected with the institutionalisation of men's dominance over women' (1985, p.592). The lack of explanation here of the reasons why hegemonic masculinity should take this form is one of the problems with this attempt to produce a new sociology of masculinity and gender relations. It is also important to note that masculinity is theorised with reference to the way masculinities are subordinated by and structured in relation to hegemonic masculinity. The authors do not seek a way of theorising masculinity in relation to femininity - the emphasis is exclusively on masculinity.[4] Another weakness is that the article does not provide a very precise or sharp definition of the concept of hegemonic masculinity. The definition that is offered is one that is defined in relation to the critique of role theory, and there is no elaboration of the composition of the type of masculinity that is both hegemonic and dominant. Instead of an adequate definition of hegemonic masculinity there is throughout the paper the rather casual assumption that it can be understood as either 'traditional' or mainstream 'masculinity'. The usefulness of this concept however is that it allows one to conceptualise not only different types of masculinities that are structured by, or have a relationship to, hegemonic masculinity, but it also enables one to grasp the ways in which this relationship can take the form of resistance, subordination, collusion, rejection, or acceptance. Whatever form the relationship takes, the concept enables one to understand the way hegemonic masculinity creates problems and contradictions (the infamous, crisis of masculinity) for different groups of men as they struggle to act as 'men' in different social contexts. In order to elaborate the concept of hegemonic masculinity and to provide an illustration of the similarities between the sex role theory and the construction of men and masculinity in the concept of patriarchy I have constructed a typology that represents an outline of this discourse. This is used purely for the purpose of attempting to present an outline of the discourses and practices that indicate the cultural beliefs that are associated with men.

Table 6.1: Typology of the hegemonic discourse on masculinity

IMAGE	OBSESSIONS	OCCUPATIONS	TRAITS
Powerful	*Sex -*	Paid *Work*	Independent
Strong	Heterosexuality	Skilled	Rational
Big	Pornography	Technical worker	Cultured
Single	*Power*	Manual worker	Competitive
Handsome		Mental labour	Brave
Hirsute	*Physical*	Manager	Virile
Muscular Body	activities	Writer	Sexually active
	Sport	Scientist	Violent
Stands in a	War	Engineer	Controlled
certain way	Outdoors	Surgeon	Repressed
	Technology		Superior
Sits with legs		Paternal authority	
apart	Public	*Power*	*Power and*
Wears Trousers	responsibilities	Control	*Control:*
(metaphorically			in relation to
and			
Figuratively)			-emotions
Stands alone			-other men
			-women
			-children

It is this discourse that organises and structures the modes and varieties of masculinities that are 'performed' by men and the one that creates confusions, contradictions and 'crisis'. This discourse tells a particular story of men and masculinity, but it is an idealised and ideological account of the social construction of masculinity. Nevertheless this typology enables one to appreciate the way different groups of men, for example, gay men, re-represented certain aspects of this discourse. The writings by gay men on masculinity opened a space whereby the difficulties with hegemonic masculinity began to be exposed. In order to provide one example of the way masculinities interact[5] with the dominant discourse on masculinity, I want to take the discourse on the male body and demonstrate both the contradictory nature and the power of the dominant discourse on masculinity. The first point to note is the relationship between body image and the other categories listed in the typology. As Connell (1987) states,

> The meaning in the bodily sense of masculinity concern above all else, the superiority of men to women, and the exaltation of hegemonic masculinity over other groups of men that is essential to the domination of women. The social definition of men as holders of power is translated not only into mental body images and fantasies, but into muscle tensions, posture, the feel and texture of the body. This is one of the main ways in that the power of men becomes 'naturalised'. (Connell 1987, p.85)

But not all men can achieve this type of body image, they may be small, fat, lack muscle tone or whatever, or they may resist the notion that their gender/masculinity is constructed through this body image. A different type of resistance and negotiation is the 'macho-style' adopted by gay men (Weeks 1985), and the emphasis on physicality in gay culture. As Richard Dyer explains:

> By taking the signs of masculinity and eroticising them in a blatantly homosexual context, much mischief is done to the security with that 'men' are defined in society, and by that their power is secured. If that bearded, muscular beer drinker turns out to be a pansy, how ever are they going to know the 'real' men any more? (Dyer, as quoted in Weeks 1985, p.191)

The concept of hegemony is useful in that it allows one to theorise the dialectical interplay between the contradictions, negotiations and resistance to this discourse on masculinity and discourses on femininity and the experiences of women and men. At the same time the notion of discourse enables one to grasp how the subjects of this interplay, the *sexed bodies* of women and men, are *fixed* by a discourse rooted in biology. It appears as if hegemonic masculinity refers to an observable stable subject - a biological body. It is this notion of the fixity of biology that gives such power and legitimation to this discourse on masculinity and to the corresponding discourse of hegemonic femininity. These discourses appear to refer to 'natural' differences, and seems 'true' and 'fitting' and thus 'common-sense', though the recent literature on bodies and technology would indicate that it is no longer possible, *if it ever was*, to conceive of biology as a fixed, or stable category (Grosz 1994; Butler 1993; Haraway 1991). The point here is that the dominant, patriarchal hegemonic discourse on men and masculinity assumes this fixity to biology. One of the distinguishing features of a man is his penis, and 'real' men engage in heterosexist sex with their penises - but as the quote from Dyer indicates - they don't. There is no stability to hegemonic masculinity either in terms of its referent - the male body- or in relation to the way men experience masculinity. Some men reject the idealised male body as part of their identity as men. Their view of masculinity will tend then to stress other elements of this discourse, for example, a particular type of occupation. It is the 'hegemonic discourse' that is always in flux or in 'crisis' and it is not longer possible, (if it ever was) to theorise men and masculinity assuming a stable hegemonic masculinity. The discourse of hegemonic masculinity is composed of a number of inter-relating but distinct discourses - discourses of the body, discourses of work, discourses of sexuality - all of that shape men's practice and attitudes towards themselves, other men and women. Thus rather than refer to the discourse of hegemonic masculinity it is necessary to consider the different discourses that it contains.

The problems with the conceptualisation of gender and men and masculinity that I have discussed thus far in this chapter did not unfortunately set the framework for my interviews with the male computer programmers. As I explained in the introduction the interviews were conducted before I had worked through all of the theoretical problems with the feminist explanation of gender segregation - a framework that had shaped the interview schedule. This meant that I was not as alert as I needed to be to the process of gendering in the various workplaces I visited. I believe now that my research method would have still present problems for exploring this process, but even within the limitations of this method - a sharper intellectual clarity of gender as process would have forced me to ask different type of questions, much more directed to issues of masculinity and sexuality at the workplace.

Two key areas of the discourse of hegemonic masculinity were discussed with the male computer programmers I interviewed - these are the social relations that constitute their paid work and their relationship and attitude to domestic labour in the home. I used these two areas to structure my discussions with men as I investigated the extent to which work is a central constituent of men's subjectivity and subject positions as men,[6] and the contradictions for their relationship to domestic labour and childcare responsibilities.

Is Paid Work a Primary Part of Hegemonic Masculinity?

One of the most consistent themes that occurs and reoccurs throughout much of the literature on masculinity is the centrality of paid work to men's working lives and to the construction and reproduction of masculinity. The importance of work identities to male identity is demonstrated by a large number of studies. David Morgan (1992) has recently revisited classic sociological accounts of men at work and produced a reading that attempts to highlight the subtext of gender 'hidden' within these texts. The studies he examined include, Weber's *The Protestant Ethic and the Spirit of Capitalism (1930)*, Whyte's *Street Corner Society (1955)*, and more recent modern classics such as Nichols and Beynon's *Living with Capitalism (1977)*. Morgan attempts to ask feminist questions of the material, and states that his reading has 'been shaped by a particular understanding of gender relations, one that has derived largely from the feminist critique of patriarchal institutions and practices' (Morgan 1992, p.70). Despite the problems, discussed above, of using this framework, some interesting ideas emerge from this account. In particular, the relevance of the separation of home and work to hegemonic masculinity is given a particular emphasis in Weber's analysis and definition of capitalism. Weber believed that the growth and development of modern capitalism is dependent on the separation of waged work from the work of the household, as the household would contain traditional and affective ways of thinking and acting as opposed to the calculating rationality necessary for the world of business and commerce. To quote:

> The modern rational organisation of the capitalistic enterprise would not have been possible without two other important factors in its development: the separation of business from the household, that completely dominates modern economic life and closely connected with it, rational book-keeping. (Weber 1930, pp.21-2)

Morgan discusses the impact of this separation for men in terms of the different contradictory aspects of masculinity that he relates to Weber's notion of the 'spirit' of capitalism. He contrasts the notion of machismo, with its underlying presumption of sexuality and sexual conquest, to the ideas of self discipline and rationality that are central components of the spirit of capitalism and are pivotal to a specific, mainly middle-class professional construction of masculinity. The contrast amongst men of different classes in relation not only to their acquisition of masculinity but also the way in that maleness is manifested within the different cultures is also discussed. Morgan suggests that the contradictory aspects of masculinity can be traced to different experiences men have at different times in their lives. So, for example, the notion of self-discipline and sacrifice separates off married and family men from single men. The latter group would place an emphasis on sexuality and virility in order to establish their masculine identity.

My research material also suggests this analysis. There are clear differences between the men in my sample in relation to the aspects of hegemonic masculinity that shaped their attitude to work and gender relations in the workplace. Of the twenty-three men in my sample, sixteen were married with children; only one was married and childless, the rest were single and either living alone or with parents. Though we never discussed sexuality, virility as an aspect of this discourse is expressed in a number of ways. We talked about cars and careers. One single man told me that he had moved around software houses because he 'desperately' needed a car. He told me about the problems he was having with his 'old banger' that he was deeply attached to, but could not afford to run. So he wanted a company car for 'running about in' but he was very particular about the type of car. Different type of cars were associated with difference hierarchies in the organisation, so this man was seeking promotion in order to acquire a 'good' car, i.e. a status car. The single men were generally more interested in money and their level of pay than job satisfaction. They were also more motivated by the excitement of 'something new' - that involved either changing companies or on the lookout for new challenges, actively seeking more responsibility than either the older men or the majority of young women in the sample. One man told me that his 'ambition was endless'. Though he was careful to point out that this did not mean that he was 'computer crazy' and though he was only 24 years of age he said that 'techies' tended to be 'the young lads, who were computer crazy, eat and sleep it and read every piece of computer thing published'. The fear of boredom and the desire to have an exciting job were continually used as a criteria for an evaluation of men's work, they were always looking for something 'different' in order to retain their interest in their work. This energetic approach to work manifested itself in acquiring useful information about the company they worked for, with an eye to changing their position in the organisation, usually by seeking promotion. The following conversation is very typical. One man, Nick, told me that after dealing with applications programming for four years he wanted to move on.

> I did it for four years and I'd had enough. I was looking to get off. ... I had a chat with one of the guys in operations, and he said that there was a vacancy going so I made all the moves, enquired about the job and it sounded very interesting. It was totally different to what I'd been doing and if I'm going to get on as far as computing terms go I think it's a good idea to have done a wide range of things.

A. F. When you say 'get on' what do you mean?

> Climb the ladder whether it's on a technical level or whether it's on a managerial level. I don't know yet, I haven't decided that route I'm taking, but the more experience you have, the more areas you know about, I believe stands you in better stead for the future. (Extract from transcripts)

With very few exceptions all of the men I interviewed were very knowledgeable about organisational details: the structure of the hierarchy, the distinctions between different work titles; and had devised a useful network for keeping in touch with what was 'new' in the organisation. For the majority, job progression, job satisfaction and intellectual excitement were critical aspects of their attitude to work. They explained that differences between men can be traced to their 'drive' and this will affect the importance they put on: (i) their level of pay, (ii) excitement and challenge of 'managing' projects or acquiring 'technical' knowledge or (iii) the intellectual stimulation of taking responsibility. One man admitted that what attracted him about taking responsibility for projects was having power. When I asked what this meant to him, he said that he liked to

> have some control over what's going on, rather than somebody else controlling what I do. (Extract from transcripts).

As will be demonstrated in the next section, men with children, especially younger men were more likely to question the contradictions of these attitudes for their domestic lives. But generally it appears that their work is central to their subject positions. Different aspects of hegemonic masculinity shape the options they choose at work but the notions of excitement, challenge, and stimulation are significant in that they can be related to the idea of 'drive' that can be associated with, as Hollway tells us, 'the production of meanings concerning sexuality' (1984, p.231) and the discourse of male sexual drive that is another critical element of hegemonic masculinity. The interview material would then appear to indicate that though work occupies a central position in hegemonic masculinity, for the majority of the men interviewed this centrality is related to excitement, power and control, and thus linked with the male sexual drive discourse. This suggests a different interpretation to the position that emerges from the 'new men's studies' interpretation of masculinity and paid work, that is usually discussed with reference to the notion of crisis, rather than sexual excitement. This material also points to the process of gendering at the workplace.

Discourses on Paid Work and Hegemonic Masculinity

In order to explain the contradictions of hegemonic masculinity for men, the writers on the topic have a tendency to concentrate on different aspects and practices within the various discourses. Some writers analyse the ways that masculine identities and subjectivities are shaped by sexuality, 'race', and class and by different cultural experiences, see for example, Brod and Kaufman (1994); Segal (1990); Connell (1983). Other writers Chapman and Rutherford (1988), Metcalf and Humphries (1985) emphasise changes in hegemonic masculinity in relation to sexuality and attempt to assess the implications of these changes for gender relations. Whereas, Brittan (1989); Tolson (1977); Morgan and Hearn (1992); Collinson and Hearn (1994) emphasise the centrality and importance of paid work and men's occupations for an understanding of men and masculinities. In their analysis of changing masculinities they stress structural changes in the organisation of the capitalist labour process. According to these writers, the pressure both for change and crisis in relation to masculinities can be traced to the same source - changes in the nature of work, both in middle class and working class occupations; changes in the structure of the labour market; the type of jobs that are available to men, the addition of women to the labour force and the lack of availability of paid work (Connell 1991; Willis 1977). The increasing demands for equal treatment from women and the development of global capitalism is discussed in terms of a loss of dignity and increased alienation at work, and as fracturing hegemonic masculinity. The shifts in public and private patriarchy that, along with the growth of women's involvement in the labour market, and the development of women's liberation are key elements in the explanation for the crisis of masculinity thesis. As Brittan explains:

> Today the 'crisis of masculinity' is, ... much more severe because of the tremendous structural changes in advanced industrial societies. Moreover, the crisis is theorized and discussed in academic journals and texts; it is given reality in the media, and it is preached about in churches. Reasons for its magnitude have been attributed to the rise of feminism, the collapse of the nuclear family, and the consolidation of a hedonistic materialistic culture that celebrates the sovereignty of individual desire. More important, however, is the belief that women are not only beginning to dominate some sections of the labour market, but that they are also moving into positions of real power in government and industry. (Brittan 1989, pp.180-1)

An analysis of the miscellaneous discourses that make up hegemonic masculinity is beyond the scope of this book. So whilst remembering the manifest connections between all the different aspects and practices that make up the discourses of masculinities, I want to concentrate on the relationship of men's paid work to their masculine identity. I want to explore the idea that it is in fact the power of this discourse that makes it difficult for some men (such as the male computer programmers I interviewed), to become more involved with household tasks.

Conflicting Discourses: Hegemonic Masculinity and Domesticity

The cultural distinction between what is considered men's work and women's work and the strong link between paid work and male identity, and hegemonic masculinity may account for the resistance on men's part to domestic labour that is indicated by the responses from men to the questions on domestic labour considered below. This in turn reinforces and reproduces hegemonic discourses on gender.

In this section I am concentrating on the responses from men who had children, rather than the single men interviewed. I found that there was a tremendous reluctance to talk to me about their involvement with domestic arrangements, particularly housework - and this contrasts not only with their ease in talking about work but also their willingness to discuss their contribution to childcare. The defensiveness and sometimes hostility to my questions on housework, was continually expressed by the faltering responses, and the constant requests for clarification on the meaning and usefulness of these questions. Very often astonishment was expressed at the fact that I was asking *men* a series of questions dealing with the issues around childcare and housework. Generally there was a lack of awareness of how much is involved with the running of a home, even when children are not present. This can be illustrated by the extract from an interview with Keith Parker, a fifty one year old with four children, only two of whom, an eleven year-old and a sixteen year-old, were still living at home:

> Talking of involvement with the family. When you say bringing them up, if they were young children, say under five then I could quite easily perceive a different direction to your question, because a woman tends more to be the primary influence. But for instance with the younger lad, the sixteen year old, we have mucked in, we go out rambling, and walks and swimming and things like that. The youngster goes swimming as well and she now is coming out on the rambles and walks so I ... try and do things with them whereas with the two older ones I was perhaps more divorced from them . . How relevant is this to programming? (Extract from transcripts)

> There are aspects within the house, for instance my wife will, ... because she's working quite a lot, she's probably working more hours, fiscal hours,

than I am. For instance, she doesn't get in until about three o'clock in the morning.[7] That's very, very tiring. She's actually shattered in the morning and of course, I would say, in the housewife terms does the washing, the ironing, the shopping. I like to go shopping with her because that's one of the tasks we can do together. She won't let me touch the ironing although I can do it. Washing, well these days it's no problem you just open the washing machine, put it on a particular programme and I'm quite capable of doing that. I'm quite capable of cooking, but being a traditionalist my wife doesn't like me to do it. Well there was a period of two years or so when I did everything, . . , I'm capable of doing it, it's a question of whether it's easier to avoid the aggro by not doing this than to try and force the issue. Does that answer the question? (Extract from transcripts)

The men usually began by telling me that I should be talking to their partners if I want to know about their contribution to the house - who they said 'would probably contradict' their interpretation of their involvement and of their appropriation of family responsibilities. They were untroubled by how little time they actually spent on housework. It was very obviously not a priority for them. They did however resist the notion that they spent very little time on household chores. Though some men looked at me apologetically the majority tended to emphasise the contribution they made. There was a general tendency, when the question was pressed for them to indicate that they contributed quite a 'fair bit' of time to the running of the home, though they spent very little time on housework. Responses to my request for details of their contribution ranged from a singularly honest 'I do the odd job' to the more typical 'I do the washing up, and I put the kids to bed when she's out'. The following sequence of quotes gives an illustration of these responses.

A.F: What about housework how many hours do you do a week?

I suppose I do a fair bit actually.

A.F. Do you?

Yes, wash the pots etc.

A.F. So, you always do the washing up?

It's shared between us, she either washes and I'll dry.

A.F. And the cooking?

Oh, yes, she cooks usually, yes ... If she's ill, I'll do the ironing and stuff . .
I mean, I get home, have my tea then there's the dog to take for a bloody
walk isn't there. I do all the dog walking practically.

A.F. Do you?

Yes, well she takes it out during the day if she's got to get the kids from
school, but normally on a night I do it.

This type of response is a good illustration of the way that these men
were oblivious to the amount of time that is needed to organise a
household. When I asked if they could provide me with an approximate
figure for the number of hours and specific tasks that they undertook, it
became clear that their input tended to be very minimal. So, for example,
David a thirty three year old with three children[8] said of his contribution
around the home:

I do the washing up. Until last week I helped put the kids to bed. Both the
kids and saw them all get into bed. Alison, that's my wife, is involved in
quite a lot of the same things in the church that I am that means we swap,
that means that I will put the kids to bed and she'll go out and do some of
the other things, so I'm as competent at putting them to bed as she is, - not
quite as competent but I would do a good job.

A.F. Not quite as competent?

Yes. Well bathing three at one time is not easy when they're sort of all
under three. It takes a fair amount of effort by yourself ... I find it hard
work. In one sense it's challenging. So I wouldn't decry that I think that
it's an important role to take on. In one sense it is more important doing
that role than me working ... because I could get a job elsewhere, whereas
bringing up the family has a more continuing aspect. (Extract from
transcripts)

A distinction needs to be made here between men's role in childcare
and their role in housework. There was an overall awareness of the need to
be more involved in childcare and from a number of men they expressed
sadness about their inability to be more actively involved. They expressed
pride and pleasure in their relationships with their children and on many
occasions expressed regret for the fact that they are missing out on their
child's development and growth. This view was more prevalent from
younger men with children, but not always, as the following indicates. Ian,
29 years old, with a 15-month-old son said they he did very little 'actual'
childcare. The majority of men then clearly operated within a very rigid

and traditional sexual division of labour and made no apology for this. Mark, aged 53, with two grown up children, whose partner worked as a full time secretary said that she took total responsibility 'for the housework and that sort of thing'. One man used the presence of domestic technology as the explanation for his lack of contribution to the domestic division of domestic labour in his home.

A.F. You said you were married. Does your wife work?

She's a dressmaker and curtain maker. She's only been doing that the last two or three years.[9]

A.F. Housework? How many hours a week do you do?

I'm trying to match with my wife but I don't know if I'm going to achieve it though. We don't seem to have a lot to do. It's reduced since the kids left. I don't know how many hours. Washing the pots, doing a bit of cooking. I don't do any washing. I don't know ... I suppose maybe about three hours a week.

A.F. How many hours does your wife do?

Well she's obviously done a lot more in the past but now we've got an automatic washer and a microwave. ... She does the washing and ironing and things. She still does a lot of things for our daughter. She does a lot more than I do, maybe ten hours a week. (Extract from transcripts)

These contradictory and ambivalent attitudes towards childcare and housework correspond to similar findings in some of the literature on men and masculinity. The research would also indicate that the 'feminist orthodoxy' on men's control of women's labour and subordination in the home is still salient. However I want to argue even from my small sample that there are differences between men especially in relation to responsibility around childcare that produces conflicts for the discourse of hegemonic masculinity. The next section reviews some of the statistical evidence on the division of labour in the household, and though the evidence is slight, there appears to be some changes amongst men in their attitude to childcare and household responsibilities. The research evidence that is outlined below would indicate some change in men's engagement with childcare, and with the day-to-day drudgery of housework.

Sexual Division of Labour in the Household

Some of the evidence on this topic is summarised by Lynne Segal in *Slow Motion* (1990). In her analysis of the changing perspectives of men to fatherhood from the inter-war years to the present day, she considers men's desire to experience a more involved relationship with their children. She quotes a number of studies that would support the view that men's domestic involvement is limited to their concern and interest in children rather than with the support of the women in caring for the home. This is despite the increased involvement of women in the labour market. The numbers of women, especially married women working have increased dramatically since the Second World War.

In America in 1948, 38.5% of all women aged between sixteen and fifty years of age participated in the work force. By 1987 this percentage had increased to 68.6.% (see Crosby and Jaskar 1993). If these figures are broken down to consider the numbers of married women with children who are working, it appears that in 1987, 66.7% of all women aged twenty five to fifty four years of age with a child 18 years or younger were employed, compared with figures of married women working in 1920 when only 9% of all household had two wage packets. Despite the increase in the number of married women with children doing paid work the research on the division of labour in the home shows that between 1965 and 1975 husbands in America increased the time they spent on housework from an average of 81.4 minutes per day to an average of 82.5 minutes per day, an increase of just over one minute a day (Crosby and Jaskar 1993, p.145).

Research by Berk (1985) that specifically examines the contribution to household tasks of men in families where both the man and the woman are working full time found little difference in the amount of housework done by the man. In 1976, 353 husbands were selected to keep diaries of how they spent their time. It was found that those men married to employed women devoted *four minutes more* per day to household tasks than did men married to housewives. By 1987, further research revealed that this figure had increased to '10 minutes more per day on childcare than other fathers if they were white, and sixteen minutes more per day if they were black' (quoted in Crosby and Jaskar 1993, p.146).

In Britain, the change in employment rates for married women shows a similar pattern. In 1951 the number in paid employment is 21.7%; by 1971 the figure had changed to 42.3% and by the 1980s the rate for married women's participation in the labour market had reached over 50% (see Beechey 1986, p.50). Ann Oakley (1974) provides a comparison of data on housework hours that show that on average in Britain in 1951 women were doing seventy-two hours of housework per week. By 1971 this figure had increased to 77 hours per week. The difficulty of interpreting the research on the domestic division of labour is due to the lack of consensus on the definition of household tasks. Also as Judy Wajcman points out,

> A major problem with most time-budget research is that it does not recognise that the essence of housework is to combine many things, usually concurrently. This has a profound bearing on the interpretation of time spent in childcare and the apparent growth of leisure time. (Wajcman 1991, p.94)

Recent figures show that, on average, a 'husband' will do 5.28 hours of housework a week where he is the breadwinner, and in the case of all couples, 'husbands' will do 6.57 hours a week. The *Women and Employment* survey collated by Martin and Roberts (1984) indicates that nearly three-quarters of 'working' wives do all or most of the housework, and this remains true even for the 54% of the women who work full time.

Table 6.2: Division of household tasks [1] 1983 and 1991 in percentages

	1983			1991		
	Men	Wm	Shared	Men	Wm	Shared
Household shopping	5	51	44	8	45	47
Makes evening meal	5	77	17	9	70	20
Does evening dishes	17	40	40	28	33	37
Does household cleaning	3	72	24	4	68	27
Does washing and ironing	1	89	10	3	84	12
Repairs household equipment	82	6	10	82	6	10
Organises household bills and money	29	39	32	31	40	28
Looks after sick children[2]	1	63	35	1	60	39
Teaches children discipline	10	12	77	9	17	73

[1] By married couples or couples living as married
[2] Data on child rearing for 1983 relates to 1984

Source: Social and Community Planning Research (*Social Trends 25 1995*)

I mentioned above that there are slight shifts in men's involvement the household, and these figures indicate how slight they are. These surveys show that men had greater involvement in some household tasks in 1991 than they did in 1983. The percentage of men who prepared the evening meal increased from 17% in 1983 to 28% in 1991, and there is an increase in men's doing the household shopping. The recent survey also attempting to discover the extent to which gender perceptions of these tasks had changed and this is indicated in the following table.

The survey does not provide a breakdown of responses according to gender, but despite this limitation it appears that people believe household tasks should be shared much more, with the exception of washing and ironing for women and household repairs for men. These tasks reflect assumptions about women's work and men's work that are so familiar in the production of meanings concerning masculinity and femininity.

Table 6.3: Gender perceptions of household tasks 1991[1]

How Tasks should be shared	Men	Women	Shared
	%	%	%
Household shopping	1	22	76
Makes evening meal	1	39	59
Does evening dishes	11	11	75
Does household cleaning	1	36	62
Does washing and ironing	-	58	40
Repairs household equipment	66	1	31
Organises household bills and money	17	14	66
Looks after sick children	-	37	60
Teaches children discipline	8	17	73

[1]All respondents were asked how tasks should be shared. Those who were married or cohabiting were asked how tasks were actually shared. Only married and cohabiting couples with children under 16 living in the same household were asked about child rearing.

Source: Social and Community Planning Research.[10]

The *British Social Attitudes Survey 1988* stated that even for couples with no children at home, the bulk of household work is still done by women and, overall, the position has hardly changed in the last few years. This is indicated by recent figures on men's contribution to household tasks. There is no information given in these surveys as to what extent these households use nannies, cleaners, etc., and figures on the number of households who used paid help for domestic labour was not available. The tables are used here simply to indicate the extent to which women continue to have responsibility for housework and childcare. These assumptions are also part of the process of gendering at work as they produce contradictions for women and men as illustrated by the following extracts from two of the women interviewed.

> I think a lot of men see their job as more important than the home and so they're looking for something that interests them and if they want they can get on and have promotion and I think men feel it's sort of about their manliness, their job, it's part of a man. I think a job is part of him. The home sort of thing, to a lot, to most women I would say it's just part of something they do, most get married and have children and when they've got children it's something they do to bring in extra money so they can go to Spain for holidays or whatever, you know. It's not so much, it's an extra to a woman rather than sort of part of her.

> A.F. Is that how you feel about your job?

> No, not really because I feel, I'm quite involved with the work, you know, I'm quite willing to put in as much overtime as I have to, if necessary, you know. I was here till half past seven last night. I started at half past seven yesterday morning and was here till half past seven last night. I'm quite involved with my job. I feel, to me it's quite an important part of my life. It's important to me to get some sort of satisfaction out of it, but I haven't' always felt like that. And my husband's quite supportive because he's told the bank he wants to stay within the area so that I can still work here because he knows I like it and I get quite a lot of satisfaction out of it, you know and he is quite prepared to say, 'I'll forego promotion'.

> I know of women I work closely with who are of the opinion that women certainly with young children shouldn't work, that it's very wrong for them to be at work, they should be at home, with the children. I don't know people who believe it's wrong for women to work, just for a mother.

> I mean we treat it as a bit of a joke, because I know their opinions and they know mine but I suppose I was surprised at the people who did feel that strongly, that it was wrong you know for a woman to have a career if she's got children, that her place is in the home, but everybody's entitled to their opinion, they know mine, and I know theirs and I would, if I had children, I would go back to work and I've made that opinion known. (Extract from transcripts)

One of the young men interviewed did not appear to be conscious of his assumption that women were responsible for the home.

> I suppose on the whole women work less hours as a rule. If they're married or aught like that it's not as easy for them to just stay behind when something wants doing until 11.00 o'clock, you know, it's not the kind of thing. It's more, because, I mean they have more to do in the home I suppose, really, so in that respect it's more demanding, but not impossible. I mean Jean for example she works, well more hours than I do anyway. I suppose she's single, so it's different. (Extract from transcripts)

Another man of a similar age stated,

> I think if you're going to have children you ought to have children and stop work until the children are at an age where they can look after themselves. (Extract from transcripts)

In a majority of interviews the discussion on the sexual division of labour in the home was analysed in relation to 'society' and 'people in general' and there appeared to be a confused awareness of the contradictions of these sentiments with working relations and practices, as the following extract illustrate:

> One of the problems I've found, well not problems, but one of the things I do find happening is quite often you're questioned by men as well as women because you're not married. You know, there's something the matter with you. You know 'why surely it's the done thing in society it's acceptable to 99% of women, why not you'? And then you get the other type of men who joke about it and say 'Oh, you've done the right thing, I should have done that' even though you know damn well they don't mean it. No, I know there's a lot of women I work with who are married and there are certain men who think that, you know, their role is at home and I suppose a lot of men's can't understand why women don't want to do the role at home like, as the norm in society. (Extract from transcripts)

Despite the changes as indicated by the surveys on the division of labour in the home there appears to be little movement in relation to housework notwithstanding the increased activity of women, especially married women, in the labour market. It is important to note here that the shift in men's involvement with childcare relates to only certain kinds of activities and generally they avoid the more monotonous, day-to-day maintenance of child rearing and feeding. It appears that many men are more involved in the leisured aspects of childcare, so they take on some of the interesting and pleasurable activities. So, for example, some will wheel the child in a pram in public, (something that previous generations of men found difficult as it challenged their notion of masculinity) and this is now a common occurrence (see Rutherford 1992). Many men will play with children in the park, take them to and from nursery, take them out for the day, bath them, read to them and generally take an interest and concern in their growth and development.

It appears to be the case that the traditional division of labour inside the home is still very strong around some areas of domestic labour and this is reflected in the responses of the male computer programmers. Martin and Roberts (1984) found that a substantial number of women and a high proportion of men thought that 'a women's place is in the home' and that 50 percent of all the respondents thought that 'a husband's job is to earn the money: a wife's job is to look after the family'. *British Social Attitudes* survey in 1988 found a similar pattern in that 63 percent of men and 51 percent of women surveyed thought that married women with children under school age ought to stay at home (Jowell, Witherspoon and Brook 1988, p.200).

It seems clear from these surveys that women are still largely responsible for the running of the household. It is women who do the cooking, cleaning, washing, shopping, and take on the major responsibility for childcare. Whilst men's contribution appears to increase marginally if a woman is in full time paid work and if there are children, the evidence indicates that men continue to consider domestic labour as women's work. Men regard their contribution as helping women rather than taking full and equal responsibility (Oakley 1985; Martin and Roberts 1984; Charles 1993). If this situation prevails contemporary developments on home working could worsen the situation.

The increased trend towards the use of technology in the home is a factor that blurs the distinction between the spheres of 'business' and the 'household' that Weber (see above) deemed to be so crucial for capitalism. Technology in what some commentators call the post-industrial society has lead to rapid changes in both the nature of work and individual experiences of paid labour. It is now possible for computer programmers to work from home, though it is still very limited. Only two of the women I interviewed worked mainly from home using information technologies. Depending on the type of occupation and on communications technology (e.g. faxes, electronic mail etc.), it is perfectly feasible for some workers to work in this way and it is a small but growing trend. The white-collar trade union MSF (Manufacturing, Science, Finance) has produced a checklist for negotiating home based teleworking arrangements with employers. Monica Blake (1994) in an article on teleworking in the nineties argues that at the present time ten to fifteen percent of the workforce is engaged in telework.

Garhammer and Gross (1993) conducted a study of teleworkers that found that they spent more time than other workers on childcare (quoted in Mundorf, Meyer, Schulze and Zoche 1995). These trends, though at present, limited to middle class professionals and the self-employed have important consequences for technologies and gender in relation to families. There are two famous example of firms using home based workers in computing in Britain - FI International that is entirely staff by home based workers and ICL that has the flexibility to support permanent staff with children to become home workers (Rubery et al. 1992).

A number of organisational practices discussed above; e.g. the practice of not allowing women to work shifts; the lack of flexibility on home working; the expectation of long and open ended working time requirements coupled with the assumption that women would not be able or willing to work these hours; the assumption that women had 'natural' helping skills that made them more suitable for support work rather than project work; demonstrates the importance of organisational discourses for gender segregation. These practices reinforced assumptions about gender attributes that had implications for men's subject positions and their resistance to housework. The relationship of these practices to the discourse of hegemonic masculinity help to explain why men are so resistant to an equal division of labour over household tasks. Yet this resistance is rarely a feature of the literature on masculinity. Rather in these texts the emphasis is on masculinity at the workplace rather than either on domestic labour or gender segregation at work and the implications of this for the study of gender at work.

Shifting Discourses: Men and Masculinities

In a manner that parallels the early production of feminist texts, from the late 1970s there has been an outpouring of books on men and masculinity largely describing how men feel, think, act, and understand masculinity. And just as it is difficult to discuss the category 'woman' without qualification in terms of class, 'race', sexual orientation, disability, age, ethnic origin, and culture, in a similar way it is equally difficult to discuss men and masculinity without talking about masculinities. Increasingly the 'new men's studies' became the study of masculinities rather than masculinity. The concept of multiple masculinities that refers to the diversity of forms of masculinity comes out of the analysis of the lived experiences of men as described in these texts. The concept of masculinities challenges the dominant discourse on masculinity and the model of men and masculinity that dominates the writing on gender, work and technology. The 'new men's studies' texts describe the problems and contradictions experienced by men as they try to negotiate, resist and accommodate the 'hegemonic' discourse on masculinity. Through the descriptions there emerges not only the idea of the multiplicity of masculinities, but also the problems and stress masculinity poses for men; and the complications of acquiring and maintaining their gender identity. The impetus for the growth of the 'new men's studies' was the reaction of pro-feminist men to the powerful critique of men and masculinity from second wave feminism. However this soon gave way to the 'crisis of masculinity' thesis and this shifts the debates away from an engagement with feminism to an exclusive concentration on men, (see the discussion in Brod and Kaufman 1994; Collinson and Hearn 1994). Many authors, especially, Tolson (1977); Carrigan, Connell and Lee (1985); (Connell 1985, 1987, 1991, 1995); Hearn (1985, 1987); Brod (1987); Brittan (1989); Hearn and Morgan (1990); Rutherford (1992); Brod and Kaufman (1994); point to a number of structural changes that occurred in industrial capitalism from the 1960s onwards that lead to this 'crisis.' The central features of these changes are usually taken to be the widespread application and ascendancy of technology; the subordination of the market to bureaucratic controls; increasing specialisation in paid work; the decline of manual occupations; deskilling and proletarianisation across a range of 'professions' the increased participation of women in waged labour and shifting values around sexuality and gender identity. As Tolson writes:

> For all men, particularly within certain fractions of the middle class, the post-war experience has been disturbing. There is a contemporary 'problem of masculinity' ... despite the institutionalization of male supremacy, and behind the masculine social presence, individual men are beginning to lose some of their self-confidence. Partly, the sheer complexity of the modern state sets firm limits on personal authority. Even at 'the top' a successful careerist cannot simply rule by personal charisma or domination. And partly, the sexual tensions of the 'sixties, effects of the 'permissive society', have undermined the masculine 'presence'. In a consumer society, sexuality is publicized, criticized, compared. It is not so easy for men to maintain the pretence of sexual bravado. (Tolson 1977, p.16)

Thus the failure of men to engage with housework and the slight changes that are evident from the research on men's involvement with childcare can be analysed in terms of shifts in the discourse of male occupations and paid work and the relationship of this discourse to the one on domestic labour. And it is the clash of these competing discourses that can explain some of the paradoxes and contradictions evident in the responses from the men I interviewed. The shifts in the discourse of men and work can be traced to the changes in the labour marker in respect of job security, deskilling, 'flexible working' and unemployment. These factors have meant that the vast majority of men can no longer expect job security or have any certainty that their chosen occupation/professional is in any way essential or significant. This according to a number of commentators has weakened men's confidence and power in relation to the public sphere of capitalism. For example, as Tolson states;

> For the disillusioned male careerist, this myth of 'domesticity' has become his last remaining source of support. Against the anxiety of his professional 'crisis of confidence' he will still make domestic plans, direct operations, project himself into the future. As husband and father, he is the subject of an ideology to that his wife and children are the objects of his concern, his protection, his authority. And his focal position is maintained by a continuing economic power - the material reality to that the ideology corresponds. (Tolson 1977, p.95)

Housework, then, comes up against two powerful discourses that shape masculine identity. The centrality of paid work for men's masculine identity (that includes strict notions of what constitutes men's work), and the organisational pressures of work in capitalist societies. Both of these occupational discourses keep in place the rigid sexual division of labour in the home. As Tolson said, ''Manhood' is achieved only at an emotional distance from the domestic world' (1977, p.50). The contradictions experienced by men in relation to their working life, make their investment in the family more acute and complex in terms of the role this plays in upholding their masculine identity.

Men, Sacrifice and Paid Work

What needs now to be explained is why this 'turn to domesticity' does not lead to equality in relation to domestic labour. It is clear from workplace studies, and there is some evidence from my interview material, that the importance of paid work for men, particularly married men, is related to the notion of areas of responsibility and self-sacrifice especially towards their children. And single men, in a similar fashion to single women, are aware that their attitude to work will have to change when they marry. The sense of responsibility and sacrifice undertaken by men for the welfare of their families is a critical factor in their self-identity and their interpretation of masculinity, and informs their views on paid work and domestic labour. To quote one of my respondents:

> We obviously decided when we had children that one day my wife would want to go back to work, but there was obviously the problem of looking after the kids, ... so she worked evenings and weekends - and then there

was this opportunity to go back into the bank, one day a week, that although it crossed our boundary of what we wanted to do, we wanted to wait until they were completely back to school both of them before we actually entertained anything on a full time basis. (Extract from transcripts)

There is a clear indication in this quote that life for this man and his partner was organised around their concern for their children. Many of the men I interview demonstrated this type of concern, interest and attention in relation to their children. For them, they fulfil their *family responsibilities* by taking on the 'sacrifice' of doing paid work. It is both this notion of sacrifice and the idea of different areas of responsibility that enables them to maintain a contradictory attitude to domestic labour. As Andrew Tolson comments,

> The extent to that definitions of gender interpenetrate attitudes to 'work', is not often fully understood. For it is not simply that sexuality enters into the division of labour, differentiating 'men's' and 'women's' jobs. Nor is it a matter merely for legislation, to be reformed by 'equal pay' and 'opportunity'. For men, definitions of masculinity enter into the way work is personally experienced, as a life-long commitment and responsibility. In some respects work itself is made palatable only through the kinds of compensations masculinity can provide - the physical effort, the comradeship, the rewards of promotion. When work is unpalatable, it is often only his masculinity (his identification with the wage; 'providing for the wife and kids') that keeps a man at work day after day. (Tolson 1977, p.48)

The interviews I conducted would not support the contention in Tolson's quote that this turn to the family is purely a response to 'unpalatable' work. The men, for the most part, clearly enjoyed their jobs. They appeared to be aware of more choices and options in the way they could combine work and family; the public and the private. One man describes the changes in his life with the birth of his son:

> My wife and I - our relationship has altered since he came along, as you would expect. She was very determined to keep her job - she has over 200 people she is responsible for. She found that very rewarding and what we tend to have - was not an open relationship in the common sense - but I don't suppose it's even strange - a relationship where we appeared to meet after work, and we happened to live in the same house, and on a weekend we happened to go about normal business in the accepted manner. And now I find I'm not willing to put the hours in as much because I do realise that I really want to get home and not only see the boy but see her as well, and relieve her of some of the stress ... I will go one of two ways, I'll either draw away from the family life and then throw myself even heavier into work or I will do the opposite, draw away from work and carry on and start

Gender as a Verb

a more full family life, but the time when men seem to run out of steam and out of ambition, all that's past. (Extract from transcripts)

The study by Theo Nichols and Huw Beynon's (1977) of men working in a chemical factory, although focused on the attitudes of the men to changes in the capitalist labour process and the impact of class relations of these changes nevertheless provides a good illustration of the contradictions experienced by men in reconciling work and family responsibilities:

Take Jack Steele. He just lives the work. You know, he has just become it. You see him outside, even at home with his wife and kids, and he is not as much at ease there as he is in the work situation here. I think it's a pity if you lose all interest in things except work but perhaps it's inevitable. I don't know. I don't really. Perhaps it will happen to me. Perhaps that's what you've got to be to be a plant manager. (Nichols and Beynon 1977, p.101)

Nichols and Beynon interviewed an Irish man named Michael who said that the purpose of work for him was to provide for his four girls, to give them a good start in life by enabling them to have a good education. In a chapter entitled, 'The Ideology of Sacrifice' they provide an illustration of how the discourse of sacrifice enables these men to invest their labour with dignity and in this way enables them to cope with the lack of dignity and esteem with which they are held by the company. The workers at ChemCo are described in the following way:

They suffer in order to get the money: to buy things. They talk of getting a nice house of their own, for the kids, and many of them have achieved this. Of taking the wife and kids away for trips in the car. Of providing a good life for their families. A good life that is based upon their sacrifice. When you're packing bags, self-sacrifice and a determination to see things through become central to your world; just as they do for wives and *their* sacrifice in the home. She sacrifices herself for her husband and her children just as he sacrifices himself for them. ... His exploitation in the factory justifies her oppression in the home: and notions of masculinity and motherhood reinforce their mutual dependence. It is only through sacrifice that a wasted life has value. (Nichols and Beynon 1977, p.193-4)

This shows an awareness of the sacrifices of the women who live with these men. Such awareness is not always evident in later studies, despite the fact that the authors endorse feminism. David Collinson's (1992) *Managing the Shopfloor: subjectivity, masculinity and workplace culture* is centrally concerned with a study of masculinity and workplace culture. His analysis of his interview material illustrates the problem of a narrow focus on masculinity for the theorising of gender relations.

The book is divided into a series of chapters that examine the self-management of men in relation to capitalist work practices in a northern factory. The central focus is the way men manage to retain a sense of manhood and masculinity that has been subordinated and oppressed by capitalism. These issues are explored through the themes of resistance, compliance, collusion and incorporation. A number of men throughout the book refer to the sacrifices and responsibilities involved with family life. One worker is quoted as saying:

> So now I try to be interested in the lad's schoolwork. I really push the youngsters. I could have made a bit more of myself than I have by being here. At the grammar school I had the chance. I didn't go any further because of myself and not being something better. (Collinson 1992, p.189)

Collinson discusses this worker in terms of his 'heroic sacrifice', that he says, is also 'tinged with resentment and a sense of constraint'. Yet another worker Frank makes a similar point and is explained in the following terms:

> Securing the respect of his children is Frank's primary motive. Sacrifice itself is not enough, he must also achieve promotion and together these actions must be perceived, recognised and valued by his family. Yet in searching to secure the respect of his family, Frank suffers numerous costs: detached relations with shopfloor colleagues, a cynical compliant orientation that "works the system" and a recurrent need to manage and deny deep-seated contradictions between various discursive practices. (ibid., p.193)

One of the stated aims of this book is that it seeks to avoid the 'gender-blindness' of previous studies of working class men. Unfortunately, another kind of 'gender-blindness' presents itself and is a weakness in the analysis of the 'various working class masculinities' explored in the text. Paying particular attention to Collinson's discussion of 'Alf' is a good way to demonstrate this point. In his comments on the theme of sacrifice with reference to Alf - one of his respondents - he says,

> Alf's sacrifice for his children does not end at the factory gates. It also involves baby-sitting every weekday evening, whilst his wife works part-time. Precisely because of his sacrifices, Alf seeks to instil into his two children the very desire and ambition that has remained unfulfilled in him. He wants them to be different from him. Alf is determined to ensure that his sacrifice is not in vain. (Collinson 1992, p.185)

The emphasis is on Alf's failure to satisfy his ambitions and the compromise in regard to his role as the main breadwinner. The significance and importance placed on this man's self-denial and the lack of

any comment on the role of his 'wife' is problematic for a feminist reading
of this text. The woman is invisible and removed in this analysis. This
neglect of any mindfulness of women's role is very salient. On reading the
passage I immediately thought about 'Alf's partner' and the 'sacrifice' this
woman made as she took responsibility for running the household, caring
for two children during the day, doing a part-time job every weekday
evening. I found it difficult to accept Alf's 'sacrifice' as purely a privation
on his part.

Collinson states that 'central to the examination of human behaviour
in organisations' (ibid., p.233) in a host of issues encapsulating culture,
history, power, social practices and subjectivity. However despite his
sensitivity to the different discourses that construct the identities and
subjectivities of the masculinities practised by the men he interviewed, his
theoretical analysis is limited because of his partial analysis of gender
relations. Of the limited number of references to women in his text, the
majority mention women only in relation to male sexuality. For example
he states:

> Within the all-male environment of the Components Division, masculine
> sexual prowess is a pervasive topic. Mediated through bravado and joking
> relations, a stereotypical image of self, that is assertive, independent,
> powerful and sexually insatiable is constructed, protected and embellished.
> By contrast, women are dismissed as passive, dependent and only interested
> in catching a man. These images contribute to the unity between men on
> the shopfloor and constitute a powerful pressure, to that shopfloor workers
> are expected to conform. (Collinson 1992, p.114)

Though he mentions the 'precarious and fragile' nature of the unity
constructed through this discourse of male sexuality, he does not attempt to
analyse the contradictions or confusions this discourse may engender in
relation to their 'lived experiences' and relationships with women and to
the process of gender segregation at work. The sexuality emphasised
throughout the study is heterosexuality. The notion that the men he
interviewed may be referring to a 'hegemonic masculinist discourse on
sexuality' in order to frame their representations of gender relations is not
considered, despite the fact that he make reference to the contradictory
aspects of the discourse of sexuality that dominated the shopfloor
discussion and practices in relation to sexuality.

Though the theoretical framework in Collinson's study is a very
useful one for understanding how a number of discourses shape the
'meanings; interpretations; relationships; culture; history; hierarchy; power;
practices and subjectivity' (1992, p.233) of masculinity on the shopfloor, it
remains however a study of men, not gender, and thus not only neglects to

consider the extent to that discourses of femininity impact on hegemonic masculinity but also only provides a partial interpretation of men's work and masculinity, as it is not possible to understand these relationships if women and hegemonic femininity are not included as part of the analysis. As Sandra Harding has argued, it is useless to analyse,

> masculinity and femininity (as) simply complementary poles of thought ... (as) two symmetrical halves of the fruit of the tree of knowledge. Both are partial, distorted, and damaged renderings of the range of male and female potential. (Harding 1991, p.13)

The neglect and exclusion of women is quite common in studies of masculinities. However if Harding is correct that masculinity/masculinities can only be understood in relation to femininity, women have to be part of the explanation and investigation of subjectivity, masculinities and workplace culture and also in order to understand the process of segregation at work.

The Importance of Segregation for Masculinity

The notion that sex segregation work roles is critical to men and to masculinity is a theme that continually appears in Cynthia Cockburn's work, for example, in her study of *Brothers: male dominance and technological change* (1983), discussing the behaviour of men in relation to women, work and technical knowledge she writes:

> If women *can't* do certain work because they are weak, unintelligent or temperamentally unsuited, the resulting economic advantage for men needs little emphasis. There are political advantages as well, however. A man, being relatively competent, becomes relatively powerful. *Much of men's self-respect depends on the idea of being able to do work that men alone are fit to do.* (Cockburn 1983, p.179) (my emphasis)

Given that the male computer programmers I interviewed were working alongside women who were doing the same job, I was interested to discover the tensions or problems this caused them in relation to their ideas on gender and masculinity. In what ways, if any, were their conceptualisations of gender relations and masculinity affected by the fact that they were doing similar jobs to women? Did the fact that they worked alongside women doing the same job reshape their views of masculinity and/or femininity? What image of masculinity did they use in order to make sense of their work situation? To what extent if any did their work situation create a 'crisis' of masculinity for these men?[11]   I was also interested to discover the difference it made to their views on women and men's roles in the home. To what extent did they hold non-stereotypical or pro-feminist views about sharing household and childcare responsibilities? These questions were prompted by; on the one hand my theoretical problems with the conceptualisation of men and masculinity that proceeds from the concept of patriarchy and on the other hand by the writings by men on masculinity.

My interpretation of the interview material is that men's notion of masculinity was not affected by the presence of women in their occupation. With a few exceptions, the men appeared to be very sincerely complimentary about women's ability as programmers and gave no hint that they felt threatened by their presence. The reason for this is that they tend not to consider their women colleagues in their discussions of work.[12] Rather they are concerned with 'getting-on', or 'getting-up', about 'getting-control' and 'getting-power'. Part of the explanation for this lies in the organisational discourses that interacted with hegemonic masculinity and hegemonic femininity and constitute male and female workers in different ways. One of the consequences of this is that men focused on male work relations rather than on work relations with women. They do not see women as competitors for their ambitions in the workplace. However some of the men interviewed did resent women's presence at the workplace. These men tended to be older and to view women as inferior workers whose presence diminished the status of the occupation.

There is no evidence from this series of interviews of the presence of the diversity of masculinities, reported in the 'new men's studies' - with the possible exception of age differences. There is also not much evidence that these men were experiencing a 'crisis' of masculinity and that they needed to do much negotiating, or resisting the discourse of hegemonic masculinity. What remains an issue is the usefulness of the concept of masculinities for the study of gendering at work. This concentration on differences between men has a tendency to divert attention away from an interpretation of the how gender segregation still continues to be such a notable feature of organisations.

In Summary

This chapter has raised a whole series of issues that are significant for any consideration of the relationship between the discourses of masculinity/masculinities and the process of gender segregation at work. It also raises the problem of women interviewing men about feminist issues concerning gender. All the men I interviewed were very embarrassed by my attempts to discuss masculinity. They obviously found very strange and novel the notion that masculinity was in some kind of flux or the idea that one could discuss masculinities rather than masculinity. Rather than the plurality of masculinities that is discussed at length in the books on men and masculinity, I found many similarities and correspondences in the way these men viewed their relationships to the sexual division of labour in the home and paid work. The language used to express their attitude to their occupation is similar to the terms that are used to denote hegemonic masculinity. They frequently referred to power and control and the competitive nature of their work. They only used these terms in relation to working with other men, so very rarely were women used as a reference point for their comments on ambitions or rivalry at work. One of the most striking similarities was the fact that they all carried with them in their head a very clear account of the structure and the hierarchy of their workplace. They could say without any hesitation who occupied what position; how many people were above them in the hierarchy; what they had to do if they wanted promotion and whom they had to replace. The majority of the women I interviewed did not have this type of knowledge of their organisation. The men all openly expressed a pride in their work, especially in the skill and technical aspects of the job. Both of these notions enabled them to experience feelings of superiority, power and control in relation to other occupations. It became evident after a number of interviews that these men were very happy and comfortable responding to my questions in an abstract and impersonal way: that is they coded their responses in terms of 'men in general'. It is this type of response that can account for the similarities in the discussions of their attitudes to work. It was only when I began to ask questions coded in a specific 'personal' style that I began to note some differences and contradictions in their relationship to their job. Whilst the centrality of work to their subject positions as men was common there were some differences between them concerning their interests and involvement with work and their views on women working. These differences were connected to attitudes towards their female colleagues; family responsibilities, especially childcare and their views on whether their work was constituted around notions of sacrifice or notions of intellectual stimulation and challenge.

Different facets of hegemonic masculinity will be foreground in different contexts, different aspects of that will be present depending on the life experiences of individual men. The manner in that the structure of organisations and organisational procedures shape the social construction of masculinity is that these practices need to form part of an explanation of gender relations. In the next chapter I seek to examine this discourse and the role of organisations in the process of gendering with reference to the different workplaces I visited during the course of my research.

Notes

[1]   The following quote from a section of Talcott Parson's analysis of the family demonstrates his view of women's role and his thinking around the impact of women's increasing participation in paid work: 'It seems quite safe in general to say that the adult feminine role has not ceased to be anchored primarily in the internal affairs of the family, as wife, mother and manager of the household, while the role of the adult male is primarily anchored in the occupational world, in his job and through it by his status-giving and income-earning functions for the family. Even if, as seems possible, it should come about that the average married women had some kind of job, it seems most unlikely that this relative balance would be upset; that either the roles would be reversed, or their qualitative differentiation in these respects completely erased' (Parsons and Bales 1956 as quoted in Beechey 1978, p.162). Beechey's article is a useful outline of Parson's functionalist analysis of women.

[2]   The notion pervades the current discussions of an underclass and the 'problem' of single mothers.

[3]   In this formulation it appears as though men control whether or not women become feminists. In my view this is giving too much power to men. Based on my discussion of the discourses of femininities in chapter nine it could be argued that it is this discourse, not men, that influence some women's perspective on feminism.

[4]   This point is critical for the distinction between men's studies, women's studies and gender studies. The concept of gender as process means that it is not possible to understanding gendering at work doing only women's studies or men's studies. The study of gender segregation needs to be explored from within gender studies.

[5]   I am using the term 'interact' here as shorthand for the forms of resistance, subordination, collusion, rejection and acceptance that I referred to earlier in the text. I would also add that these practices create confusions and contradictions.

[6]   I was trying to switch between the assumptions of the 'work' model for men, and the 'gender' model for women (Fledberg and Glenn 1984) discussed in chapter three. Therefore I inverted the work and gender models, presuming a 'gender' model for men and a 'work' model for women.

[7]   His wife is a manager at a night-club.

[8]   His wife used to be a schoolteacher and was not a full time housewife. He said that they had discussed the possibility of part-time work for her when all the children were at school.

[9]   His son in at Cambridge university and his daughter lives nearby.

[10]   See Jenny Church and Carol Summerfield (eds) (1995) *Social Focus on Women*, London, HMSO, published 8.8.1995.

[11]   The theme of a crisis of masculinity is a strong element of the growth of the literature on men and masculinity (see Brittan 1989, pp.181-93) for an elaboration of the notion of crisis.

[12]   This is discussed further in chapter eight.

Chapter 7

Discourses of Science and Technology

In the previous chapters I discussed some of the discourses that shaped occupational segregation in the computing industry, in particular the gendered culture of computing and the links between this discourse and the discourses of science and technology. This chapter seeks to explore the impact of these discourses further by outlining the themes in feminists' debates on the relationship between technology and gender. This is followed by an analysis of the responses from the women I interviewed to a question on their view of the technology which tried to capture the extent to which they were aware of the maleness of the computing industry.

The feminist literature on women and technology and gender and technology contains the following themes. First is the recovery of women's involvement in the development of science and technology, and the reconstruction of the historical development of women's 'absence' from the culture of technology showing that women were not simply passive in its development. The second theme is the identification of technology with masculinity and the extent to which technology is either a liberating force for women or an instrument of male power and control. This debate is central to feminist arguments on reproductive technologies and domestic technologies. There is a tendency in these accounts to present women as victims of technology. This is because these debates are shaped by the concept of patriarchy that means that the problems of essentialism, universalism and ahistoricism that affect this concept pervade much of the literature. One of the first feminist texts that examined technology in women's lives begins by stating:

> To talk about women and technology in the same breath seems strange, even incongruous. Technology is powerful, remote, incomprehensible, inhuman, scientific, expensive and - above all - male ... Ultimately, the power of modern technology emanates from the powerful people in our society, and reinforces their power. (Faulkner and Arnold 1985, p.1)

This formulation of the relationship between women and technology is very similar to the feminist orthodoxy on gender segregation at work -

and as explained in the previous chapters, the similarity is due to the conceptualisation of gender embedded in the concept of patriarchy. Differences between feminist's writings on technology can be explained in part by how they attempt to reconcile these problems and the conceptualisation of gender from which they frame their arguments.

Feminist Perspectives on Technology

The feminist perspective referred to as eco-feminism by Gill and Grint (1995, p.4) whose theoretical framework is a variant of radical feminism, makes a very strong link between masculinity and technology. In this perspective technology is used by men to oppress and subordinate women. Examples of this perspective on the relationship between gender and technology can be found in a number of texts on reproductive technologies (see for example Corea 1985a, 1985b; Arditti et al. 1984). In these studies the patriarchal nature of the technology is expressed in vivid and highly charged language, which makes it very exciting and interesting to read. Christine Delphy (1992) provides an interesting discussion of some of the problems with these texts, especially the issue of biological determinism. She argues that they tend to repeat conservative and sexist notions of women's 'nature' in relation to biological motherhood and in this way reinforce the myths that uphold discourses on motherhood and nature. Though these accounts demonstrate the lack of power experienced by women in organisations dominated by men they also fail to challenge the discourses of motherhood which structures women's identity and subjectivity.

The liberal feminist position on technology concentrates on the problem of access in science and computing in the education of girls. In this account technology is not gendered, the problem is one of equal opportunities rather than the gendered culture of the industry.

The feminist perspective that attempts to understand the processes and practices by which technology embodies gender is central to this chapter. The writers in this tradition, such as, Cockburn (1983, 1985); Wajcman (1991); and Green, et al. (1993), evaluate the historical development of cultural notions of gender and technology. The perspective developed by these writers trace how the social shaping of technology is gendered. In these studies technology is treated as a culture, rather than as a set of objects or mechanical operations. The thrust of these accounts is to demonstrate the connections between the gendered nature of technology and the growth and development of this representation. The slight differences in interpretation between these writers can be explained by the problems of joining two theoretical frameworks: the system of patriarchy and the system of capitalism. As a recent discussion of this literature states:

> The debate about the origins of the cultural association between masculinity and technology is part of a much wider set of issues concerning whether 'patriarchy' can be said to pre-date Western capitalism, and to what extent asymmetrical gender power relations are necessary to, or are part of the logic of, capitalism itself. As a whole, it can be understood as part of the engagement of feminism with Marxism, and has been particularly valuable in highlighting the (frequent) invisibility of gender divisions within Marxist accounts. (Gill and Grint 1995, pp.9-10)

The value of these accounts, despite the theoretical problems, is that they illustrate the extent to which technology is saturated with masculinity rather than femininity. By demonstrating the relationship between technology and masculinity this helps to explain some of the problems posed for women in the way they relate to aspects of technology. The distinctiveness of these accounts is that they are attempting to formulate a feminist strategy around technology that attempts to shift its cultural representations so that the development, design and organisation of technology will be either accessible, women user friendly and less controlled by men. The tension in this perspective can be demonstrated by the following question. Is it actually men who control women through technology or is it that the culture of technology is saturated by masculine values? In some accounts, for example, Wajcman (1991) the emphasis is on the power of masculinity in the shaping of technology. In others, as in the quote above from Faulkner and Arnold (1985), the stress is on men controlling women. There are very few case studies of computer programming that concentrate on the gender aspects of the occupation. A short piece in *Technology Review* (1984) is indicative of a liberal feminist approach that examines the different qualities men and women bring to computer programming. The emphasis here is on the contribution women can make to the industry and how more access to computer technology can help to increase women's representation in science more generally. The case study by Game and Pringle (1984) on the computing industry is located within a Marxist-feminist framework. The emphasis in their paper is on the impact of de-skilling for the structure of occupations in computing. They point to the predominance of women in the data preparation area, one of the least prestigious jobs in the industry and the over representation of men in the high status positions. They state that the position of computer programmer is the occupation that is most difficult to assess (1984, p.87) given its position in the centre of the occupational structure of the industry. They examine the underlying cause of the increase in the number of women programmers and the extent to which this represents the process of de-skilling and the feminisation of the occupation. Though they comment that the presence of women programmers cannot be explained simply in terms of this process, they do not develop this point in any detail. My discussion of the different programming jobs, and the segregation of women into the role of programming support rather than development which is outlined in chapter five, may help to explain the aspects of femininisation referred to by Game and Pringle. Their study then shifts to a discussion on the relationship between sexuality and the computer. They point to the representation of masculinity and machinery stating the 'computer is the ultimate in machines, the giant phallus' (1984, p.89). Men are represented as both sexually powerful and yet 'gauche', and this is explained by reference to men's biological sex not to gender. They state:

> Men see it as an extension of the social power they are allocated through possession of a penis. Indeed they see it as an extension of the penis. And just as they regard their dicks both as supremely powerful and as playthings, so they do the computer. Simultaneously, they regard women as toys and as objects to have power over ... Men in computing, particularly those who work for the computer companies, seem to combine a gaucheness about sexuality with an immense capacity for objectification. (Game and Pringle 1984, p.89)

There are a number of problems with this study and this conflation of male sexuality with technology. The quote implies that all men actually view technology as an extension of the phallus. This charge cannot be sustained as not only is there no empirical evidence to support such a statement but also, what is implied is that all men think and act in similar ways in relation to technology: an assumption which can only be based on biology. Rather than theorising the connection between men and technology in this way, it is important to concentrate on the discourse that permeates the culture of technology and the implications of this for the gender technology relationship. There is a similar problem with their tendency to conflate the terms gender and sexuality in their references to masculinity. In this account gender becomes transmuted to sexuality. Men's relationship to computer technology is connected to their sex as though through a seamless web and women are positioned as the objects of male power. The problem here is that this characterisation of the relationship between gender and technology positions women computer programmers as passive victims of male power and evades the issues of the processes and practices of gender relations in the occupation in which women have an active part. This study assumes a relationship between masculinity, men and technology that also infers a subordinate correlation between women, femininity and technology. This characterisation of gender and technology fails to develop the impact of women working as programmers on gender relations in the industry and overlooks the contradictions, conflicts and negotiations surrounding technology and gender at the workplace.

The study of computer programming by Anne Lloyd and Liz Newell (1985) points to some of the contradictions for women working as computer programmers. The article is especially valuable as the writers are both programmers and the impetus for their writing comes from their personal experiences of the industry.

The paper begins by describing the contribution of a number of women from Lady Ada Lovelace, to the ENIAC 'girls' and Grace Hopper to the history of programming. The historical references to women and computing help to counter the myth that women are not part of the history of the industry. However the growth and development of computing after the Second World War lead to it being predominantly a male occupation. The factors that contribute to the scarcity of women's programmers is explained by the male dominated structure and organisation of the industry. The barriers facing women's entry to computing is explained by women's lack of technical and scientific qualifications and the limited access to computers at school. Though reference is made to the cultural connotations of computing, the emphasis is on the strategies used by men to exclude women. Women are portrayed as lacking in confidence around technology. This however, repeats the stereotype of femininity and does not explain how they, as women, feel confident and competent. This representation of women's relationship to technology is static and framed by a conceptualisation of gender that is linked to the sex-role theory discussed in chapter seven. This has the effect of reproducing a stereotype of women's relationship to technology: - women as technologically incompetent - which takes the discussion away from an exploration of the actual experiences of women who are programmers.

These contradictions can be neatly demonstrated by the remarks directed at Lloyd and Newell when they tell people (they don't say whether the comments are from mainly men or women) they are computer programmers. They write:

> Women who do step out of their designated role and into the computing industry are often greeted with surprise, dismay and incomprehension. We ourselves have often been the objects of comments such as: 'You don't look

like a computer person'; 'Isn't that rather an odd thing for you to do?';
'What do you do, type things in?' and spoken with utter disbelief -
'Heavens, you must be brainy' (Lloyd and Newell 1985, p.246)

When I conducted my research I was interested to find out if these
type of responses were a common occurrence for the women in my sample.
I was also interested in trying to explore whether they experienced any
contradictions and conflicts with the notion that being a women computer
programmer is considered an 'odd' occupation for a woman. I asked a
number of questions in order to try and draw out the type of experiences
documented by Lloyd and Newell. I had deliberately left these questions
towards the end of the interview as I was hoping that I would have
established a degree of trust and relaxation with the interviewee. However
despite this intention, this section of the interview produced a great deal of
hesitancy and confusion. One woman got very angry saying that the
questions I was asking were very strange and that she could not understand
why these questions were important. She said:

> I dislike these sweeping statements. I don't believe the world is black and
> white and therefore I tend to look at people as people rather than women.
> (Extract from transcripts)

In particular the women did not experience any 'oddness' about their
occupation. They accepted their confidence around programming easily,
taking it for granted and tending to diminish the 'technical' aspects of the
job and talking up the 'logical' side and problem solving elements of
programming. Only two men from the sample stereotyped women's
relationship with computing. They did not say that women were incapable
of being good programmers rather they told me that women were not
interested in computing, that they felt that women would find programming
boring.

The principal response from both men and women was framed in
terms of individual differences between people in relation to qualities they
mentioned as necessary for the job. The most frequently mentioned
qualities were logic, patience and individual effort. There were some
spontaneous responses that linked technology with gender making
reference to the cultural representations of technology as male.

> Well it seems that very few women choose computing as a career. I know
> on my course in Sunderland there were about 50 on the course and there
> were only about 4 women. Now I've always failed to understand why
> because the women on the course were equally as good and in a lot of cases
> better, they were all pretty good. It just seems to be a male dominated
> thing. I think it probably goes back to the connection people make between

computers and mathematics, which is again something that men tend to go
in for. (Extract from transcripts)

Many more of the programmers did not view computer programming as
technical. A very common response to this series of questions was as
follows.

> There's nothing particularly technical about computing. If anything it's
> more a logical thing, it's so you've got to be able to follow things logically.
> You've got to think, to do things orderly, it's a logical sort of orderly type
> of thing, more like ... accounting than say mechanics or engineering if you
> see what I mean. (Extract from transcripts)

There was however a number of contradictions between this
assessment of programming and remarks made in other sections of the
interview. Quite early on in the interview I asked questions about previous
employment and education qualifications in order to uncover the routes into
programming and their expectations of the job. Some references were
made at this stage to the view that before they became programmers they
believed that it was a very technical job, that you have to be a 'brain box' to
be a programmer, and how this assumption had been challenged by the
actual process of programming. There were however no connections made
between these assumptions and gender. My questioning of differences
related to gender were interpreted as questions about sex discrimination
rather than attempts to elicit views on the gendered culture of computer.
Some awareness of this process was mentioned but only with reference to
schools and college, not with reference to their immediate working
environment. So, for example, they were quite happy to talk about gender
and computing in relation to events that happened on their college or
training courses, or as anecdotes and stories from friends in other
companies but found it difficult to translate this awareness to their
immediate work situation. When I pressed the issue one woman, Sam, told
me:

> At college, some of the females tend to sort of sit there and say, 'No, I can't
> do it', and tend to panic rather than sit down with somebody and say, 'Look
> can you just go over this'. They tend to think 'I know I can't do it', you
> know, 'I'm not clever enough', type of thing. I found that in a couple of
> them, whereas the men that are on the course, if they find it difficult, they'll
> say 'I'm having a bit of trouble with this' and they'll go and see somebody
> or sort it out more than the women will. (Extract from transcripts)

There was a tendency to think about differences, not in terms of
gender, but in terms of age. So the implication from the quote is that
'young' women may have experienced problems because of their gender

but this is seen as a feature of adolescent behaviour that disappears when 'boys' and 'girls' grow up - adults behave differently. This type of reasoning was very common, with both women and men differentiating between young men and women and older people. There was however general agreement from both the men and women interviewed that a small minority of men, never women, became addicted to the terminal – 'terminal addicts' one woman called them. In the literature on computing they are usually referred to as 'techies'. These are the people who spend all their working time and leisure time working with/playing with a computer. Both men and women said that they had never met a women 'techie' and explained this gender difference by saying that women have more responsibilities than men, which meant they had less time to play with the computer. Thus a common response when asked about gender and computing was that yes, there are differences but these are only slight and only applies to a small number of men. So, for example, Sam (Samantha) said,

> I don't think there's many in our section but certainly some will work on the computer all day at work and go home and either work or play all night on a computer and, sort of, their life revolves solely around computers. But I think as women, especially if they're, you know got commitments or family or whatever, you know, that type of thing then they tend to leave their work more at work, simply because they have got commitments out of work. (Extract from transcripts)

The men mentioned a small minority of 'people they know' who were terminal addicts, and said that they did not know any women who 'eat and drink' computers. This was viewed very much as a very small 'extreme' minority of those working in the computing industry. The men did not extol the technical aspects of the job. Rather they repeated the remarks expressed by the women, stressing the need for logical thinking rather than technical ability. For example one man, John, admitted that he was not interested in the 'technical' side of his job:

> I'm not really interested in the technical side of computing. I like the business side of it. I don't like anything technical at all. (Extract from transcripts)

He did consider that men are generally more interested in the technology than women, but this type of response changed when the he began to generalise about gender and technology, as in the extract below:

> I think a lot more men are more interested in the technical sort of programming side of it. I know a lot of people that are in computing, a lot of the male people anyway can get very enthusiastic about software, writing

programmes, only I don't get enthusiastic about that at all, but some people do and they tend to be mostly male, the people that do. (Extract from transcripts)

From the interviews it is clear that the programmers distinguish between 'techies' or 'terminal addicts' and 'normal' workers, the former group, they all nominated to be a small minority of men in the industry. None of the people I interviewed were 'addicts', and though many of them, especially those in software houses worked for long hours, through evenings and weekends, they viewed this as simply the requirements of the job rather than connected to the pleasure of the technology. However there is one important difference between the responses from the men and women I interviewed. Men tended to be vague in their responses to questions concerning gender and technology as they inevitably answered these questions as though gender equals women. As I argue this vagueness is caused by men's lack of interest in women as colleagues: they were concerned with the men they worked with, not with women. The women however, answered the questions around gender and technology by rejecting the 'technical' aspects of the job. Neither they, nor the men I interviewed, viewed the technology itself as gendered. There was an awareness of gender issues in relation to the organisation's power structures and the lack of equal opportunities for women due to gender stereotyping, but this analysis was not extend to the notion that computer technology held representations of gender. On the contrary the technology was regarded as neutral. In an earlier section of the interview schedule I asked why they liked their job and the majority of both women and men in the sample spoke of the pleasure and satisfaction they experienced in the problem solving and creative aspects of programming. The phrases 'intellectual challenging', 'stimulating' and 'exciting' were regularly used but these expressions of pleasure were not related to the technology - the computer - rather to the status of having an occupation which was primarily mental rather than manual labour.

I enjoy sort of using my brain and being set something and having to sort of work it from the beginning to finish, having to think about it and decide what do I do here and, yes, I enjoy that side of it. I like to get my brain working. (Extract from transcripts)

The majority of the computer programmers I interviewed did not view their work as technical largely because they made a distinction between the type of programming they did - that is, programming software applications and the programming involved with computer communication systems. Interestingly the few women who did programme in the area of communication systems did not regard their job as technically more demanding than programming applications. I interviewed two men who also worked with communication systems. In contrast to the women in the same area they stressed the technical aspects of the job. These men stated that they did not consider that the technical aspects of programming would be any less difficult for women. The men and women who worked in this area of programming both stressed individual aptitude and ability over gender.

On the basis of the interviews it could be argued that one aspect of the orthodox feminist discourse on technology was supported. This is that women deny or negate the technical aspects of their jobs. It could also be argued that they do this in order to avoid the conflict this raises for their subject position as women. This subjectivity being structured by the discourse of hegemonic femininity. It was also the case that men were more inclined to stress the technical aspects of the job. However the distinction here is very slight. The majority of men I interviewed did not discuss their jobs as technical. The terms they used to describe their work was very similar to the women programmers. The interviews do not support the feminist perspective which posits men as strategically organising against women in the workplace and which argues that technology is being used as part of this project. The men I interviewed did not feel threatened by the fact the women were working alongside them as programmers. Though it was clear that men felt more comfortable than women in the work environment, they did not feel the need to prove themselves as workers in organisations. In this sense, computer programming is easier for men than for women.

Overall I was struck by the lack of acknowledgement and awareness of gender issues surrounding computing from the majority of the people, both men and women, that I interviewed. However this lack only appeared to operate with reference to their immediate workplace. As I mentioned above, they did generalise about gender stereotyping, and how men and women are viewed in the industry, but believed that they and their colleagues operated on the basis of individual abilities and attributes. It could be argued from this that the discourse on individualism which is central to the capitalist ideology of liberal democracies produces tensions and contradictions for women and men whose subjectivity and identity is also structured by the other discourses discussed in this book. The notion that human beings are constantly negotiating these discourses and that these discourses are fluid and not fixed or static means that there are spaces for constructing competing discourses or, if that sounds too ambitious or optimistic, there is movement within discourses so these discourses can be changed.

Women Power and Technology

Elizabeth Grosz argues that the aim of feminist theorising is to construct alternative theoretical strategies and that there is a need to go beyond simply criticising either existing theory or practice. She states,

> if it remains simply reactive, simply a critique, it ultimately affirms the very theories it may wish to move beyond. It necessarily remains on the very ground it aims to contest. To say something is not true, valuable, or useful without posing alternatives is, paradoxically, to affirm that it is true, and so on. (Grosz 1990, p.59)

By focusing on gender and technology, I want to examine the extent to which the feminist critiques on technology are constructing either theory or strategies for change, or to what extent they produce the type of negative or reactive project discussed by Grosz. The feminist critique of science and technology which stresses the male dominance of science would appear to reproduce and thus affirm the theories which it criticises, given the attribution of power and dominance to men, which characterises these critiques. The debates on gender and science have structured the debates on gender and technology, as technology is rarely discussed without reference to science. As Judy Wajcman explains:

> The development of a feminist perspective on the history and philosophy of science is a relatively recent endeavour. Although this field is still quite small and by no means coherent, it has attracted more theoretical debate than the related subject of gender and technology ... feminists pursued similar lines of argument when they turned their attention from science to technology. (Wajcman 1991, p.1)

The feminist critique functions on a number of levels. One dimension concerns the articulation of the scientific project: scientist's own conception of their enterprise. Elizabeth Fee in her article *Critiques of Modern Science: The Relationship of Feminism to Other Radical Epistemologies* (1986) provides a number of examples of this bias including the now infamous statement from Richard Feynman who called the idea that inspired the work for which he won a Nobel prize an:

> old lady, who has very little that's attractive left in her, and the young today will not have their hearts pound when they look at her anymore. But we can say the best we can for any old woman, that she has become a very good mother and has given birth to some very good children. And I thank the Swedish Academy of Science for complimenting one of them. (Fee 1986, p.45)

Moreover, the emphasis on objectivity and rationality within scientific methodology legitimates not only scientific knowledge but also men's involvement and women's exclusion from science and technology. From the emergence of modern science, science has been conceived as the control of nature. The characteristics which denote science in our culture link the high status of scientific knowledge with men and the control of nature. Men are characterised as closer to culture versus women as closer to nature. Men and science are deemed rational in contrast to women who are defined as emotional illogical, and irrational. As Weininger (1906) stated:

> A being like the female, without the power of making concepts, is unable to make judgements. In her 'mind' subjective and objective are not separated; there is no possibility of making judgements, and no possibility of reaching, or of desiring, truth. No woman is really interested in science; she may deceive herself and many good men, but bad psychologists, by thinking so. (cited in Tuana 1989, p.v)

The masculinity of science has not only been manifest in its conceptualisation of itself; scientific knowledge has been used to legitimate the confinement of women to the sphere of the 'natural' not simply because of mistaken male bias and lack of understanding but, according to some writers, in order to control and dominate women. According to, Cockburn (1985); Corea (1985); Hanmer (1983), (1987); Faulkner and Arnold (1985), this involves male dominance in the real sense of actual men having power and control of women, and the use of scientific reasoning and practices to legitimate this control.

For some writers, the problem of science and therefore technology would be solved by the involvement of more women in the scientific community - the 'adding women on' approach. For others, (Harding 1986; Rose 1986) the problem is much more fundamental and requires a reassessment of scientific methodology. The issue I want to concentrate on is the link between the feminist critique of science and the feminist critique of technology in relation to male dominance and male power. In the literature on women and technology, there appears to be a borrowing of and concentration on, the idea that technology is used by men to subordinate and control women and the conflation of science with technology. As Wajcman state; 'technology, like science, is seen as deeply implicated in the masculine project of the domination and control of women and nature' (1991, p.17). In order to deal with the question of power, I want to begin by providing some examples from the literature to demonstrate the notion of power that underpins the feminist critique of science and technology. For example, Margaret Low Benston in *Inventing Women* writes that:

power is the most important message that male use of technology communicates. Power over technology and the physical world is just one aspect of men's domination of this society ... Male power over technology is both a product of and a re-enforcement for their other power in society. Even at the household level, every time a man repairs the plumbing or a sewing machine while a woman watches, a communication about her helplessness and inferiority is made. (Benston 1992, p.37)

As I indicated earlier there is a long list of books and articles that discuss women's relationship to the power of science and technology in these terms (see Corea 1985; Arditta et al. 1984). The problem with this is that women are positioned as passive victims of male dominance and male control. Women are cast as the dominated, as powerless. 'Power is associated firmly with the male and masculinity. Commentators on power have frequently remarked on its connections with virility and masculinity' (Hartsock 1990, p.157). The discourse around technology is thus shaped by these discourses on science and power. So, for example, when feminists write of 'power over our bodies', 'power over our lives', they are using the concept of power and domination that pervades the traditional discourses on power. Thus there is as Grosz argued (see above) an affirmation of this conceptualisation of power rather than the posing of an alternative. It provides little, if any, room for manoeuvre from conceptualising the relationship between women and technology in ways other than those of domination and hinders the creation of a strategy for change.

The notion of power used to theorise the gender/science and technology debates imitates the traditional approach best exemplified by the work of Steven Lukes in his book *Power: A Radical View* (1974). Power here is considered in three dimensions that characterise the exercise of power in modern society. Here it is important to differentiate between coercive power and legal-relational power, and Lukes explores the ways in which this clear cut distinction is blurred. The first dimension is

the ability of A to prevail over B in formal political decision-making (normally in government) on one or more key issues; where there is a direct and observable conflict between A and B over outcomes. (Lukes 1974, p.16)

Power here is taken to mean the ability of one formal office holder to shape the final outcome of government. The second dimension is defined as 'the ability of A to prevail over B in determining the outcomes of conflicts of interests and also in determining what is to count as a formal issue where there is a conflict of interests over policy preferences' (ibid., p.16). Here the argument is that all decisions are likely to be of importance to some group or interest in society. However some groups are

144 *Gender as a Verb*

strategically placed so that they can ensure that all issues that threaten them are resolved in their favour. In other words, elite groups in society either inside or outside the political system can continuously use their influence or presence in the system to determine the outcome of those issues that are important to them. The third dimension of power is defined as 'the ability of A to prevent B from realising his 'real interests' or from articulating them effectively due to the mobilisation of bias resulting from the institutional structure of society' (ibid., p.17). In this view, power is equated not just with who decides but with the way in which the economic and social structure of modern society conditions human thought and action, so that individuals never understand their 'real interests' (ibid., p.17). In this formulation power can only be analysed by first asking the questions of where people's ideas of reality and their desires come from. This points one to the underlying structure of the capitalist system which structures individual thoughts and actions such that fundamental threats to the system are not only contained, but that people are diverted from using their power to change the system. This third dimension corresponds to a Marxist analysis of bourgeois power. This approach maintains that there is a class structure in Britain made up of those who own the means of production and those who have only their labour power, and that this structure of ownership and control is reflected in not only the state but also the intellectual life of a society. Here power is exercised through the state that is the instrument of those who have economic power. Parliamentary politics would be viewed as 'ideologically' significant rather than being of any fundamental significance, as it gives the illusion that people can exercise real political choices. Power is viewed as repressive, as emanating from the top downwards, either through governmental and social elites, state and/or class interests. Foucault says of conceptualisations of power such as these, that:

> it allows power to be only ever thought of in negative terms: refusal, delimitation, obstruction, censure. Power is that which says no. Any confrontation with power thus conceived appears only as transgression. The manifestation of power takes on the pure form of 'thou shalt not'. (Foucault 1979, p.53)

Arising from his critique of this way of formulating power in society, Foucault outlines a different way of thinking about power. If power is always about domination posed

> only in terms of constitutions, sovereignty etc., hence in juridical terms; (and) on the marxist side, in terms of the state apparatus. (Then) The way in which it was exercised concretely and in detail, with its specificity, its techniques and tactics was not looked for; one contented oneself with

denouncing it in a polemical and global manner, as it existed among the 'others' in the adversary's camp: power in soviet socialism was called totalitarianism by its opponents, and in Western capitalism it was denounced by marxists as class domination, but the mechanics of power were never analysed. (Foucault 1979, p.34)

Rather than concentrating on the negative, repressive aspects of power, Foucault argues that if this was the only story about power, it cannot explain what he terms the productivity of power. The way power 'produces things ... induces pleasure ... forms knowledge ... produces discourse' (1979, p.36). Foucault's critique and analysis, allows a more emancipatory analysis of power that enables the establishment of a framework for examining women's relationship to technology.

Feminists have long talked about power in much more diverse ways than those discussed within mainstream academia. By talking about gender relations in terms of power, feminists put on the agenda the idea that the whole of social relationships involves notions of power. This includes the recognition that whenever two or more people are engaged in some activity, power conflicts and struggles are involved. This means, however, that women are also involved in the exercise of power. Rather than viewing power with unease, or simply in terms of male dominance, as coercion, as a negative concept, the fact that women have and exercise power means that power cannot simply be located with men. Foucault's 'new' concept of power provides the possibility of enabling a productive discourse on power that could be used to explore the empowerment of women in ways that could be progressive and liberating. Nancy Fraser (1989) also puts forward a positive reading of Foucault on power, arguing that his analysis enables power to be analysed at the micro level, at the level of everyday practices, and turns the focus away from power as residing with the state or with the economy. Jana Sawicki (1991) makes similar points in her discussion of Foucault and power. She analyses the ways in which his concept of power differs from traditional conceptions that concentrate on power as dominance, as repression, and discusses the exercise and productivity of power in relation to identity and sexuality and the body.

In this next section I want to perform a similar exercise in relation to gender and technology. In order to begin to recast this debate, it is necessary to separate analytically science and technology. As was explained at the beginning of the section, much of the literature draws on the debate around science to discuss technology. This has meant that the same restrictive analysis of power and dominance that pervades the debates on science also saturates the debates on gender and technology, and as I hope to demonstrate, both limits and restricts our understanding of technology. The principal argument for my support of Wajcman's (1991) contention that feminist analysis of science and technology need to be separated out, is that the vast majority of women have access to technology in term of *use*, in contrast to their relationship with science, and this means that the study of gender and technology needs to be approached differently.

If you take a long historical view you find that women were closely involved with the earliest technologies, both in terms of technique, e.g. knowledge and know-how, and design and use. The historical evidence would appear to suggest that women in Western industrialised societies, continued up to, and during the industrial revolution, to be as involved as men were with technology. Gradually they were moved out of this arena either because women were deemed to be unable to cope with technology or because women's skills were not recognised, and/or the concept of technology narrowed, so that only male activities were designated technological and women's activities and skills were devalued. It would appear then that, though Cynthia Cockburn is correct to argue that:

> Technological competence is a factor in sex-segregation, women clustering in jobs that require little or none, men spreading across a wider range of occupations which include those that call for technical training. (Cockburn 1985, p.9)

This is only correct in relation to a specific historical period. It also only represents one dimension of women's relationship to technology and obscures the more complex involvement of women both historically and present day. The history of computing provides a clear example that women can take the lead in technological involvement. Women were the first computer programmers (Kraft 1977; Lloyd and Newell 1985; Wajcman 1991). These women worked in the department of defence for the American government, and in my research on computer programmers I interviewed women who did similar programming work for the British ministry of defence. It is only when the importance of computer programming was recognised and thus status entered into this occupation that the type of changes referred to by Cockburn occur. In other words it is not technological competence which is paramount as such, but the status, power and control which goes with this competence. It follows then that Cockburn is incorrect to argue that 'only very recently have women begun to aspire to technical training and work' (1985, p.8). The historical picture is much more complex.

Following the models proposed by Keller (1992) and Long and Dowell (1989) I would propose that technology has moved through a number of stages historically. Firstly, the craft stage, where product invention and use were designed for a specific purpose and women took part in all of these activities. This stage can be put on the long historical path from hunting and gathering societies through to the beginnings of industrialisation. Women had the techniques and the know-how. Cynthia Cockburn (see her discussion 1985, p.21) would disagree with this picture, as she argues that women were excluded from craft production, but the historical evidence from Stanley (1983); Griffiths (1985), would appear to indicate that women were engaged in specific crafts and trades, and that during this stage women designed, made and used technology. Cockburn's analysis of this stage is, I would argue, based on a limited use of the term 'technology'. Three different layers of meaning of technology are identified by MacKenzie and Wajcman (1985), (see also Wajcman 1991; Bush 1983). These are: technology as a form of knowledge, technology as a form of practice, and finally technology as physical objects.

The debates on gender and technology have tended to concentrate on the first layer of meaning: on knowledge and know-how. Cockburn uses technology in this way to refer to a very specific type of technological knowledge that she terms 'essentially a transferable knowledge, profitably carried from one kind of production to another' (1985, p.26). Ironically it seems that she is using a definition that refers to a later stage (applied science) where technological knowledge is exclusively the property of a small number. During the industrial revolution a number of processes acted to exclude most women in terms of technique and use, though some historical examples are available of women who were involved in both. For example the work of Lillian Moller Gilreth (Trescott 1983) in engineering and the first women computer programmers who work on ENIAC - Electronic Numerical Integrator and Calculator (see discussion above) could be included in this stage. Gender and technology in the present day is shaped by the 'Applied Science' model. Essentially technology and science during this stage is controlled mainly by rich white men, which excludes practically all women and the majority of men in terms of technique, but not of use. The latter categories include the consumers and users of technology. As Cockburn writes:

> women are to be found in great numbers operating machinery, and some operating jobs are more skill-demanding that others. But women continue to be rarities in those occupations that involve knowing about what goes on inside the machine. (Cockburn 1985, p.11)

Many times in the literature on women and technology the role of women as 'simply' consumers and users of technology is discussed, and this is usually presented in a negative way. However if we pay attention to the historical relationship of women to technology and understand technology so as to include all three layers of meaning we can see that there is no *necessary* antagonism between women and technology; and that women's relationship to technology is not necessarily that of passive victims. This historical perspective aids our project of redefining women's (actual and potential) relationship to technology via reconceptualising the relationship between technology and power. It is here that we need to make use of an alternative concept of power to one associated with control and domination. In the light of the arguments outlined above about the micropractices of power, in terms of pleasure and control and the importance of these dimensions of power in upholding a macro level of power, it is important to acknowledge some element of personal power within the 'user' relationship to technology. For example, people who can drive a car, an aeroplane, a tractor, who can work a computer, a camcorder, a mixing desk seem to have more control, authority and autonomy than those who are unable to use these technologies. Highlighting the pleasure and power that can be exercised through the use of technology prepares the ground for a distinct way of theorising around gender and technology which is specific to technology and marks out the distinction between science and technology. Through the identification of technology with applied science, and a particular mode of conceptualising science, women are constructed as passive recipients of technology. In this model women don't make, control, understand technology and thus are dominated and controlled by it. This simplifies the reality of the different ways in which women relate to technology, and by encouraging this particular discourse feminist analysis is perpetuating the myth of a female subject who is situated within the discourse of technology as a controlled and passive user. The implication of this for a feminist analysis of technology is that a fundamental starting point needs to be the specific social interests that structure the knowledge and practice of particular kinds of technology. Incorporating the conceptualisation of power as suggested in this chapter, could provide a framework for a positive theory of power, unlike the traditional approach which views power as negative, as aggressive, as destructive, as 'male', and which excluded women's participation in the exercise of power in areas of social life. This is not to deny the exclusion of women from the exercise of power at a macro level, or to deny the ambiguity of Foucault's analysis of power for women. He never discussed the gendering of power, but then again according to Meaghan Morris and Paul Patton (1979), Foucault's aim was never to provide a theory of power but rather a description of the various techniques of power. From these descriptions, this 'genealogy' of power, one can extract a positive, even an optimistic discussion of power. Foucault does not dispute the coercive and repressive aspects of power but whilst accepting these dimensions, he also explores, what he calls the 'productivity' of power. As he says:

> if power was never anything but repressive, if it never did anything but say no, do you really believe that we should manage to obey it? What gives power its hold, what makes it accepted, is quite simply the fact that it does not simply weigh like a force which says no, but that it runs through, and it produces things, it induces pleasure, it forms knowledge, it produces discourses; it must be considered as a productive network which runs through the entire social body much more than as a negative instance whose function is repression. (Foucault 1979, p.36)

I would argue that whilst it is true that Foucault's analysis does not provide in any way a complete or properly theorised analytical model of power that feminists can use, he does however provide a framework from which one can start to build a model of gender and power, which may help to recast the debate on gender and technology. This framework would enable the construction of alternative feminist strategies rather than continuing to use theories of male dominance based on a notion of power which:

> is limiting because it detemporalized the process of social change by conceiving of it as a negation of the present rather than as emerging from possibilities in the present. In so doing, it restricts our political imaginations and keeps us from looking for the ambiguities, contradictions and liberatory possibilities. (Sawicki 1991, p.86)

In Summary

This chapter explored the trend in feminist writings on technology that positions women as dominated and powerless rather than active and participating. I have argued throughout this book that this positioning of women as oppositional to men around questions of power can be traced to the concept of patriarchy and the conceptualisation of gender which flows from this concept. By conceptualising gender as a process of negotiating and resisting a number of discursive fields it is possible to interpret the contradictions and conflicts of women's relationship with different aspects of technology. This concept of gender also challenges the position that equates men automatically with power and dominance. Using Foucault's analysis of power it is possible to analyse the relations between gender and technology that not only gives women more agency in their interactions with technology but also provides a theoretical framework from which to devise feminist strategy and policy around technology. It would appear that the discourse of hegemonic femininity, in contrast to the discourse on masculinity, militates against women being taken seriously in organisations. This chapter explores the contradictions of these discourses for women computer programmers, especially in relation to their gendered subjectivity. I am interested in exploring how women computer programmers negotiate, resist and transform this environment, and maintain their feminine subjectivity. In order to address this issue, I construct a typology of hegemonic femininity and use this to suggest some features of this discourse. There are two principal discourses that constitute hegemonic femininity: the discourse of sexuality and the discourses of domesticity and the family. I am using the term domesticity to signify the reproductive and productive relations expected of women in the home. The power of the discourses that constitute women's place in the home is based on the 'naturalness' of women's capacity to bear children. Women's subjectivity is critically constituted by the idea (1) of wife and mother and the notion that it is only through these 'roles' that women can be fulfilled. I begin by outlining a typology of this discourse (see next page) that should help to illustrate the dilemmas and contradictions facing women computer programmers in the light of the competing discourses of femininity, technology, masculinity and organisations.

Chapter 8

Discourses of Femininity

It would appear that the discourse of hegemonic femininity, in contrast to the discourse on masculinity, militates against women being taken seriously in organisations. This chapter explores the contradictions of these discourses for women computer programmers, especially in relation to their gendered subjectivity. I am interested in exploring how women computer programmers negotiate, resist and transform this environment, 'in such a way as to create a position for women within technological work that allows them to be both technological and feminine' (Henwood 1993, p.45).

In order to address this issue, I construct a typology of hegemonic femininity and use this to suggest some features of this discourse. There are two principal discourses that constitute hegemonic femininity: the discourse of sexuality and the discourses of domesticity and the family. I am using the term domesticity to signify the reproductive and productive relations expected of women in the home. The power of the discourses that constitute women's place in the home is based on the 'naturalness' of women's capacity to bear children. Women's subjectivity is critically constituted by the idea (ideal) of wife and mother and the notion that it is only through these 'roles' that women can be fulfilled. I begin by outlining a typology of this discourse (see next page) that should help to illustrate the dilemmas and contradictions facing women computer programmers in the light of the competing discourses of femininity, technology, masculinity and organisations.

Conflicting Discourses: Femininity and Organisations

As has been discussed in the preceding chapter the central beliefs of organisational discourses are: (i) the presumed gender neutrality of a worker; (ii) that organisational rules and expectations are gender neutral; (ii) the expectation that work is separate from home, and consequently (iii) that the organisation has first claim on the worker's time. Pringle's book *Secretaries Talk* (1988) addresses some of these issues and problematises the study of organisational discourses by focusing on power and pleasure in

Table 8.1: Typology of the hegemonic discourse on femininity

IMAGE	OBSESSIONS	OCCUPATIONS	TRAITS
Slim	Body	Housewife	Dependence
Attractive	Beauty	Mother	Emotional
Petite	Clothes	Carer	Close to nature
Beautiful		Volunteer	Maternal
Tall	Love	Domestic Work	Open
Well groomed	Romance	Paid Work	Caring
	Desire		Domestic
Sexually	Passion	Nurse	Devious
attractive to		Teacher	Sly
men	Sex	Secretary	Competitive
Sexually		Typist	with women
inexperienced	Looking for a	Cleaner	over men
Virginal	man/to father:	Shop Assistant	Bitchy
		Unskilled factory	
Fertile	Babies	work	Not
	Children		trustworthy
In a	Food	Part time worker	
relationship	Home		
Maternal	House	Cooking	Emotionally
Domestic		Sewing	strong
Stands in a			Courageous
certain way	Private/Domestic	Subordinate	
Sits with legs	responsibilities	Lacking ambition	
together		Powerless	
	Keep Fit		
	Sport		
Wears Frocks			
Lipstick			
Never alone			

relation to the discursive practices of gender in organisations. Her work provides a different approach from the traditional accounts of women's working lives. As she states:

> The focus here is on the relationship between secretaries as an identifiable social group and the discursive construction of secretaries as a category; on the relationship between power structures and the day-to-day negotiation and production of power; on the connections between domination, sexuality and pleasure. (Pringle 1988, p.x)

She questions the assumption of 'rationality' that ideologically structures organisational discourse and explains the relationship between a boss and a secretary as 'irrational' in Weber's 'ideal-type' characterisation of organisations. She argues that the boss/secretary relationship is similar to traditional, affective ways of thinking and acting which she equates with familial relations. There is however a lack of clarity in the discussion of the 'irrational' nature of the relationship, between familial relations and the discourse of sexuality. She also has a tendency to collapse the two discourses into each other, which obscures the explanation of these relationships. For example she argues:

> It may be argued that 'rationality' requires as a condition of its existence the simultaneous creation of a realm of the Other, be it personal, emotional, sexual or 'irrational'. Masculine rationality attempts to drive out the feminine but does not exist without it. 'Work' and 'sex' are implicitly treated as the domains of the 'conscious' and the 'unconscious'. But far from being separate spheres the two are thoroughly intertwined. Despite the illusion of ordered rationality, workplaces do not actually manage to exclude the personal or sexual. Rather than seeing the presence of sexuality and familial relations in the workplace as an aspect of traditional, patriarchal authority, it makes more sense to treat them as part of modern organisational forms. I am concerned here not with 'actual' families but with the family symbolism that structures work as well as personal relationships. The media, advertising and popular culture are saturated in such imagery, which provides a dominant set of social meanings in contemporary capitalist society. (Pringle 1988, p.89)

Pringle (1988) is correct to point to the complex interplay of the various discourses on sex that get played out in the workplace. Using a Foucaultian framework she also argues that 'male power' is not simply imposed on women but is a contradictory and complex part of the process of gendering at the workplace. The text provides a case study of the strategies and counter-strategies used by secretaries in organisations, and the way they negotiate their way through the conflicting discourse of femininity, sexuality, domesticity, and organisations. Pringle's concentration on the discourse of sexuality tends to obscure the other aspects of hegemonic femininity that inform the gendering process. The discussion of feminism is a good illustration of this. In the text, she discusses how secretaries are portrayed by feminists as either the 'victims' or 'dupes' of men. She mentions this characterisation in her interviews with secretaries, and reports on the dilemma this characterisation posed for them. She concludes that, whilst most wanted equal pay and equality of opportunity, they were wary of the label feminist, that they perceived as either 'man-hating' or as women attempting to become 'men'. She writes:

> Feminists are seen as both strident and joyless, obsessed with 'finding a rapist behind every filing cabinet'. In seeking to remove sexuality and femininity from the workplace they threaten to remove not only dangers but also *pleasures*. (my emphasis) Secretaries do not necessarily want to take on 'masculine' work profiles and career goals, develop new skills, or perpetually be off on training courses in order to become part of management. (Pringle 1988, p.100)

A number of questions are posed by this. Firstly, why not? What is it about these aspects of work which secretaries, women, reject? Is it simply the 'masculinity' of the work profiles, or do the conflicts and complexities of other discourses which shaped women's subject position as workers also need to be considered? So, for example, the reasons why 'secretaries do not want to take on 'masculine' work profiles and career goals' could also be explained through the discourse of domesticity. It would be difficult for a woman with household responsibilities to 'perpetually be off on training courses'.

The studies on women returnees, both to work and education, would indicate the enormous difficulties encountered by women in attempting to combine household management, child care and a career. There is some indication of the difficulties experienced by the women I interviewed and there is also research in the 1980s that outlines how women's working lives are different to men's (Martin and Roberts 1984). Women tend to have a two-phase pattern of economic activity, of working before they get married and have children, and going back to work when the children either go to school or go to nursery. Both the number of children and their ages affect a women's participation in paid work. Overall it is the age of the youngest child, and particularly a child under five, which is the main determinant of whether or not women work outside the home and whether or not they work full time. Women also experience a sequence of caring responsibilities. One in five women between the ages of 35 and 49 is looking after an elderly person, and one in four between the ages of 50 and 64 is looking after a sick or elderly relative (Martin and Roberts 1984). A lot of women's energies are sapped by the conflicting demands of these various roles. As the studies of women and work argue, 'full-time women workers still regarded themselves primarily as "housewives", their husbands as "workers"' (Pollert 1981, p.115). So whilst I am very drawn to an analysis of women's paid work which analyses how discursive practices mediate gender and work, there is a problem with explanations that simply concentrate on the discourse of sexuality and neglect other aspects of hegemonic femininity. However the way in which women interpret the meaning of 'housewife' and 'mother' cannot be simply assumed.

Managing Femininity: Differences and Similarities

None of the women programmers I interviewed defined themselves as primarily mothers. Despite the small sample, an analysis of the women's living arrangements shows seven different practices. Of the nine women who were single, one lived with her parents, two lived alone and the rest with their partners. Eight of the women were married with children. There were five married women with no children. Of the six women who were divorced or separated, two had children, and one woman was widowed with two children. When the women discussed their individual connection to paid work and domestic responsibilities, a complex relationship is revealed. The simple dichotomy presented in the Pollert quote could not be applied here. Rather, what was revealed was the different ways these women struggled to maintain their subject position - a way of being a woman - of dealing with their domestic responsibilities while at the same time managing the contradictions and conflicts of the organisational discourses encompassing computer programming.

The concept of 'contradictory subjectivity' discussed by Henriques et al. (1984, p.118) is a useful conceptual tool for analysing the impact of these competing discourses on women's subjectivity. This concept alludes to the way the experience of conflicts and contradictions in subjective positionings need to be managed by women continually. This management process is part of the way women perform gender at the workplace, and by these practices gender both the occupation and the organisation. Using this type of analysis it is clear that women are active agents in the process of gendering at work. Women negotiate, resist and manage the contradictory and conflictual discourses they encounter in organisations. At the same time, they reconcile the conflicts these practices produce for their subject position as women. The ways these discourses are 'managed' by women are, however, structured by the discourse of hegemonic femininity. This discourse shapes the manoeuvrability women have in reconciling the different discourses.

As demonstrated by the typology of this discourse, women are defined as primarily domestic and maternal. This assumption is based on men and women's biological differences. The strength of the discourse of hegemonic femininity and hegemonic masculinity lies in the supposed naturalness of the sexual division of labour. As Weedon states:

> Being a good wife and mother, as these roles are currently defined, calls for particular qualities, thought to be naturally feminine, such as patience, emotion and self-sacrifice. These expectations about natural femininity structure women's access to the labour market and to public life. Common

sense tells us that women are best suited to the service industries and 'caring' professions and that the 'aggressive' worlds of management, decision-making and politics call for masculine qualities even in a woman. Yet are masculine qualities in a woman quite natural? (Weedon 1987, p.3)

A number of the women used this type of 'common-sense' to explain their relationship to work. Almost all the interviews reiterated these views on women's work and men's work, but did not see their own work in these stereotypical ways.

Well I think a lot of men see their job as important and so they're looking for something that interests them and if they want they can get on and have promotion and I think men feel it's sort of part of their manliness, their job. It's part of a man - I think a job is part of him. The home is a lot to most women I would say; it's just something they do. Most get married and have children and when they've got children it's something they do to bring in extra money so they can go to Spain for holidays or whatever, you know. It's not so much, it's an extra to a woman rather than sort of part of her, part of them.

A.F. Do you feel like that about your job and your wage?

No, not really because I feel I'm quite involved with the work. You know, I'm quite willing to put in as much overtime as I have to, if necessary. You know, I was here till half past seven last night. ... I feel, to me it's quite an important part of my life. (Extract from transcripts)

The material from the women computer programmers I interviewed suggests how they try to reconcile their occupation with notions of femininity and motherhood. The inconsistencies and contradictions revealed by their responses indicate their struggle to reconcile the contradictory discourses that shape their occupation. One of the key responses to my questions about childcare and household arrangements was the theme of choice. The majority of the women talked about their decision to work or stay at home. They felt they had choices and that this distinguished them from men and gave them a privileged position. Women used this notion of choice to feel that they were more 'equal' than men in that they had the freedom either to work or not, which they felt men did not have. Whilst at work however, they were aware that this 'choice' did not provide them with status. They also were conscious of the lack of status of housework and childcare in organisational discourses. Women managed the tensions produced by these competing discourses in different ways.

Karen had acquired the status of a 'heroine' at *Business Systems Department* as she is the only woman from the data preparation department who moved into programming. She was continually being referred to in interviews, by both management and the other programmers, and is generally held in high esteem by the majority of people in the department. I interviewed her at home, as she had just given birth to her second child, and she had this to say about how she viewed women's relationship to work:

> Women will leave anyway and have families. Men go to work because to a certain extent they've got to and they're looking to get on as well as they can, in whatever area they've chosen. I would say a lot of women go to work for the company, you know, for the little bit of extra money, but to a certain extent they have a choice, or most women have a choice. I think that's the only difference in attitude and that obviously could colour the way ... the effort they put into it. (Extract from transcripts)

In common with a number of other studies, it is notable that Karen, when speaking in the abstract, about women in general, repeated a common discourse on women's attitude to paid work (see Collinson 1992). When speaking of her own work, Karen said:

> Alright I've always had a choice but I would always choose to work. It isn't just the company, it's the stimulus. I think that I don't find being at home stimulating enough. ... Certainly, I mean, the money is an added attraction but when you've got kids you've got to pay for somebody else to look after them. Obviously the money side of it, you know, dwindles a bit - you're not sort of getting as much extras as you would say without children. I think if I was a millionaire I would still work so, well I don't think money so important as I find it stimulating and I find that I need to work, as if were, for that reason. (Extract from transcripts)

The issue of 'choice' is related to the attempt to reconcile the conflicting discourses of work and home, whilst maintaining a subject position as a woman and a worker. I asked if they thought that programming is more a 'man's' job than a 'woman's', and they appeared to find this question difficult to understand. Their responses indicated that they did not interpret computing programming as a particularly masculine occupation, or as particularly technical. Rather than mention the different types of programming women do in comparison to men, they tended to respond in terms that were very similar to the descriptions given by the men in my sample. They used terms like 'challenging', 'stimulating', but their main emphasis was on job 'satisfaction'.

It is interesting to consider how these women are able to use generalised notions about women's work and men's work and reconcile these ideas with their desire to work, particularly since they were forced at times to defend their presence in their organisations. The next section attempts to suggest some of the ways women manage these contradictions.

Coping With, Rather Than Resisting Femininity

In particular women with children were forced to defend their decision to take on paid work. They encountered hostility from male colleagues and from partners when they continued to work. The fact that a woman is held in high regard as a co-worker, as in the example of Karen, did not shift the antagonism expressed towards her by some men and some women workers. She told me that some men had said to her that 'it was greedy for married women to work as it meant two wage packets in one house" and "why have children if you are not going to look after them'?

> When I first got pregnant and said I would be returning to work, some men tried to talk me out of it.
>
> A.F. What did they say?
>
> Well, one chap said he believes that maternal instincts are so strong that there's no way that any woman could possibly come back to work. He was a complete idiot, mind. So there was a bit of that until I did come back. And I found up to then I was never taken as seriously as the other blokes ... but I think I was seen as a woman, that is probably likely to leave and have a family and that's the end of it, sort of thing. Once I came back it was completely different. Once they realised I was serious, then a different attitude was displayed altogether. I think I was almost a different person coming back, in that I was more responsible. I was different and I don't think it was necessarily having a child that did it, it was just the fact that, you know, they saw me differently and I responded. (Extract from transcripts)

Some men (and some women) felt confident expressing these traditional views principally towards women with young children. The women who had children but no husbands, despite the fact that they may have partners, were generally exempt from criticism. The women said that they took little notice of these remarks, saying that the men who voiced this opinion were the older men in the organisation. Similar comments from women were received more problematical, the women admitting that they felt deeply hurt by their remarks. The following quote illustrates this problem.

> I hear the suggestion that women with children shouldn't work ... I'm certainly aware of people here that don't approve. I don't think you've got the particular person I'm thinking of on your list. There are people I know of, who I work closely with, who are of the opinion that women, certainly with young children, that it's very wrong for them to be at work. They should be at home, with the children. I don't know so much that just by the

fact that you are a woman you shouldn't work. I don't know people who
believe it's wrong for women to work, just for a mother.

A.F. How do you feel when you hear that kind of comment?

Well I mean we treat it as a bit of a joke, because I know their opinions and
they know mine, but I suppose I was surprised at the people who did feel
that strongly. ... but everybody's entitled to their opinion ... (Extract from
transcripts)

Another women said that if women choose to have children, then they must
be prepared to suffer the consequences of this 'choice' for their position
and status in the workplace.

Women do leave to break their career up or whatever; to have children, to
bring their children up and when they come back they can't expect to be at
the same place as they were when they left or the same place as the men
were when they left, if you see what I mean. You obviously make the
decision to leave and have children, then you sacrifice something in your
career ... I don't think that you can expect things to be put on a plate for
you. (Extract from transcripts)

There was no collective response to this problem by women. They
each had devised their own individual answer. Some shrugged it off,
taking little notice of the remarks and dismissing the people who made
them. Others felt hurt and upset and responded to the comments by
'keeping their head down' and working hard. As mentioned above for one
woman, Karen, her determination to return to work after the birth of her
second child had unexpected consequences.

Managing Work and Childcare

Karen encountered a number of oppositions in her determination to
continue working full time as well as caring for her two children. She
spoke to me of the difficulty with some of the men she worked with, when
they realised she intended to return to work after her maternity leave. She
also commented on the unexpected consequences of her return: the effect
on her attitude to her work, and on the changed perceptions of her work
colleagues, and the manager of the section. Once Karen decided that she
was not prepared to take their opposition seriously, this changed both her
male colleagues and the management's attitude to her as a worker. By her
actions in relation to child care, she felt that she was taken seriously as a
worker. Karen did not view this shift as either a threat or a reversal to her
femininity, because she has taken into her subjectivity - her sense of self -

the notion of the gendered neutral worker. While she was aware of the difficulties of her position as both mother and paid worker, she did not see her actions as contradictory or conflicting.

Other women were angry about the hostility they encountered in relation to their role as mothers. Some women with children were conscious of the tensions produced by the choices they were making, but generally expressed the belief that attitudes towards women working had changed. They explain this change either by reference to shifts in the discourse of hegemonic femininity or to the view that the gender neutral stance of organisational discourse had changed. The sentiments expressed in the following quote are indicative of some of these views:

> Women are changing their attitudes now, because 'why should they stay at home', or certain ones are objecting to staying at home. They want a career as well as a home life bringing up a family. I found I was only at home for five months and I was bored to tears. It just wasn't stimulating enough and my husband didn't want me to come back to work and I said I'm sorry I can't stay at home, I've got to come back to work. It was destroying me. (Extract from transcripts)

The quote above indicates that women also encounter opposition from their partners in relation to the time and effort they expend on their paid work. They deal with this in a number of ways, from 'training' men to take on more housework or more usually by doing most of the work themselves, either early in the morning before they go out to work, or in the evenings and weekends. Karen was one of the few women who had struggled with her partner to have a more equitable sexual division of labour in the home. She told me how she had 'trained' him to do his share of the work.

> I trained him. He's very good with children for a start. That's a natural thing but it was always understood from the beginning of our marriage that everything was down the middle and I have to do, you know, some of the horrible jobs, like mowing the lawn and messing about with the car, if necessary. ... I mean he didn't like the idea at first but it was that or not having children. (Extract from transcripts)

The majority of the women I interviewed, cope with, rather than challenge their responsibilities for domestic labour. They were expected to do it, and they did. They attempted to square the circle of running a home and keeping a full-time job. Their lives were tightly scheduled and organised with very little space for leisure or pleasure. The following quote indicates the tensions and stress involved:

The times I've gone home and I've thought 'Oh, God. I've forgotten to do this, shall I ring him up at home and tell him'? and I'd think, 'No, it can wait while the morning'. He's at home as well, so. Hubby does tend to nag at me sometimes saying 'you spend too much time at work, you know, slow down a bit you're not doing yourself any good by working all the hours you are doing'. I don't think married life has changed me so much as the job's changed me, you know, the new job. Certainly before that, it was half past eight to five and that was it. Now it's nothing unusual if I'm here Saturday, Sunday some weeks. (Extract from transcripts)

There were four types of responses from women to the tensions produced between their 'work' lives and their 'family' lives. As I have shown (i) some women concentrated on organising and reconciling the demands by adopting a 'work' model in their organisation and a 'gender' model at home. They appeared to rationalise this by referring to the fact that they had made a 'choice' and there were certain consequences to that choice. (ii) A few women tried to negotiate shared responsibilities in the home. (iii) Women bringing up children on their own were the group most likely to adopt a strategy of careerism, which is very similar to the male model described by Collinson and Hearn (1994) and Tolson (1977). This means that they attempt to operate inside organisational discourse by concentrating on their careers, and paying somebody else to clean the house and look after the children. From this group there was a lack of awareness of the contradictions this discourse creates either for themselves or other women. They tended to be unaware or refuse to acknowledge the gendered nature of either the organisational culture or the computing industry. (iv) The last group of women are those who attempt to challenge these discourses by struggling against the culture they encounter at work, by asserting their position as women workers in organisations rather than 'passing' as organisational men. They do this by asserting their femininity. One woman explained how she used her femininity to give her an 'edge' in the organisation.

A woman in a totally male environment, well ... [it depends on] . . the woman. I think most women in a totally male environment can handle [men] because all your life you're used to being flattered by men and you've grown up with it so you've learnt to backchat and you've learned to cope. Whereas you put a boy, a sixteen year old boy down in data prep with all those women, he'd die because you know, they just can't handle it because they're not brought up like that. (Extract from transcripts)

There are then a number of positions that women adopt in managing the competing discourses that constitute their gendered position in the workplace. One of the consequences of the different practices adopted by women means that alliances between them are difficult as some women are 'attending' to domesticity in a manner that contradicts other women's attempts to develop a career. The first group help to keep in place a critical aspect of hegemonic femininity, especially the notion that domesticity is women's primary responsibility. None of these women resisted the discourse of domesticity, rather they accommodate and cope with the demands of both domestic and paid labour. While some felt that men should 'help' in the home, others voiced the opinion that women must reconcile the conflicts between the different jobs by working harder. If all the work at home is 'attended to' in this way, then their presence at work is not incompatible or problematic for their subjectivity as women. Nor is their work conflictual for the gendered culture of either the occupation or the organisation.

Another contradiction is that because domesticity is not challenged and continues to be a strong element of the discourse of hegemonic femininity, women have to work very hard in order to be taken seriously as workers. Even for those women who are divorced and separated, or who choose to live on their own, their position as paid workers is structured by this element of the discourse of hegemonic femininity. Women are working hard to keep up with what they consider to be their domestic responsibilities, but they also work hard to be 'organisational men' in order to maintain their status as workers in the computing industry. Thus in order to prove to their colleagues and to their management that they are 'serious' workers, the women work much harder than men.

Working Hard to be Taken Seriously

The men and women I interviewed casually informed me that women worked harder, and were more conscientious, than men. Women were also aware that they had to work hard in order to justify their presence in the organisation. These differences between the behaviour of women and men were explained to me, generally by referring to stereotypical notions of masculinity and femininity.

> Men seem to have a different way of looking at work. Work is a part of their life, that is accepted. You go out to work. You earn money. With women they look on it far more seriously. It isn't a matter of course, it's something you fight for and just being a woman you have to fight harder than a man. You're more hungry. If you want promotion you're more hungry than men generally, I think. You seem to have to persuade people that you're serious, you're not playing at it. (Extract from transcripts)

The women are very aware of the fact that they work harder than men, but they expressed this in terms of irritation and annoyance rather than anger. With one exception:

> It bugs me that sometimes they'd rather talk to a man, but it's only because they're not used to talking to women and then they see me as the typist. I find it annoying but it's a very male orientated industry this one. (Extract from transcripts)

This is the only example I have of a woman who was very keenly conscious of gender inequalities and the problems facing women working in 'male' organisations. She also told me that 'she was not a feminist', but she believed in equal opportunities. The implications of being viewed, as 'not serious' means that women have a constant struggle to become valued members of their organisation. As Burton (1991) points out:

> To fit in, woman have to take on some of the values and preferred ways of doing things in work organisations, which are grounded in men's, not women's experiences. (Burton 1991, p.33)

Karen had a very long struggle to move from the data preparation room to become a programmer. It did take her nearly two and a half years to make this move. When she finally shifted in the systems section, she had very little work for a further six months, until she began to 'fit it'. The following quote from Karen provides some indication of this struggle:

> Well yes, I think that's the main problem, getting on, you know - starting. Being taken seriously to start with I think is the main thing. Once you are, then you obviously got the opportunities to sort of make your opinions known and you've got the contacts then. Once you get higher up the ladder as it were, ... I don't know, I don't suppose they'd ever really consider at the moment having a woman as head of department for business systems, but you never know in ten years time they might. (Extract from transcripts)

It is difficult for small numbers of women in occupations dominated by a male culture to the extent that computing is, to change discriminatory practices in any dramatic way. Especially as initially, some women are struggling to overcome the notion that they are not as committed to their job as their male colleagues. An additional problem is that it is not only men who hold this view as was illustrated by the quote from Jean, the Applications Development Manager at *Radola*.

The view that women are not committed workers or that they are transitory, impacts on their working lives in a number of ways. For example, this attitude will affect women's chances to become a project leader. This will directly affect their salary, status and power in the organisation. The following account demonstrates the impact of this attitude on one of the women I interviewed. Unfortunately, in this case, the man who was treating this woman so dismissively, was also her line manager.

> He'll deny it, but I'm always arguing with him about it, telling him that he doesn't treat me the same as the men. I'm a woman and I'm just like a skivvy.

A.F. What does he do?

> Just generally the way he is to me, the way they are to me. I feel as if I'm just used as a skivvy but to be truthful I aren't as clever as some of those lads.

A.F. How do you know?

> Because I know the work they're doing and I aren't as clever and I aren't as interested. ... I just don't have the knowledge.

A.F. Are you sure?

> It's too complicated really and I think it's enough for me, you know, what I'm doing. I'm quite happy, you know, at the level I'm at. I feel that if I wanted to get on working for George and the way things are I'd find it hard because I'm a woman. I feel that, because I think that's the way he looks on women. And sometimes, I mean, I've had a big argument with him because sometimes he's horrible. He doesn't mean it, he's a Greek and he doesn't mean what he says, he doesn't know but he says some horrible things to me. And I applied to get out of the department one day because I was that fed up with the way he talked to me, how rude he was to me and everything, just putting me down all the time, as a joke, you know, making it funny, and I just felt that he was making me look stupid and showing me up in front of everybody.

A.F. So he was saying these things in front of everybody?

> Oh, yes, and I said that I was going to leave the department and find a job somewhere else. He apologised and said he didn't mean to say it and he wouldn't say it any more but it starts creeping in again. He really insults me, but I don't think he really means to do it. I'm sure it's because I'm a woman and it's partly to do with it, but as I say I don't think I could get on a real lot even if I wanted to because of his attitude, but I don't particularly want to get on that much anyway. (Extract from transcripts)

I interviewed George quite soon after this account - two days later in fact. Despite my best efforts, I felt antagonistic towards him. I was aware that my manner was cold and distant, though I have no doubt that he interpreted this as academic objectivity, and accepted my demeanour as that of an impartial researcher. I did my best to play this game as I was anxious to maintain the confidentiality of my interview with Gillian. His position as a group leader in the production control area, meant not only is he involved with interviewing and hiring staff, but he also co-ordinates the work of the sixteen programmers in his section.[1] George, for his part, was charming, convivial, courteous. Throughout the interview he used the male pronoun (he) to refer to the staff. When I mentioned this to him, he replied 'sometimes it is difficult to understand whether I say she or a he'. He was, however, very complementary about the women computer programmers in his team, he said he found them very 'hardworking' people and that they 'worked harder than men'.

A.F. So why do you think women are more hardworking?

It must be in them, it's something, I haven't thought about it, but it's an observation, it's not an analysis, it's just an observation. I mean if you go to any office in here you'll see that women mostly have their heads down working. ... I think it's in their nature to work harder. Don't you find that? (Extract from transcripts)

The comments on women working harder than men contradicts Burton's (1991) argument that men 'cannot afford to believe that women, doing both [domestic work and paid work], can perform as well or better at the work-place' (ibid., p.8). My research would indicate that men could easily afford to comment on the fact that women worked harder than they did. The men did not appear to feel threatened or apprehensive about the differences between their work and their female colleagues. They were largely indifferent. I believe this is because, in the main, they do not perceive women to be a threat. They are competing with other men, not with women. Therefore they are concerned with cultivating male networks, with noting other men's activities, interests and ambitions. This suggestion would also be supported by the research on men in organisations conducted through the 'new men's studies', which indicates that men 'often seem preoccupied with the creation and maintenance of various masculine identities and with the expression of gendered power and status in the workplace' (Collinson and Hearn 1994, p.8). This is due in part, as Burton points out, to the fact that men's work tends to be rated higher than women's, by both men and women. As she states: 'good female performance is perceived as due to effort, and good male performance as due to ability' (1991, p.18).

Yet, the presence of women computer programmers, who manage a home and a full time job, working alongside men becomes part of the process whereby this discourse shifts and changes, though these shifts may appear to be imperceptible and uncertain. So for example, none of the women I interviewed described themselves as feminists, and not one of them expressed any anger that they were expected to take on domestic responsibilities, or appeared to consider it in any way problematic that men occupied all the powerful positions in their organisation.

Part of the explanation for this could be the centrality of child bearing and child rearing for hegemonic femininity. Unlike the men in my sample, they couched their attitude to children by using the term 'responsibility' rather than 'sacrifice'. Though a few women resisted,

> No, I've never want to get married and I certainly don't want children.

A.F. Why?

> I think probably the reason for it is ... my mother was divorced, both my sisters have been divorced, one of them twice, and I've seen so much hassle with marriages and one thing and another. I suppose deep down inside me that's probably got something to do with it. (Extract from transcripts)

Femininities

The 'ideology of sacrifice' that characterises men's attitudes to work, (see Nichols and Beynon 1977; Collinson 1992) is largely absent in the women's discussions of their paid work. The women spoke of the stimulation and satisfaction they obtained from their work. I expected this theme of 'sacrifice' to be applied to the family and the home but few of the women used this expression though they were very conscious of duties and responsibilities around children. The different responses by women to these 'duties' indicates the ambivalence produced by the hegemonic discourse on femininity, a discourse which gets its power from 'its claim to be natural, obvious and therefore true' (Weedon 1987, p.77). The majority of the women I interviewed used this discourse to rationalise and interpret their position in paid work using a 'biologically based common-sense'. As Weedon explains:

> Common sense consists of a number of social meanings and the particular ways of understanding the world that guarantee them. These meanings, which inevitably favour the interests of particular social groups, become fixed and widely accepted as true irrespective of sectional interests. ... it looks to 'human nature' to guarantee its version of reality. It is the medium

through which already fixed 'truths' about the world, society and individuals are expressed. (Weedon 1987, p.77)

All the women and men I interviewed used this type of discourse to explain why women do not occupy the same positions in the industry as men. This is also used to explain how women's relationship to work is different from men's. However, this shared discourse on hegemonic femininity and hegemonic masculinity did not establish the basis for solidarity and shared interests amongst the women. Just as the preceding chapter demonstrated, with reference to the discussion of masculinities rather than masculinity, in a similar way, hegemonic femininity creates femininities rather than femininity. As mentioned above differences can be detected amongst the women I interviewed in the way they coped with the discourse of domesticity and hegemonic femininity.

Conflicting Discourses

The three distinct ways that the women I interviewed, cope with, rather than challenge hegemonic femininity produced three types of femininities. The women who worked hard at combining their domestic responsibilities with their paid work resisted the element of hegemonic femininity which involved dependence - though there is an issue here of emotional rather than financial dependency. Women who have no child care responsibilities and adopted a strategy of careerism, which is very similar to the male model described by Collinson and Hearn (1994) and Tolson (1978), resisted the discourse of domesticity and relied on a 'ideology of individual choice' (Burton 1991, p.14) to explain their relationship to paid work. This group of women cope with the contradictions of their position by explaining the gendered nature of either organisational culture or the computing industry with reference to the problems caused by 'individual' men. The last group of women are those who attempt to challenge these discourses, by struggling against the culture they encounter at work, by asserting their position as women workers in organisations, rather than 'passing' as organisational men. However, there are differences here between the extent to which a woman 'uses' her sexuality, to give an 'edge', an advantage in the struggle between the conflicting discourses encountered at the workplace. An example of the way this process works is provided by the following extract from Weedon:

> Many women acknowledge the feeling of being a different person in different social institutions that call for different qualities and modes of femininity. The range of ways of being a woman open to each of us at a particular time is extremely wide but we know or feel we ought to know

what is expected of us in particular situations - in romantic encounters, when we are pandering to the boss, when we are dealing with children or posing for fashion photographers. We may embrace these ways of being, these subject positions whole-heartedly, we may reject them outright or we may offer resistance while complying to the letter which what is expected of us. Yet even when we resist a particular subject position and the mode of subjectivity that it brings with it, we do so from the position of an alternative social definition of femininity. (Weedon 1987, p.86)

Sexuality and Organisational Discourse

There are two strong discourses that critical to hegemonic femininity: the discourse of domesticity, and the discourse of sexuality. In the interviews I conducted, I attended to the relationships between gender, computer programming and domesticity. My aim was to provide an account of the dichotomies between formal/informal and public/private in the process of gendering at the workplace. My neglect of sexuality can be explained by the fact that the literature of the early 1980s on women's work and gender at work said very little about sexuality and organisations. References to women, sexuality and work, usually changed to discussions of sexual harassment. (Cockburn 1991; MacKinnon 1979). Sexual harassment was mentioned by a number of the women I interviewed. One woman would only talk to me about her personal experience of harassment, if I stopped the tape recorder. Another woman spoke of the difficulty she had in getting the management to take the harassment she had suffered seriously. This problem was compounded by the fact that the harasser was also her line manager. She told me the story in the following way:

> I mean, it was a small thing, but, he was a bit, well twice I reported him for sexual harassment, so you know, I wasn't very happy. I mean I quite liked him and everything but he was just, he wouldn't take me seriously.   I got fed up ... I felt I should have been on a higher grade than I was. I wasn't very happy with my career path either.

> A.F. What kind of sexual harassment?

> He just used to pat me on the bum now and again. You know, nothing excessive really, just annoying stuff that you know. And he used to make jokes - sexist jokes in meetings, you know, with the users, and to a certain extent belittle me in meetings which I took offence to.

> A.F. What happened when you made the complaint?

Well, they knew what he was like and they were quite [pause], I think, on both occasions they talked to him and told him, you know, he had to stop and take things a bit more seriously. He was just told, you know, to buck up a bit, that's all.

A.F. Did he take any notice?

Well, he didn't take hardly any notice the first time. I think the second time, actually ...they talked to him so it went a bit higher and he told him, that it was serious and they would have to do something about it if he carried on, so.

A.F. What happened then?

I think he was annoyed and he was probably a bit angry - he couldn't understand why I'd complained about it. You know, he just couldn't understand what I was making a fuss about. (Extract from transcripts)

This woman was moved into a department that was managed by a woman, soon after this experience. Sexual harassment is a major problem facing women in organisations. Cockburn (1991) found that nearly every women she interviewed experienced some form of harassment. Examples ranged from men commenting on women's bodies, on women's dress, to touching, to using pornographic literature and sexist language and sexual banter (see also Sedley and Benn 1982; Wise and Stanley 1987). Sexual harassment is now recognised as an aggressive act from men towards women. The majority of this type of abusive behaviour is directed towards women: there is a very small amount of evidence that suggests that women can also harass men. Therefore very little comparison can be made between women sexually harassing men, and men harassing women. The rarity of these incidents has not however prevented the huge commercial success of the play *Ollenna* (1994) and the film *Disclosure* (1995), two productions that deal with men as the 'victims' of harassment. There are no comparable (in terms of commercial success), plays, books or movies that treat the subject from the perspective of working women. I do not want to diminish the ubiquity of sexual harassment and the problems caused to women; however, I want to argue that by concentrating only on sexual harassment, other aspects of women and 'sex' at work fade and become invisible.

Sexuality at work tends to be discussed in one of two ways. If the focus is the problems women encounter at the workplace, there is a tendency to collapse discussion of sexuality into a discussion of sexual harassment (see Cockburn 1991). If 'sex' at work is discussed in relation to men's workplace studies there is little mention of sexual harassment, rather 'sex' at work is mentioned with reference to sexual banter, sexual jokes. This approach is a common feature of ethnographic research of male workplace culture (Willis 1977; Collinson 1992), and features in some studies of women's work (Cavendish 1982; Pollert 1981; Westwood 1984). Cockburn (1991) suggests two functions for sexual banter. Firstly, that this practice can be used in male bonding and secondly it's role as a form of resistance to control at the workplace, both at the expense of women (see Burrell 1983). There are, however, very few studies which deal specifically with sexuality and gender in the workplace. The seminal works of Hearn and Parkin (1984), Hearn et al. (1989;) and Pringle (1988), on the issues raised by this topic are exceptional as they retain a sense of the importance of sexual harassment as a problem for women at work, and manage to separate out sexual harassment from discussions of sexuality. Pringle (1988) makes the point that it is too easy to characterise all relations between men and women at the workplace in terms of sexual harassment. She writes:

> In naming and theorising sexual harassment feminists have drawn attention to the centrality of sexuality in workplace organisation. However, they have largely restricted sexuality to its coercive or unpleasurable dimensions. Radical feminists have emphasised sexual aggression and violence as the basis of men's power. If women experience pleasure it is treated as 'coerced caring' (MacKinnon, 1979:54-55). In these accounts either virtually all heterosexual activity may be labelled as sexual harassment or a line has to be drawn between what is harassment and what is 'acceptable'. (Pringle 1988, p.95)

These texts are not arguing that men exercising power over women in a sexually abusive way should be ignored, but that the literature on sexual harassment appears to be making the argument that sex can be eliminated from men and women's working lives. Part of the tension here is that 'sex' in organisations is constituted through the discourse of heterosexuality.

Sexuality is a powerful element of organisational life, for women as well as for men. Women have a number of particular problems with 'sex' at work, not simply in terms of sexual harassment, but because women's bodies are objects of sexual desire, for men but also for women. Men's bodies are also objects of sexual desire, for women and for other men. The pleasures of bodies and desire in the discourse of sexuality, particularly given the key place this discourse plays in constituting hegemonic femininity means that 'sex' at work is particularly problematic for women.

The contradiction this poses for women is that organisational discourses constituted them as gender neutral, yet in hegemonic masculinity and femininity their bodies are 'sexed'. All human beings come with sexualised bodies to the workplace, and some of these bodies provide pleasure just in the gaze. It is not only men who are extracting pleasure from the gaze, by simply looking at women. Women are also women looking at men. Men's bodies are also sexualised by women. Women are also looking at other women, and men are looking at other men. How people are dressed is noticed, and commented on; the way people talk to each other is noticed and commented on; the sexual activity between people at work is watched and spoken of. All of these activities provide a source of pleasure. Given the body as a site of pleasure, fantasy and desire, it is not possible to eliminate the connotations of sexuality and sex from the workplace, despite the fact that the discourse of organisations is premised on the separation of the private work of sex from the public world of work. Sex at work cannot be discussed simply in terms of sexual harassment. Nor is it possible to shift the sexualisation of bodies. It may also be strategically useful for sexuality discourses to become more overt in organisations as this would further expose the myth of the gender neutral worker.

Burrell's (1992) article *Sex and Organisational Analysis* is a useful study which provides an historical examination of the attempts which were made to try to desexualise the workplace and the resistance by workers to these measures. Burrell outlines the rationalisation process that governs these attempts to suppress the sexuality of workers in organisations. He mentions one of the problems as the lack of clarity around which activities can be designated as sexual activities. He asks:

> How are we to recognise *sexual* activity? Are we to restrict ourselves only to that genital more generalized eroticism of touch and phantasy? Clearly there is the possibility of conceptualizing a continuum of sexual relationships in which full genital sexuality involving penetration is near one end of the scale whilst the other end is marked by a plurality of polymorphous pleasurable sensations and emotions. (Burrell 1992, p.72)

This raises the interesting question of the example of sexuality at work that I referred to above: is 'looking' a sexual practice? Burrell's account emphasises the importance of the elimination of sex at work for organisations as part of the attempt to discipline and control workers. In light of his account, I would suggest that one of the mechanisms for the control of sexuality was to move women from the workplace.[2] The reason for this is, that through the discourse of hegemonic femininity, women's subject position has sexual connotations in a different way to men. As Burrell explains:

> Suppression of sexuality, therefore, involved both eradication and containment, inside and outside work respectively.   And these twin processes have continued to influence the lives of the worker since that time to this. Today then, we are presented with a situation in which human features such as love and comfort are not seen as part of the organisational world. In popular ideology, rightly or wrongly, they are associated with the home and the family. But this translocation is not accidental. Human feelings including sexuality have gradually been relocated in the non-organisational sphere - the world of civil society. Their expulsion back into the family, into private life and away from the world of work has been achieved   by   a   whole   variety   of   organisational   forms. (Burrell 1992, pp.73-4)

However, as Foucault's *History of Sexuality* helps to elucidate, the process of repression and resistance created a form of discourse on sexuality in organisation. Part of this discourse is the myth that sexuality and work are not compatible, but there is increasing evidence that organisations are saturated with bio-politics (Hearn and Parkin 1987; Hearn, Sheppard, Tancred-Sheriff and Burrell (eds.) 1989; Pringle 1988), and this has implications for women, the process of gendering at the workplace and occupational segregation.

In Summary

This chapter shows the conflicts produced by the conflicting discourses of organisations and hegemonic femininity in relation to women's paid work. Women have to manage their domestic responsibilities away from the gaze of the organisation. The lack of a company policy on maternity and paternity leave, in any of the companies I visited, is another indication of the power of this discourse in contributing to the problems women encounter when they return to work after the birth of a child.

The different and inter-related discourses that affect the women and male computer programmers I interviewed are not fixed. The elements of these discursive fields are constantly shifting, being managed and negotiated. The way individual men and women use aspects of these discourses to give meaning to their experiences (their subjectivity), and to their identity as gendered individuals is therefore often precarious and contradictory. To maintain that women are always the 'victims' of male sexuality is to overlook the process of resistance, control and coercion between women and men, and also between woman and women and men and men in relation to the discourse of sexuality. In the next chapter I examine the discourse of science and technology in order to suggest how this discourse works in the computing industry to further marginalise the discourses of femininity.

Notes

[1] Only two of these sixteen were women.

[2] The historic segregation and exclusion of women into jobs which are separate from those of men and which are less well paid is generally explained with reference to patriarchy and capitalism (see Walby 1986). The extent to which the discourses of sexuality and hegemonic femininity has shaped these practices is explained only in relation to male dominance, not in terms of the discourse of organisations.

Chapter 9

Conclusion

The main focus for this research is to contribute to feminist theorising in the area of women's paid employment by suggesting how the meanings attached to various discourses can form part of the explanation for the persistence of gender segregation at work. Though it explores one dimension of the problem the study suggests an explanation for the persistence of gender segregation; shows how a variety of discourses operate to reproduce the phenomenon and illustrates how resistance and compliance can occur. The theories that explain segregation; e.g. sex role theories, human capital theory, labour market segmentation, patriarchal exclusion, and so on all explain some aspects of segregation. The usefulness and novelty of the approach taken in this book is that, rather than simply identify discourses, it shows how discourses work in the creation of the material reality of both gender and employment relations. Thus it broadens the topic of occupational segregation to include the impact of gender discourses on the phenomenon in order to investigate how segregation is accomplished and reproduced, demonstrating that the maintenance of gender identities is a factor in the reproduction of occupational segregation. This perspective can illuminate the practices and meanings within which women and men live, as well as point to the active nature of occupational choices, thus demonstrating the complicated ways by which gender structures occupations. A further novelty in this study is that it explores occupational segregation in an occupation that is interchangeable by women and men unlike the majority of studies on the topic that examine how women are clustered into particular occupations.

Though I believe I have formulated some ideas that would help with any future research in the area, I think I only partly completed the task I set myself at the beginning of the project. To some extent this book portrays a personal route through the feminist perspective that informed my ideas for the last twenty years and is itself a product of two distinct theoretical paradigms. The first part of the work is framed by feminist-Marxism, as it was this theoretical position which informed the focus of the research through the accounts of women's work established by writers such as Cavendish 1982; Pollert 1981; Westwood 1984; Beechey 1983; Cockburn

1983, 1985; and Hartmann 1981. These accounts had emphasised the relationship between women's position in the labour market and the sexual division of labour in the house. Women workers were confined to low-paid jobs, with few opportunities for promotion, conditions that ensured their dependence on men and thus secured their unpaid work in the home.

Many of these studies were concerned to demonstrate how the intersection of patriarchy and capitalism structure women's oppression, subordination and exploitation and resulted in gender segregation at the workplace. Though this proved to be an extremely complex exercise. However the large amount of literature that resulted from this endeavour has greatly contributed to an understanding of the centrality of gender for workplace organisations. A vast amount of empirical and theoretical work about women has been accumulated. However I argue throughout this book that one of the cornerstones of the feminist paradigm is flawed. Largely because of the problem of essentialism that had dogged the concept of patriarchy, an attempt was made at the beginning of second- wave feminism to develop additional concepts. This lead, especially in the area of paid work, to an engagement with Marxism.

The attempt to feminise Marxism happened in a number of ways. Some writers examined traditional Marxist texts for references to women and attempted to interpret the extent to which Marx and Engels were aware of gender as an aspect of the social relations of capitalism (Vogel 1984). Others uncovered the history of women in various socialist and labour movement organisations, and outlined the contribution of these women to revolutionary politics and debates (Rowbotham, 1973). A large number of writers engaged with Marxist analysis of capitalism (Gardiner 1975, Kuhn and Wolpe 1978; West 1982), especially with the contribution of domestic labour and women's position in the labour market to both capitalist accumulation and the reproduction of the system. These debates became paralysed by problems of Marxist economics and this effectively side-tracked any real progress in the feminist analysis of women's paid employment. This also weakened the popularity of this theoretical and intellectual position. I have tried to show that one of the problems with these accounts is related to the static concept of gender that is embedded in the analysis of patriarchy. This directs the analysis of gender away from an interpretation of the process of gendering and towards a fixed idea of gender sex roles and categories, rather than towards an exploration of gender as being continually in a process of production and negotiation. A further weakness with this tradition is that within the Marxist analysis, labour is only analysed with reference to its use as a commodity. Therefore the subjectivity of labour is not a factor in this account. However, the relationship between human beings as both subject and object in capitalist social relations means that their subjectivity will influence, shape, and interact with the social relations of production, and this subjectivity is gendered. Studying the links between subjectivity and paid labour is a recent phenomenon in industrial sociology, and is due in part to the impact of Foucault's work on the social sciences. His work provides a critique of the unitary and rational subject that has dominated sociology. Foucault's analysis of the relationship between power, discursive practices and subjectivity provides a number of conceptual tools from which to re-examine the contradictions of women's experiences of paid work.

Undoubtedly women are objectively oppressed in capitalist society, but the processes and practices through which this occurs are complicated and contradictory for both women and men. It is extremely difficult to explain this complexity using the conceptualisation of gender that is embedded in the notion of 'patriarchy'. Although patriarchy is a concept of enormous resonance and power, - given that it points to the long historical process of discrimination and oppression suffered by women in all recorded societies, - it has become a way of expressing gender asymmetry and gender inequality, and in this sense it is a political concept for feminists on both a practical and a theoretical sense. However when used as a theoretical concept it impedes the development of feminist analysis over a wide range of topics, including some of the critical questions raised by feminist analysis of women and work. These questions converge on the extent to, and the ways by which gender shapes paid labour. The concept of patriarchy answers these questions by analysing the oppression of women in employment with reference to male domination in the home and at the workplace. Consequently the position of women in the labour market tends to be 'read off' (Beechey 1983, p.43) the sexual division of labour that operates in the household. Occupational segregation and women's role in production are explained with reference to women's reproductive role. Women's oppression both in the home and in the workplace are explained in terms of male dominance. The power, positions and roles of men tend to act as an overarching explanation for gender segregation, whether vertical or horizontal, and in this scenario, women lose their agency. The processes by which waged work becomes gendered are not analysed, but rather are obscured by the positioning of men as dominant and women as dominated. This approach is also unable to explain the contradictions and conflicts experienced by both women and men at the workplace.

Despite the fact that the concept of patriarchy has been the subject of a number of criticisms from feminists, a static conceptualisation of gender still continues to frame studies of women's employment, and this has consequences for understanding the extent to which women exercise power and control in relation to the process of gendering at work. One of the principal problems of the theorisation of gender in Marxist-feminism and also radical-feminism is that analytically women are positioned as powerless and men are powerful, and this ignores the existence and reality of *women's power*. It is not the case that all men are absolutely dominant in every situation, nor does the reverse situation apply in the case of women. Just as gender is a process, so too is power, and in order to analyse gender at work and women's power as an aspect of this process, it is necessary to use Foucault's notion of power rather than the way power is conceived in both Marxist analysis and political philosophy more generally. There has been an overestimation of men's power in the workplace that has obscured the impact of their domestic commitments and interests on their subject position as men.

Male dominance is not complete whether in the home or workplace. Conventional industrial sociology and Marxist sociology had marked off the organisation of the factory as a separate area of study, and there is little consideration given to the connections between the workplace and the home on the part of men. Women's domestication of the shopfloor is stressed in ethnographic studies of women's paid labour (see Cavendish 1982; Pollert 1981; Westwood 1984) but this is represented as related to the sexual division of labour in the home and not analysed either as a demonstration of women's power or agency. Many of these accounts slide over the complications of the process of gendering in the workplace, and though women's resistance to their subordination has been noted in all these studies this data has not been used to challenge the orthodoxy of women's powerlessness and subordination. Critiques that discuss the problems of this account of women's paid work and recognise the fact of women's power make the mistake of locating it within the family (see Grieco and Whipp 1986) rather than examining women's power at the workplace.

Historical Shifts in Discourses of Femininity

From the historical evidence (see Bradley 1989) it is clear that the ideology of female domesticity was a critical aspect of job segregation in the workplace and that this ideology provided the basis for men's exclusionary tactics against women workers. Rather than arguing, as Hartmann does, that men actively and deliberately organised as a sex against women, I argue that because of the relationship between the discourse of femininity and the discourses of masculinity - i.e. the relational aspects of gender -

men's actions and practices are shaped by discourses of masculinity. As women were restricted by the ideologies of femininity to the sexual division of labour in the household, men were also restricted to paid work. There are numerous studies that demonstrate the ideological work of gender that accompanied the industrial revolution and resulted in the historical separation of the home and the workplace and the gendering of the public and the private (Hall 1982, Alexander 1982, Barrett and McIntosh 1982; Poovey 1989). The responsibility and care of women and children through paid work was a vital aspect of hegemonic masculinity. Similarly the care and responsibility for children and the home were the dominant aspect of hegemonic femininity. Therefore, if we reflect on the historical evidence of men actively and strategically resisting women's presence in the workplace, this can be explained by the salience of work for the construction of masculinity for men. Poovey however point to the unevenness of this ideology, and she demonstrates what she terms:

> the other face of this ideology - the extent to which what may look coherent and complete in retrospect was actually fissured by competing emphases and interests. ... that the middle-class ideology we most often associate with the Victorian period was both contested and always under construction because it was always in the making, it was always open to revision, dispute, and the emergence of oppositional formulations. (Poovey 1989, p.3)

Ideologies, just like discourses, are constantly shifting, and I would argue that whilst historically the discourse of domesticity was a critical aspect of the discourses of femininity other aspects of these discourses have now become more dominant. In the contemporary discourses the emphasis has shifted from domesticity, and the discourses of motherhood, sexuality and work now have to be negotiated by women. Historical changes have occurred within these discourses for a variety of reasons. There are two important shifts for women that have diminished the strength of domesticity in the discourse of femininity. These can be related to sexuality and equal opportunities. The debates around equal opportunities, whilst not having much practical impact in terms of women's jobs and occupational segregation, have introduced the notion of equality in relation to masculinity and femininity, and thus have implications and consequences for women's subjectivity. Sexuality has always been an important aspect of hegemonic femininity, but historically it has been relegated to the private domain, not the public. Sexuality as an aspect of feminine subjectivity was always contradictory and complex for women, but historically these contradictions were not so apparent. Thus the shift from domesticity as the signifier of women's acquisition of womanhood, of a feminine self, has exposed the contradictions and complexity of the discourses of gender for public disclosure rather than private torment. The notion of contradiction is useful here as it indicates that there are always spaces, alternatives and thus options for the construction of alternative discourses of gender. Foucault's statement about contradiction provides support for the interpretation of my research material that refused to be interpreted by a neat and tidy analysis. He wrote:

> The history of ideas usually credits the discourse that it analyses with coherence. If it happens to notice an irregularity in the use of words, several incompatible propositions, a set of meanings that do not adjust to one another, concepts that cannot be systematised together, then it regards it as its duty to find, at a deeper level, a principle of cohesion that organises the discourse and restores to it its hidden unity. This law of coherence is a heuristic rule, a procedural obligation, almost a moral constraint of research: not to multiply contradictions uselessly; to be taken in by small differences; not to give too much weight to changes. (Foucault 1972, p.149)

Contradictions

Theoretically I believe that in order to change the position of women in society, one had to understand the process of gender and the practices that constitute femininity. Femininity however was not constructed in the abstract. Femininity was/is constituted in relation to masculinity: the two are intertwined; one only understands what is meant, what is represented by the term women, by understanding, men and masculinity. However, the 'new men's studies' have not interpreted gender studies in this way. Rather as I discussed in chapter seven, they deal solely with masculinity and men and have failed to include women in their studies of gender. The shift from women's studies to gender studies has also had the effect of sharpening the existing divisions inside the women's movement by strengthening antagonisms and suspicions between women who still use a women's studies perspective. Mary Evans in her article 'The problem of gender for women's studies' (1990), argues that the shift has allowed the study of differences to replace the study of gender inequalities and women's oppression; that using the concept of gender rather than women allows the unequal nature of the relationship between men and women to be disguised. In other words the shift to gender has produced some contradictory effects and these could obscure the 'fine meshes of the web of power' that subordinate women and produce male bodies and masculinities organised around control and domination.

Ending

Giddens (1987) has argued that ideas about how societies work has a 'reflective relationship' with the social processes they seek to explain. The existing paradigm in feminist thought which is shaped by the concept of patriarchy produces a discourse that is not helpful to women. A paradigm consists of the 'orienting assumptions and conceptual frameworks which are basic to a discipline' (quoted in Acker 1989). The conceptual framework that has been used in many feminist studies of segregation has established an orthodoxy where it is difficult to perceive how change might occur. In order to begin to change the situation for women at work, it is necessary to understand and interpret it. It is essential to grasp the process of gendering at work in order to begin to change it. This process is full complex and contradictory - but this is where attention is needed. The task of creating a new conceptual framework is immense but in order to bring about meaningful change to gender segregation at work it is necessary to begin to develop a new discourse about gender relations. Talking about gender means talking about women and men, not women or men separately. The process of gendering is constituted through the interactions of the discourses that shape gender in Western societies. Throughout this book I have suggested we need such an approach to the old problem of unequal gender relations at the workplace.

However there are a number of refinements that I would make if I was embarking on a similar piece of research. Some observations have been made in chapter four concerning the research method adopted in the study. It seems to me that in order to study processes and practices in the workplace it is essential to have a period of observation, preferably participant observation. It would also be useful to provide case studies of similar occupations; similar in that the occupation is interchangeable by women and men; in order to build up a sample of firms and occupations that show the workings of the internal labour market. The extent and dimension of segregation in different occupations needs to be continually assessed in order to provide quantifiable data on the effectiveness of government legislation and equal opportunities programmes in reducing segregation. There is also a need for the collection of observational data concerning the processes of segregation and the responses of individuals and organisations to the phenomenon.

The book suggests that a wider remit is needed to equal opportunities policies in that simply providing opportunities for women to enter different types of occupations and enhancing promotion opportunities is only the first step in the process of reducing segregation. Equal opportunities policies and initiatives need to be coded in the language of gender as process in order to understand the dynamic that shapes the process of segregation as well as retaining the concept of gender as static in order to quantify the extent of the phenomenon. Thus in examining occupational segregation by gender it is necessary to avoid presentations of the contrast between women's and men's experiences of work and concentrate more precisely on the meanings of gendered experience. The production of case study approaches to occupations need to include information on specific personnel policies and practices in order to enable more effective policies to be developed. This would provide the basis for political and educational campaigns, albeit in a political and economic conjuncture that is far from favourable to the prerequisite social movements that are required in order to bring about positive changes. Previously sections of the women's movement, with limited trade union support, were in the forefront of challenging occupational segregation but the weakness of feminism in maintaining an active movement concerned with work based issues has seriously reduced the possibility for serious qualitative transformations.

Appendix

Research Methodology

Approach to Research

The methodological approach adopted in this book is that the researcher is not a neutral observer standing outside social relations and social structures. Hence the approach to knowledge is one that is embedded in the following quote by Dale Spender who wrote:

> at the core of feminist ideas is the crucial insight that there is no one truth, no one authority, no one objective method which leads to the production of pure knowledge, but there is a significant difference between the two: feminist knowledge is based on the premise that the experience of all human beings is valid and must not be excluded from our understandings, whereas patriarchal knowledge is based on the premise that the experience of only half the human population needs to be taken into account and the resulting version can be imposed on the other half. This is why patriarchal knowledge and the methods of producing it are a fundamental part of women's oppression, and why patriarchal knowledge must be challenged. (cited in Reinharz 1992, p.8)

The assumption that the researcher should strive to be a neutral observer is made by many who use quantitative and qualitative methods in a natural science model of social science enquiry. This assumption is challenged by the feminist critique of social science that documents the male bias of theory and research (Stanley and Wise 1993). Feminist scholars have analysed male bias in the social sciences (Delphy 1984; Roberts 1981; Smith 1988; Stanley and Wise 1983, 1993) and have made a distinctive contribution to long-standing debates about the nature of science and its epistemological foundation (Ramazanoglu 1989). These analyses have led to an important debate around the problems of doing empirical work within a feminist perspective (e.g. Roberts 1981; Stanley and Wise 1983, 1993; Reinharz 1992). There is now available a considerable literature that debates issues on the existence of a feminist methodology. As Stanley and Wise (1993) have noted, feminist researchers have variously denied and affirmed the existence of a specific feminist methodology. Questions about the modes of thinking, data collection and analysis which are more appropriate for studying the situation of women from a feminist perspective were raised early in the contemporary feminist critique of the social sciences (Smith 1988) and are still being explored and developed (Fonow and Cook 1991; Maynard 1994; Reinharz 1992).

However the problem still remains in feminist methodology of the relationship between the researcher and the researched. (Wilkinson and Kitzinger 1996). The problem of the researcher imposing their own definitions of reality on those researched still remains, as does the issue of transforming those researched into objects of scrutiny. Ideally in this research I would have preferred to have the object of the research enter into the process as an active subject, but this was not possible because of the conditions of access on the research process imposed by the management of the organisation studied. However as various writers have pointed out, there is an ongoing contradiction with the notion of the active subject. In that the attempt to translate and analyse the experiences of others means that the researcher objectifies and abstracts their experiences in an attempt to make general statements about, it this case, social processes and structures (Ramazanoglu 1989; Oakley 1981).

Researching as a Feminist

The feminist methodological literature centres on four issues. These include, the issue of the distinctiveness of a feminist research method and secondly what does this mean. Thirdly, the usefulness of the attempt to construct a feminist research method rather than adopt and adapt the plurality of social research methods. Finally, what constitutes the relationships between other research methods and feminist ones. In this book I am not claiming that the research method I use is particularly feminist though Hilary Graham points out (1984) that

> The use of semi-structured interviews has become the principal means by which feminists have sought to achieve the active involvement of their respondents in the construction of data about their lives. (ibid., p.26)

Rather I used a research method as a feminist as Reinharz (1992) writes:

> Feminist research methods are methods used in research projects by people who identify themselves as feminist or as part of the women's movement. (ibid., p.6)

This raises the question of how I perceive the relationship between being a feminist and the research process.

I have been involved in the women's movement in England for twenty years both as an activist and as an academic. As an academic I have been teaching women's studies and more recently gender studies for the same period and until recently I was the review's editor of the *Journal of Gender Studies* whose editorial board struggles to operate as a feminist collective.

As Reinharz suggests, taking the criterion of self-identification allows one to

> reject the notion of a transcendent authority that decides what constitutes 'feminist', consistent with the antihierarchical nature of many feminist organizations and much feminist spirit. (Reinharz 1992, p.7)

However I am aware of the criticisms, especially from black women writers such as bell hooks and Alice Walker that this criterion is inadequate and so I attempt through my involvement with women's organisations in my locale to avoid the charge against

> Women who teach, research, and publish about women, but who are not involved in any way in making radical social and political change, women who are not involved in making the lives of living, breathing women more viable [...] If lifting oppression is not a priority to you then it's problematic whether you are part of the actual feminist movement [...] to me racist white women cannot be said to be actually feminist. (cited in Reinharz 1992, p.8)

The Reinharz text has particular relevance in the context of the debate on the association between a feminist perspective and the use of qualitative methods (Fonow and Cook 1991; Maynard 1994), as this book surveys a large amount of feminist research, and analyses the methods used by feminist researchers. Reinharz provides numerous examples of feminist research that uses an interview approach, ethnography, survey or statistical methods, experimental and cross-cultural approaches, oral history, content analysis, case studies, action research, multiple approaches and original research methods. The conclusion in her survey is that feminists use a multiplicity of methods. Thus, there is no feminist method as such, rather there are a number of interpretative, qualitative and positivist, 'objective' methods and researchers who attempt to combine the two approaches. Thus there is no unique feminist methodology but the experiences, awareness and knowledge of the ways in which sexism acts on women's lives enable feminist researchers to be acutely aware of gender as a process in the structuring of women's life chances and experiences. It was this perspective that informed the methodology adopted for this study. The choice of research method was also determined by the type of access I was able to obtain in a number of organisations.

Gaining Access

After an initial lack of success I was lucky enough to get into various computing software houses. In particular, I gained access, through contacts with the University with which I was now working, to a very large engineering company in the area. In total, 52 interviews were conducted of which twenty-three were with men and twenty nine with women, across a number of computing software companies and computer programming departments in two major manufacturing organisations in the city of Kingston upon Hull. I wrote to all the companies in the Humberside area that produced computer software and from sixteen letters sent, only five companies replied. The number of programmers in these organisations was very small and I was only able to organise a small number of interviews from this method of approach. The bulk of the research was carried out finally at *Business Systems Department*, on the outskirts of Hull. It had not occurred to me to write to them as its' reputation is based on the fact that it is a military aircraft manufacturing company so I did not consider it to be part of the computing industry. A friend with whom I was sharing the problems I was having in setting up some interviews with programmers, mentioned the Business systems division of a local company and the programming work that went on there. She introduced me to people who had personal contacts within the organisation and they provided me with an introduction to the divisional heads of the different computer sections of the factory. Because of its military and defence work I was vetted by a government agency before I was able to enter the premises. This meant waiting for six weeks before I was 'cleared' to conduct the research. I used this interval to negotiate some time away from my full time job in order to conduct the interviews and was eventually given three months study leave. The various companies who had agreed to let me conduct my research had insisted that the access would be limited to interviews with programmers and stressed that these should only take an hour. Part of these negotiations involved them 'vetting' the interview schedule. I constructed a list of questions that would not alarm the managers of the various organisations. The schedule of questions was arranged in order to facilitate a discussion on programming and gender, and also to appear mediocre and non-threatening to both the women and men I interviewed, the management in the various companies and to the Home Office.

Designing an Interview Schedule

The interview schedule was produced in order to illustrate to the companies the type of questions I would cover during the interview. In effect I tended to use the schedule as a guide, as a list of points to cover, so that the manner, order and language in which the questions were asked could be flexible. However there are a number of factors that influence the design. The key concept that organised the schedule is the concept of gender segregation. The meanings given to this concept is explained in chapter two. The case studies outlined in chapter three brought forth a number of elements which shaped gender segregation such as family and household structure and responsibilities, education, cultural notions about gender, traditional organisational practices and procedures, local employment market, type of occupation, class, 'race' and so on. Thus a series of questions was designed in order to cover most of these elements.

Rather than attempting to measure gender segregation, in other words rather than viewing the phenomenon of gender segregation as something that could be quantified, the aim of the interview was to uncover the operation of the process. Thus the concepts were used as a way of directing the interview towards a particular kind of shared experience of an occupation, so the object of the interview schedule was to turn attention to this experience. In order to facilitate this a number of steps were taken. Firstly, a letter outlining the framework for the research was distributed to the companies alongside the interview schedule. This paper was also distributed to the respondents in order to provide a framework for respondents. Secondly, the choice of open rather than closed questions were used in order to help the respondents to give responses that were not anticipated by the use of response options for closed questions. Open questions were chosen in order to allow respondent to convey the fine shades of their attitudes to their own satisfaction instead of forcing them to choose one of several statements that may all seem more or less unsatisfactory. In order to avoid frustration as to the intent of the question some probes were provided, for example, 'how do you mean that?' 'tell me more about that?' 'anything else?' 'why' or 'why not?'.

The series of questions were chosen to enable the respondent to tell about their entry to the occupation; their work experiences and the ways it shaped their life outside the organisation. The respondents were not viewed as passive agents, rather as being engaged in joint 'sense-making' with the researcher. Thus the interview was based on the model that both the researcher and the respondent exhibit a kind of reflective intelligence as they negotiate the meaning of questions on the one hand, and the meaning of answers on the other.

Interviewing Women and Men

The schedule was divided into two sections. One section covered job description, training and experience, the other, leisure/outside work activities and family situation. I had some experience of interviewing as I had been employed on a research project for a couple of months that had involved interviewing women and men who were doing shift work. Interviewing has some obvious advantages over silent observation. Firstly, it allows questions to be directed at people about themselves and their behaviour and activities. Secondly, it enables questions to be asked not only about what people do and are, but also what they think and feel; in other words interviewing facilitates the gathering of subjective opinions as well as factual information. Thirdly, it allowed me to ask people how they perceive and interpret their personal circumstances and histories and the actions of others. Finally, it gave people an opportunity to explain the motives and reasons for their own behaviour; allowing them to join the researcher in the process of analysis and interpretation. I attempted to be a 'good' interviewer. (Thompson 1978, p.165) states that the 'good interviewer' is a person with

> an interest and respect for people as individuals, and a flexibility in response.

> [...] an ability to show an understanding and a sympathy for their point of view: and a willingness to sit quietly and listen.

Though at times I fell into Prewitt's characterisation of bad interviewing in that I was

> perhaps too aggressive in pursuing the interview and thus antagonise the respondent: or ... too friendly and accommodating [...] or too hurried and cut the respondent off before he (sic) has really provided all the information necessary. (cited in Pons 1988, p.109)

Despite this, these interviews were one of the most exciting and challenging things I've ever done as a sociologist, and radically changed my theoretical approach and ambitions for the project as I explain in the introduction.

I began by collecting information through semi-structured interviews, using the schedule, (a copy of which I handed to the interviewee), as a way of putting the person at ease. I used the specific questions on the schedule as a base from which to invite the interviewee to talk about, describe, and discuss their working lives. My main task was to set and keep the interview going, providing the minimum of direction, asking for occasional clarification, and thus becoming more of a listener than a questioner. I interviewed the 'respondents' using a semi-structured format for approximately an hour and taped the interviews, which I later transcribed.

The management in each organisation had selected a number of computer programmers to be interviewed and usually provided me with a quiet space in which to record the interviews. This meant that I was unable to establish any criteria for selection and so the interview material is based on a group that is random, self-selected and volunteers. The option of interviewing people outside of work time was met with unease by those to whom I broached the idea, though in one instance I was able to record 'off site'. A number of writers (Becker and Geer 1960, pp 321-2; Hammersley 1983), all suggest that interview data is less sensitive than participant observation to enable one to record the context and personnel involved in the development and operation of departmental typifications and boundaries. Interview material provides different after-the-event accounts that need to be unravelled in order to provide a coherent explanation of the particular topic being investigated and this is approach that shaped this book.

Review of Research Method

My open-ended approach to the interviewing process did enable the research respondents to suggest what they defined as significant, and this proved to be very important when I began to interpret the material. What they stressed was their subjective experience of work and gender relations on the shopfloor, and I was forced to find a method to explicate the contradictions of the meanings they related. However, because I was restricted to a formal interview, I was unable to study the workplaces over an extended period of time. This would have given me more time in which to check out some issues, especially the apparent lack of awareness over gender relations in the workplaces. It would also have given me an opportunity to interpret the meanings, relationships, culture, history, hierarchy, power and practices of gender relations on the shop floor. I needed to supplement my interviews with observation and group discussion, and this was not available. I was also unable to be around for extended periods of time, which meant that I was unable to build up relationships of trust and relaxation. David Collinson, in his discussion of the research methodology used in his *Managing the Shopfloor* (1992), states that because of his gender he was able to integrate himself into the 'highly masculine, sometimes relaxed, sometimes aggressive informality and joking relationships that characterises most shopfloor interactions' (ibid.; p.235), but I was unable to develop this level of informality and acceptance. He mentions how his decision not to use a tape recorder helped to achieve this familiarity, though there is no evidence that my decision to use this method of collecting the data hindered the interviews. I found the fact that I had recordings of all the interviews invaluable. The transcripts, besides containing biographical information of each of the people I interviewed, also provide a collection of descriptive interpretations of the role of a computer programmer, as well as a range of conflicting and contradictory views and opinions on gender, work, leisure and domestic arrangements. With transcripts I had available a substantial quantity of data that I could continually review. However I do regret very much that I did not keep a field diary or supplementary notebook to record my impressions not only of the people I interviewed, what they were wearing, how they looked, but also a description of their workplaces and workspaces. At odd moments, I did record my impressions on tape, when I look at the transcripts and see these comments their impact is striking in that I am immediately reminded of the person, the day, the place. The disadvantage of relying on taped interviews is that I neglected to consider the importance of this type of information. However, despite this limitation, the material I had gathered did provide insights into people's experiences both of their working lives and the process of gender segregation.

The Status of the Interviews

The approach to the interview transcripts taken in this book is not that the material could provide 'facts' or 'truths' about the world; or that the transcripts could be used in a comparative sense in order to establish a criterion for the validity of the responses. Rather the transcripts were examined and various passages selected in order to use pieces of text that provide clues to the institutional practices and discourses that shape the occupation under review. This means that the interview material used in this book cannot be taken to be valid descriptions of a person's private beliefs, attitudes, opinions or values. Rather the book attempts to make sense of the interview material by tracing the discourses that inform the phenomenon of gender segregation in a particular occupation. It takes prevailing discourses of gender, organisations and computing and examines these in order to present an account of segregation that explores how discourses are part of the process through which segregation is produced. I am not arguing that the discourses I focus on are the *only* discourses in the culture that shape gender segregation. These were the ones that were chosen, mainly because of the amount of literature that discusses these discourses and because they provide a good starting point in order to explore the usefulness of this approach to occupational segregation. Other prevailing discourses, concerning age, education, sexuality, could be an area for further study.

Becoming Different

It was then, as a result of the interviews that the real change began, especially around my thinking on the concept of gender. The first and most startling stimulus for this change was that I found that the men I met were much easier to interview than the women. The women tended to be suspicious, wary, and generally defensive and distrustful of me. Because I had permission to interview them, courtesy of the management, there always appeared to be the suspicion that I was simply a management spy,[1] and that I would report back any criticism the women had of the firm, men and management. The men I interviewed were much more confident. Initially there was some suspicion, but once I explained my research in more depth, they relaxed and began to enjoy themselves. They were, in the main, very open and revealing about their fears and ambitions for themselves and their families. The men did not feel threatened by my presence, but the women did.

The impact on the interviewing situation was a wariness that was uncomfortable and not very productive, though it would be a mistake to characterise all the interviews with women as operating with these undercurrents. Some of the women I interviewed were very relaxed, friendly and forthcoming: indeed very honest about their relations at work and the way they had to juggle the demands of home and work. Despite this, the impact on my research was such that I began to explore the discourses of masculinity in some depth. I realised that despite my critique of patriarchy I had not examined the way men were positioned by the concept of patriarchy. Rather I had incorporated the critique of men as the enemy into my view of masculinity. Just as my conclusion on feminist theorising was that it was no longer possible to discuss women as a unitary category, I realised that I was still carrying around in my head the view of men as a unitary category, and the view of men as 'the enemy'. Men were constructed in many of the works I had examined as patriarchal - meaning dominant, powerful and dangerous for women to know. However, I was now discovering that the men I interviewed could not be understood with this type of explanatory framework. The operation of gender at the workplace was much more contradictory and complex. I turned then to the literature on organisations, in order to determine the extent to which the structure of organisations shaped the antagonisms and sharpened the gender differences between men and women. If it was no longer possible to 'blame men' as it were, for all the problems facing women at work, then perhaps the solution lay in the way work was structured in capitalist social relations, and this lead me to Foucault's work on discourse/knowledge and power. It was then in the period of collating, editing and typing up the taped interviews that the themes of the book began to assume more structure and organisation.

Why Foucault?

In the previous chapter I have sought to show how the theoretical framework of Marxist feminist that dominated key ethnographic studies of women's work and gender segregation in the workplace obscured the power, resistance and agency of women at the workplace. The key factor that emerged from my reading of these works is the fact that gender identity is both constructed and lived. Though much of contemporary social theory addresses this problem of the relationship between the individual and the social, the analytical link between structure and agency is still very difficult to develop. With gender, as with other aspects of the structuring of human social life, the problem of how individuals lead collective lives emerges and re-emerges as one of the more urgent problematics for contemporary social science. Foucault's work has however been hugely important for the reformulation of the place of the individual/subject within structures of power and dominance. One important theme of the women and work studies discussed in the previous chapter is the notion of resistance; but referred to less directly is the theme of complicity with segregation and that theme is of central interest to this book. At this point I would like to provide an example of 'resistance' from the interview material. In chapter nine, the section entitled 'coping with, rather than resisting femininity' discusses the remarks made by men to Karen who was pregnant with her second child. Despite the suggestion by some of her male colleagues that 'it was greedy for married women to work' and that it was selfish and irresponsible to have children if one did not intend to stay at home, Karen resisted these attempts to persuade her to stay at home.

What determines individual resistance and complicity is very difficult to analyse, and with the development of psychoanalytic theory it is clear that one cannot address this problem only in term of sociological theory. The questions of desires, identity, fantasy and fear all have to be addressed, as would the ways in which individual personal histories intersect with both structures and discourses. In this way subjectivity and agency is marked with difference.

Subjectivity

My use of the term subjectivity is based on the article by Wendy Hollway (1984), entitled 'Gender difference and the production of subjectivity'. She provides a concept of subjectivity that helped me to understand that the 'meanings' that embodied individuals give to their practices, in this case, the meanings they give to their gender identity, are critical aspects of the process of gender identification and gender difference. Her work then, demonstrates gender as process, and the relationship between this process and the subjectivity of women and men. Using this understanding I was able to interpret the research data as evidence of the maintenance and the re-production of gender differences. Though her article is concerned with understanding the 'site' of gender difference, which she locates with the discourse of heterosexuality, her analysis demonstrates the ways in which the discourses of femininity and masculinity are not fixed, but fluid; not distinct but relational. She provides an analysis that is theoretically significant for understanding the relationship between gender differences, subjectivity and change, and is 'at pains to stress that discourses coexist and have mutual effects and that meanings are multiple. This produces choice, though it may not be simple or conscious' (Hollway 1984, p.239). She makes the connection between subjectivity and discourses in the following way:

> Foucault's use of the term discourse is historical and this is crucial to the analytical power of the concept. For my purposes the emphasis must be shifted in order to understand how at a specific moment several coexisting and potentially contradictory discourses concerning sexuality make available different positions and different powers for men and women. (Hollway 1984, p.230)

Her article is wholly concerned with interpreting the discourses which structure heterosexuality, but the model she constructs provided a framework for considering the multiplicity of discourses which operated in the workplaces I had visited, which included the discourses that shaped masculinity and femininity, discourses of work and organisations, and science and technology. This variety of discourses was making available positions for subjects to take up, and producing choices, though these may not be simple or conscious. However Hollway emphasises that men and women are not positioned equally in discourses concerning sexuality. She says: 'taking up subject or object positions is not equally available to men and women' (1984, p.236). The discourses of sexuality are a critical part of the discourses of femininity and masculinity, and in this way the discourses that constitute gender permeate every aspect of social life. Discourses do not stand alone, they can only be abstracted for the purpose of study and analysis but in practice there are a wide network of discursive fields that overlap and intermingle.

Gender Segregation and Gender Discourses

In order to provide a starting point for a discussion of the issue of gender segregation I take as my starting point the issue of the relationship between gender segregation and gender discourses, between gender as it is lived and gender as it is constructed. Foucault's notion of discourse helped me to understand how discourses frequently construct women and men as different sorts of individuals or persons who embody different principles of agency. For instance, in many western cultures male sexuality and masculinity is portrayed as active, aggressive and powerful, and women are viewed as essentially passive, powerless and submissive. These dominant representations and categories that I elaborate as hegemonic discourses later in the text bear only a slight relation to the behaviours, qualities, attributes and self-images of individual women and men. *It is critical to the way that I use the concept of discourse in my analysis to point out that discourses about gender are not powerful because they provide accurate descriptions of social practices and experiences, but rather because, they engender women and men as persons who are defined by difference.* These forms of difference are the result of the workings of discourse, and when brought into play they give rise to the discursive effects that contribute to the production of gender segregation. Gender discourses that construct gender difference is not merely an effect of language, rather these discourses are involved in the production and reproduction of notions of personhood and agency. These discourses are used by individuals to generate the process of constructing themselves as persons and as social actions. It is for this reason that the categories woman and man, and the difference inscribed within and between them, have something to do with day to day practises of individual women and men.

It is not the case that individuals are duped into believing in these discourses, in other words it is not a problem of 'false consciousness'. So, what are discourses, how do they work, at what levels do they operate, how are they reproduced? Foucault's work on the emergence of discourses goes some way to address these questions though the problem of the dominance of some discourses in relation to others is not resolved in his work.[2]

The term discourse is used in the book as knowledge. That knowledge is constructed in response to the interests of a particular group or class (the Marxian use of the term ideology), is a position rejected by Foucault, so that he can be read as treating *fields of knowledge, discursive formations*, *discourses*, as if they were independent of both real objects and interested subjects. This however is another tension in Foucault's work. In his early work, it is quite clear that the interests of those in power play some role in the production of prevailing discourses, but this perspective disappears in the later texts.

The Concept of Discourse

There are a number of approaches to the study of discourses; and the terms 'discourse' and 'discourse analysis' will have very different meanings depending upon the theoretical approach of the writer. For example in the work of Potter and Wetherell (1987), *Discourse and Social Psychology: beyond attitudes and behaviour,* they focus on the performative qualities of discourse, that is, what people are doing with their talk or writing. This approach is informed by speech act theory, conversation analysis and ethnomethodology. Potter and Wetherell state that their focus is on 'the detail of an exchange', how discourse is put together and 'its construction in relation to its function'; that discourse analysis is about 'language use rather than the people generating the language' (1987, pp.160-1).

Rather than discourse analysis, the concept of discourse that is used in the book is one that is based on Foucault's view of discourse as knowledge. Rather than concentrating on the distinction between discourse and language, the aspect of discourse that informs the analysis in this book is one that seeks to elaborate the ways in which discourses shape practices, activities, social relations and the lived experience of gender. I want to show how a number of discourses impact on the process of gender segregation. The analysis of this complex and contradictory social process uses a concept of discourse that attempts to preserve the relationship between structure and agency without reducing discourse to individual 'utterance' or 'speech acts' (Smith 1988, p.161). Discourses are used to explore:

> the relationship between what we do, what we are obliged to do, what we are allowed to do, what we are forbidden to do. (cited in Barrett 1991, p.131)

The emphasis is on the practices of discourses that produced 'discursive regimes' of knowledge/power, or power in discourse. Posing the concept of discourse in this way allows one to ask, how does discourse serve, explain, assist in an understanding of - in this case gender segregation? This interpretation of discourse is supported by other writers' reading of Foucault.[3] The linkage Foucault makes between discourse and power means that discourses have effects and implications for social processes as well as social practices.

Thus discourse is used here as an attempt to produce an analysis that can provide an account of gender segregation that refers to the constituting subject rather than to the determination of the economic, to ideology and the relationship of superstructures and infrastructures. I also try to situate the problem (gender segregation) as relational to the constitution of the subject within a specifically local context. In order to understand these relationships, it is essential to link the concept of discourse with Foucault's conceptualisation of power. His analysis of power is in contrast to one that views power as something that is possessed, something that some people possess, and not others and is a sharp contrast to a Marxian notion of power as the possession of a particular class that is based on their relationship to a mode of production. Rather than viewing power as a possession, Foucault views power as running through the social network; producing effects; as productive, rather than negative. He says that:

> What gives power its hold, what makes it accepted, is quite simply the fact that it does not simply weigh like a force which says no, but that it runs through, and it produces, things, it induces pleasure, it forms knowledge [savoir], it produces discourses; it must be considered as a productive network that runs through the entire social body much more than as a negative instance whose function is repression. (interview in Morris and Patton (eds.) 1979, p.36)

Based on this formulation this book aims to explore the effect of a number of discourses on the production of gender segregation in the workplace. This is to provide a contrast to the accounts of gender segregation that pose the problem in terms either of the economic, the State, or the ideological functioning of the family. This is not to deny the power of these structures or their impact on the process of occupational segregation.

I would also like to make it clear that by using Foucault notion of discourse in order to elaborate how a series of discourses are productive (of gender segregation) I do not wish to suggest that the 'world' can wholly be read 'only in virtue of the discourse or text' (Soper 1991, p.121). I am not in other words to use Foucault's phrase dispensing with 'things' (cited in Barrett 1992, p.201). Rather as - Foucault says 'I don't want to say that the State isn't important',

> The State is superstructural in relation to a whole series of power networks, that invest the body, sexuality, the family, kinship, knowledge, technology and so forth. True these networks stand in a conditioning-conditioned relationship to a kind of "meta-power" which is structured essentially round

a certain number of great prohibition functions; but this meta-power with its prohibitions can only take hold and secure its footing where it is rooted in a whole series of multiple and indefinite power relations that supply the necessary basis for the great negative forms of power. (ibid., p.39)

Appropriating Foucault's emphasis on the productivity of discourse and attempting to apply it to a study of gender segregation at work does not mean that I have abandoned structural or materialist explanations of gender oppression.

Thus the way the term discourse is used in the book is taken to mean practices and narratives through which people live, think and speak. They are the stories or scripts through which people understand and operate in the social world. The discourses that form individual identity are intimately tied to the structures and practices that are lived out in society from day to day, and it is in the interest of relatively powerful groups that some discourses and not others are viewed as legitimate. Thus my use of the term hegemonic discourse throughout this book is an attempt to hold on to the notion that some discourses are more dominant than others, and that this is related to the power: ideological, political and economic of the capitalist class.

In an essay (Fitzsimons 1987) I distinguished the concept of ideology from hegemony by arguing that ideology referred to a system of ideas and beliefs whereas hegemony refers to the *process* by which ideas, beliefs, practices and meanings are maintained and constructed in the interests of capitalism. The idea of process contained in the concept enabled me to understand how meaning is constantly being reproduced and negotiated, and thus can have unexpected and contradictory effects. This provided a framework for understanding social change and how individuals through this process of negotiation with meaning constantly constitute their world. Foucault's notion of discourse emphasises more clearly this process of construction, negotiation, power and resistance, and demonstrates the impact of a number of discourses on subjectivity, and as such is an advance on Gramsci's concept of hegemony. The notion of hegemonic discourse provides the means for interpreting the practices which structure people's understanding of themselves in relation to the world, and suggests how subjectivity is being constructed and negotiated by individuals whilst pointing up marginality and dominance in relation to discourses. Marxism does help to explain why some discourses are more powerful than others and Althusser advances a conception of subjects as constituted in and through ideology, so why did I use a concept of discourse when the concept of ideology would have helped me to achieve a coherent theoretical framework? There had been a distinct shift in feminism thought from the late 1980s onwards, whereby the concept of discourse rather than the concept of ideology is used to explore femininity and sexuality. Was I merely jumping on a new trendy bandwagon? This question prompted me to investigate the distinction between discourse and ideology.

Discourse and Ideology

The article by Trevor Purvis and Alan Hunt (1993) contrasts the concept of discourse with the concept of ideology by suggesting that:

> if 'discourse' and 'ideology' both figure in accounts of the general field of social action mediated through communicative practices, then 'discourse' focuses upon the *internal* features of those practices, in particular their linguistic and semiotic dimensions. On the other hand, 'ideology' directs attention towards the *external* aspects of focusing on the way in which lived experience is connected to notions of interest and position that are in principle distinguishable from lived experience. (Purvis and Hunt 1993, p.476)

Another way of formulating this is to talk about different levels of analysis. *Ideology* belongs to a level of analysis that is concerned with how the system works - at the level of mode of production. So, for example, Marxist analysis of capitalism can be used to analyse capitalism in an abstract way, but the specifics of different forms of capitalism - American, Japanese, French, English, etc. - need a different level of analysis. *Discourse* could then be concerned with analysis at this level - the level of social formation.

Ideology is part of the modernist debate on knowledge and truth, and it is associated with Marxism - especially Althussian Marxism. Whereas the concept of discourse is connected to the works of Michel Foucault and is part of the postmodernist *oeuvre*. Though it is still a matter of debate as to whether Foucault can be regarded as a postmodernist, and though his work is set against Marxism as a meta narrative it is interesting to reflect on the influence of Althusser on his work given that he was both his teacher and friend.

Althusser had moved the concept of ideology from a crude and simplistic understanding of ideology as false consciousness or as a set of ideas that are simplistically imposed on the working classes by the bourgeois class, to one that is much more complicated and contradictory. Ideology for Althusser was not a set of mistaken beliefs or lies: it represented a particular understanding of the world; a particular interpretation that legitimated a particular view of society. Ideology in Althusser's work represents a shift from a strict determination of the economic base to the notion that ideologies have an autonomy, and are only determined in the *last instance* by the economy. 'How autonomous is this autonomy' was one of the debates of the 1970s and 1980s in Marx's literature. Althusser's concept of ideology helps one to understand how sets of ideas - i.e. ideology of masculinity and femininity - are linked to a system of power and control. However, despite the notion of autonomy, the concept still retains the notion that these ideas are imposed (even if that imposition is consensual rather than coercive), and that ideologies act on people rather than people acting on ideologies. The human subject is passive rather than active in this theoretical framework, and this means that it is difficult to explain shifts and changes in ideologies. How, for instance, can the notion of an ideology of masculinity explain many different masculinities rather than masculinity in the singular?

The concept of discourse helps one to examine this plurality. It also provides a framework from which to trace historical changes in discourses. However given that the use of this concept is usually taken to signal a postmodernist stance it is now necessary to outline my position in relation to this perspective.

Postmodernist?

There are a number of reasons why I refute the charge of postmodernism, despite the fact that I use concepts from this *oeuvre*. This refutation is obviously based on my understanding of this theoretical approach that I will briefly outline.

Postmodernism refers to a body of theory that is also sometimes called post structuralism. The word post modernism is now more frequently used since it carries with it some of the ideas of the second usage - that old certainties have gone and therefore a new mode of theorising is appropriate. The structuralism to which this theory is 'post', and from which it often takes its point of departure, concerns ideas about the structures underlying all human language and culture: for example Saussure's' structural linguistics. It is also 'post' another form of structural explanation, Marxism, and its adherents and sympathisers include many who used to call themselves Marxist feminists.[4]

The modernism to which this body of theory is 'post', and from which it distances itself, is usually defined in relation to ideas that emerged from the 18th century, in the period known as the Enlightenment. This is a useful starting point since most postmodernists define their project in opposition to what they identify as Enlightenment thought, questioning ideas about language, the self, and truth that derive from that period. The basic tenets of postmodernism are concerned with language, the fragmented self, and the notion of universal truths and rationality.

I would agree with the view that language does not simply *transmit* thoughts or meaning. Thought and meaning are constructed through language, there can be no meaning outside language, and that is in some way relational. A word, for example, means something only in relation to other words. Meaning is never fixed. Nothing has a stable, unambiguous meaning. Hence the word 'woman' does not of itself mean anything, except what it is constructed as meaning in the culture. It is defined in relation to its opposite 'man' (which also has no fixed meaning) and means different things in different contexts.

I would also accept the view that there is no fixed, unitary, subject. There is no essential self that exists outside culture and language. Subjectivity is created through language and culture and is fragmented and fluid. As Jackson explains:

> There is no place from 'outside' language and culture from which we can 'know' anything (including ourselves). Our identities and knowledges of the world are products of the way in which we are positioned (or position ourselves) within knowledge and culture. Subjectivity then is culturally constituted, there is no fixed identity; one's identity can shift, can be contradictory. (Jackson 1992, p.26)

The view that there is no possibility of objective scientific 'truth' that exists out there waiting to be discovered is one that is shared by feminists. As McNay states:

> The poststructuralists philosophical critique of the rational subject has resonated strongly with the feminist critique of rationality as an essentially masculine construct. Moreover, feminists have drawn extensively on the poststructuralist argument that rather than having a fixed core or essence, subjectivity is constructed through language and is, therefore, an open-ended, contradictory and culturally specific amalgam of different subject positions. (McNay 1992, p.2)

The rejection of *universal* truths then, is one that is familiar to feminism, and had lead to the notion of situated knowledges.

The idea that knowledges are 'discursive constructs' is used by Michel Foucault to indicate how discourses produce the things we know rather than describe already existing objects. This perspective allows one to view knowledges and discourses as texts that can be deconstructed. Post modernist suspicion of metanarratives, raises questions not only about the possibility of any theory of subordination, whether economic, political, sexual but of any systematic description of it or even that 'it' exists at all. From a postmodernist position, a statement that 'women are oppressed' is problematic, for what is meant by the category 'woman', and by whose criteria are they/we oppressed? Therefore at its most extreme this scepticism implies a denial of *any* material reality, and I would agree with Kate Soper (1991, p.123), who labelled this a 'self-indulgent' position and one that potentially undermines the political project of feminism, which is based on overcoming the material oppression and subordination experienced by women. I am aware that it is not possible to isolate the problem of 'truth' from the postmodern stress on meaning as something that is not fixed in objects or events, but is a product of language and discourse. So meaning shifts, and can be contested. But if no one set of meanings is more valid than any other, what is the basis for arguing that one interpretation has more truth than another? Regarding meaning as entirely fluid can mean denying even the starkest of material realities.

This dilemma is critical for feminism in that it also shares a scepticism about knowledge, truth, language and the self. Feminists have long questioned what counts as knowledge and have revealed the androcentric bias underlying much of what passes for truth in, for example, scientific 'proof' of women's inferiority (Lennon 1995). It would also be accepted that language is not a neutral medium of communication, which is why feminists have been concerned to challenge linguistic sexism. As meanings are not fixed: what it means to be a woman can shift, and hence feminists have contested essentialist understandings of gender. Feminists also accept that there is no unitary, consistent self - a feminist can experience desires and feelings at variance with their political ideals. Despite the fact that on the basis of these commonalities a case can be made for postmodern feminism, at the present time I wish to distance myself from this position for the following reasons.

Firstly, the postmodern critique of the Enlightenment's notion of the unitary subject and the substitution of the notion of the fragmented subject means that it is difficult to understand how individuals exercise agency and change the conditions of their existence. For example, collective and individual involvement in social change. Secondly, the problem of relativism in postmodernism means that the dismissal of value judgements, as well as notions of truth and rationality, makes it difficult to assert political demands on behalf of women.

Finally, as I have argued above, drawing on Foucault's work does not through association mean that I am a postmodernist. Indeed it could only mean that if it was firmly established that this was Foucault position, which is disputed. In order to make this argument I rely on a distinctive feminist interpretation that argues that Foucault is not a post modernist. That rather than dismissing the Enlightenment concepts of truth and reason, he does attempt to reconcile his view of the subject with these aspects of modernism. The reading of Foucault which I rely on to make this claim is the one provided by Lois McNay in her text *Foucault and Feminism* (1992) where she argues that though in his earlier works Foucault does appear to coincide with the postmodern account of subjectivity and agency; in his later books, particularly *The Use of Pleasure* (1985) and *The Care of the Self* (1986), he develops a concept of the self that contradicts this. As she explains:

> Foucault's final work on the self represents a significant shift from the theoretical concerns of his earlier work, and also seems to overcome some of its more problematic political implications. Individuals are no longer conceived as docile bodies in the grip of an inexorable disciplinary power, but as self-determining agents who are capable of challenging and resisting the structures of domination in modern society. (McNay 1992, p.4)

McNay convincingly shows how

> Foucault's theory of practices of the self, rather than representing a rejection of Enlightenment values, represents an attempt to rework some of the Enlightenment's central categories, such as the interrelated concepts of autonomy and emancipation. This reading of Foucault's work is not, as some commentators may argue (Poster 1984; Rajchman 1985), an attempt to force his work into inappropriate categories, because Foucault himself saw his final work as running in a tradition of Enlightenment thought rather than running counter to it. By establishing such a continuity between Foucault's work and the Enlightenment, I also wish to cast doubt on a predominant trend in recent Foucault commentary that argues that his work is a paradigmatic example of 'postmodern' thought (e.g. Harstock 1990; Hekman 1990; Hoy 1988). (McNay 1992, p.5)

As Barrett comments, the extent to which feminism has commonalities with the postmodern critique of Enlightenment views of rationality and equality and freedom is 'part of a broader debate as to whether feminism is 'essentially' a modernist or a post modernist enterprise'. She claims that there is a third position that allows feminism to 'straddle[s] and thus destabilize[s] the modern-post-modern binary divide' (1992, p.216); and that this position can be used to justify and legitimate feminist theory and practice. Though she does not provide an elaboration of this position my version would be that such a position would contain the perspective that gender is culturally and structurally situated and embodied. Hence my use of Foucault's notion of discourses as productive is one that is strategically selective and is used to explore the persistence of occupational segregation from a different perspective to that offered by studies of the labour market.

In Summary

The study was conceived as a specifically feminist sociological account intended to make a contribution to the existing literature on women's work. This meant that both the theoretical framework of the study and the conduct of the empirical research are from the outset informed by a critical awareness of the literature. The major task I identified was one of filling a gap in the research on women and work; to investigate Cockburn's (1988) 'embarrassing fact' as discussed in chapter two, and attempt to find out why women were apparently deliberately choosing their positions in the labour market rather than being controlled or coerced by men.

My project then, grew out of previous studies, especially those discussed in chapter three, and I was particularly sensitised, not to the problems of meanings and their interpretation and analysis, but rather to the theoretical models that had informed the studies. However the interviewing experience and the process of analysing the interview material forced me to evaluate my epistemological stance and my understanding of the sociology of knowledge, which had been defined by Marxist-feminism. Unconsciously the perspective that shaped the research initially saw the role of social scientists as being to discover/uncover the 'ideologies' (usually capitalist) that shaped the actions and meanings of human beings in workplace settings. As was mentioned in chapter two and chapter three certain problems impaired the attempt to establish a framework for a Marxist-feminist analysis of women's oppression, and this failure had resulted in what Michèle Barrett refers to as 'developing feminist theory whose intention is to destabilize' (1992, p.1). Marxist feminist had become side-tracked into a search for a mono-causal explanation of women's oppression which, when found, could usually be charged with providing a functionalist analysis. These explanations usually turned out to be one of the categories in Marxist analysis, e.g. division of labour, ideology, class, alienation, reproduction and so on. Another problem with this perspective was that the level of abstraction at which the debates were conducted diverted attention away from the process of gendering at the level of social formation. Though these debates cleared the ground and prepared a path for a new and alternative approach to the study of women's position in the labour force, the conceptual tools with which to begin such a study were lacking, especially in reference to the concept of gender. The critique of the concept of patriarchy had not exposed the static nature of gender that characterised the accounts of women's work, both paid and unpaid. Men remain untheorised not only in Marxist-feminist analysis but also in radical-feminist work. The position of men in relation to women, the nature of their power, their role in reproduction and production and how they understand their role, needed to be explored, and the writings by men on masculinity which took off in the 1980s switched attention from a focus on women to a focus on gender.

The emphasis on gender facilitated an approach that viewed gender as process rather than as a sex-role category. There was a renewed interest in viewing people as active agents in their own lives and as such constructors of their social worlds. In taking this approach this book is not a search for individual psychological sources of feelings or actions but an attempt to understand how gender discourses are productive of gender segregation at the workplace.

I set myself the task of interpreting the discourses that impact on and shape women's experiences at work by exploring how a number of discourses shape the processes and practices by which gender segregation occurs within computer programming with the aim then of presenting an interpretation of how segregation occurs within a number of discursive formations. Rather than attempting to ask respondents what it might feel like to experience that formation each of these discourses are then explored for the strategies and techniques of discipline and resistance that allow the control and exercise of power.

> although one starts any effort at thick description, beyond the obvious and superficial, from a state of general bewilderment as to what the devil is going on - in trying to find one's feet - one does not start (or ought not to) intellectually empty handed. (Geertz 1975, p.27)

Notes

[1] Ramazanoglu (1989) records a similar problem with her 1960s study of shiftworking women.
[2] In order to signal this dominance the term hegemonic discourse is used as explained on page 136.
[3] My use of Foucault's concept of discourse is based on a number of sources as discussed in chapter 1, pp.9-10.
[4] One such is Michèle Barrett who has recently announced that she is 'nailing (her) colours to the mast of post-marxism'.

Bibliography

Aaby, Peter (1977), 'Engels and Women' in *Critique of Anthropology*, Women's Issue 9 and 10, Vol.3, pp.25-53.

Abbott, Pamela and C. Wallace (1990), *An Introduction to Sociology: feminist perspectives* (London and New York, Routledge).

Acker, Joan (1989), 'Making Gender Visible' in Wallace (ed.) *Feminism and Sociological Theory* (Newbury Park, Sage Publications) pp.65-81.

Acker, Joan (1991), 'Hierarchies, Jobs, Bodies: A Theory of Gendered Organizations' in Lorber and Farrell (eds.) *The Social Construction of Gender* (Newbury Park, Sage Publications), pp.162-179.

Acker, Joan (1992), 'Gendering Organizational Theory' in Mills and Tancred (eds.) *Gendering Organizational Analysis* (Newbury Park, Sage Publications), pp.248-260.

Adam, Alison, Eileen Green, Judy Emms and Jenny Owen (1994), *Women, Work and Computerization: breaking old boundaries – building new forms* (Amsterdam, Elsevier).

Adkins, Lisa (1992), 'Sexual work and the employment of women in the service industries' in Savage and Witz (eds.) *Gender and Bureaucracy* (Oxford, Blackwell), pp.207-229.

Adkins, Lisa (1994), *Gendered Work: sexuality, family and the labour market* (Bristol, Open University Press).

Alexander, Sally (1976), 'Women's Work in Nineteenth-Century London; a Study of the Years 1820-50' in Mitchell and Oakley (eds.) *The Rights and Wrongs of Women* (Harmondsworth, Penguin), pp.59-111.

Alexander, Sally (1982), 'Women's work in nineteenth-century London: a study of the years 1820-50' in Whitelegg et al. (eds.) *The Changing Experience of Women* (Oxford, Martin Robertson), pp.30-44.

Alexander, Sally and Barbara Taylor (1982), 'In Defence of Patriarchy' reprinted in Evans (ed.) *The Woman Question: Readings on the Subordination of Women* (London, Fontana), pp.80-83.

Althusser, Louis (1971), *Lenin and Philosophy and Other Essays* (London, New Left Books).

Alvesson, Mats and Yvonne Due Billing (1997), *Understanding Gender and Organizations* (London, Sage).

Anderson, Alan and Anton Hersleb (1985), *Final Report of the Manpower Sub-Committee of the Electronic Computers SWP and Computer Manpower in the '80s*, National Economic Development Office (London, HMSO).

Anthias, Flora (1980), 'Women and the reserve army of labour: a critique of Veronica Beechey', in *Captial and Class*, Vol.10, Spring, pp.50-63.

Archer, John and Barbara Lloyd (1985), *Sex and Gender* (Cambridge, Cambridge University Press).

Arditti, Rita, Renate Duelli Klein and Shelley Minden (eds.) (1984), *Test Tube Women: What Future for Motherhood* (London, Pandora Books).

Armstrong, P. (1983), 'Class relationships at the point of production: a case study' in *Sociology*, Vol.17, No.3, pp.339-358.

Association of Professional, Executive, Clerical and Computer Staff (APEX) (1979), *Office Technology: The Trade Union Response*. First report of the APEX Word Processing Working Party (London, APEX).

Association of Professional, Executive, Clerical and Computer Staff (APEX) (1985), *New Technology: A Health and Safety Report* (London, APEX).

Barrett, Michèle (1980 and 1988), *Women's Oppression Today: Problems in Marxist Feminist Analysis* (London, Verso Books).

Barrett, Michèle (1984), 'Women's Oppression Today: A Reply' in *New Left Review*, July-August, No.146, pp.123-128.

Barrett, Michèle (1991), *The Politics of Truth: From Marx to Foucault* (Cambridge, Polity Press).

Barrett, Michèle (1992), 'Words and Things: Materialism and Method in Contemporary Feminist Analysis' in Barrett and Phillips (eds.) *Destabilizing Theory: Contemporary Feminist Debates* (Cambridge, Polity Press).

Barrett, Michèle and Mary McIntosh (1979), 'Christine Delphy: Towards a Materialist Feminism?' in *Feminist Review*, Vol.1, No.1, pp.95-105.

Barrett, Michèle and Mary McIntosh (1982), 'The "family wage"' in Whitelegg, et al. (eds.) *The Changing Experience of Women* (Oxford, Martin Robertson), pp.71-87.

Barrett, Michèle and Anne Phillips (eds.) (1992), *Destabilizing Theory: Contemporary Feminist Debates* (Cambridge, Polity Press).

Barron, R.D. and G.M. Norris (1976), 'Sexual Divisions and the Dual Labour Market' in Barker and Allen, *Dependence and Exploitation in Work and Marriage* (London, Longman), pp.47-69.

Becker, Harold S. and B. Geer (1960), 'Participant observation: The analysis of qualitative field data' in Adams and Preiss (eds.) *Human Organization Research: Field Relations and Techniques* (Illinois, Dorsey).

Beechey, Veronica (1977), 'Some Notes on Female Wage Labour in Capitalist Production', *Capital and Class*, No.3, pp.45-66.

Beechey, Veronica (1978), 'Women and Production: A Critical Analysis of Some Sociological Theories of Women's Work' in Kuhn and Wolpe (eds.) *Feminism and Materialism: women and modes of production* (London, Routledge and Kegan Paul), pp.155-179.

Beechey, Veronica (1979), 'On Patriarchy' in *Feminist Review*, No.3, pp.66-82.

Beechey Veronica (1983), 'Studies of Women's Employment', *Feminist Review*, No.15, pp.23-45.

Beechey, Veronica (1987), *Unequal Work* (London, Verso Books).

Beechey, Veronica (1988), 'Rethinking the Definition of Work: Gender and Work' in Jenson et al. (eds.) *Feminization of the Labour Force: Paradoxes and Promises* (Cambridge, Polity Press), pp.45-62.

Beechey, Veronica and Teresa Perkins (1987), *A Matter of Hours: women, part-time work and the Labour Market* (Cambridge, Polity Press).

Beechey, Veronica and Elizabeth Whitelegge (ed.) (1986), *Women in Britain Today* (Milton Keynes, Open University Press).

Benston, Margaret L. (1992), 'Women's voices' men's voices: technology as language' in Kirkup and Keller (eds.) *Inventing Women: Science, Technology and Gender* (Oxford, Polity Press with Open University Press), pp.33-41.

Berger, Peter L. and Tom Luckmann (1966), *The Social Construction of Reality* (Harmondsworth, Penguin).

Berk, S.F. (1985), *The Gender Factory: the apportionment of work in American households* (New York, Plenum).

Bilton, Tony (et al.) (1987), *Introductory Sociology* (Basingstoke, Macmillan Education).

Blackburn, R.M. and J. Jarman (1997), 'Occupational Gender Segregation', in Social Research Update, No.16, Spring, http://www.soc.surrey.ac.uk/sru/SRU16.html.

Blake, Monica (1994), 'Teleworking in the Nineties: A Look at Current Views' in *Managing Information*, Vol.1, No.4, pp.24-27.

Blau, Peter and R. Scott (1963), *Formal Organizations: a comparative approach* (London, Routledge and Kegan Paul).

Bleier, Ruth (ed.) (1986), *Feminist Approaches to Science* (New York, Pergamon Press).

Bologh, Rosa (1990), *Love or Greatness: Max Weber and Masculine Thinking; a feminist inquiry* (London, Unwin Hyman).

Bradley, Harriet (1989), *Men's Work, Women's Work* (Oxford, Polity Press).

Brenner, Johanna and Maria Ramas (1984), 'Rethinking Women's Oppression' in *New Left Review*, March-April, No.144, pp.33-71.

Brittan, Arthur (1989), *Masculinity and Power* (Oxford, Basil Blackwell).

Brod, Harry (ed.) (1987), *The Making of Masculinities: the new men's studies* (Boston, Mass, Allen and Unwin).

Brod, Harry and Michael Kaufman (eds.) (1994), *Theorizing Masculinities* (London, Sage Publications).

Brown, Richard (1976), 'Women as employees: some comments on research in industrial sociology' in Barker and Allen (eds.) *Dependence and exploitation in work and marriage* (London, Longman), pp.21-46.

Bruegal, Irene (1982), 'Women as a Reserve Army of Labour' in Evans (ed.) *The Woman Question: Readings on the Subordination of Women* (London, Fontana) pp.273-288.

Buchanan, David, David Boddy and James McCalman (1988), 'Getting in, getting on, getting out, and getting back' in Bryman (ed.) *Doing Research in Organizations* (London and New York, Routledge). pp.53-67.

Burman, Sandra (ed.) (1979), *Fit Work for Women* (London, Croom Helm).

Burrell, Gibson (1992), 'Sex and Organizational Analysis' in Mills and Tancred (eds.) *Gendering Organizational Analysis* (Newbury Park, London, New Delhi, Sage Publications), pp.34-89.

Burris, Val (1982), 'Dialectic of women's oppression' in *Berkeley Journal of Sociology*, Vol.27, pp.51-74.

Burton, Clare (1991), *The Promise and the Price: the struggle for equal opportunity in women's employment* (New South Wales, Allen and Unwin).

Bush, Corlann Gee (1983) 'Women and the Assessment of Technology: To Think, To Be; To Unthink, To Free' in Rothschild (ed.) *Machina Ex Dea: Feminist Perspectives on Technology* (New York, Pergamon Press), pp.151-170.

Butler, Judith (1989), *Gender Trouble: feminism and the subversion of identity* (New York and London, Routledge).

Butler, Judith (1993), *Bodies that matter: on the discursive limits of sex* (New York and London, Routledge).

Butler, Judith and Joan, W. Scott, (eds.) (1992), *Feminists Theorize the Political* (New York and London, Routledge).

Campbell, Beatrix and Val Charlton (1980), 'United we Fall' in *Red Rag*, No.11. p.12.

Campbell, Beatrix and Val Charlton (1978), 'Work to Rule – Wages and the Family' in *Red Rag*, No.5, p.8.

Carrigan, Tim, Bob Connell and John Lee (1985), 'Towards a new sociology of masculinity' in *Theory and Society*, Vol.14, pp.531-604.

Cavendish, Ruth (1982), *Women on the Line* (London, Routledge and Kegan Paul).

Chapman, Rowena and Jonathan Rutherford (1988), *Male Order: Unwrapping Masculinity* (London, Lawrence and Wishart).

Charles, Nicki (1993), *Gender Divisions and Social Change* (Hemel Hempstead, Harvester Wheatsheaf).

Church, Jenny and Carol Summerfield (eds.) (1995), *Social Focus on Women* (London, HMSO).

Clatterbaugh, Kenneth (1990), *Contemporary Perspectives on Masculinity: men, women and politics in modern society* (Boulder, Colarado, Westview Press).

Cockburn, Cynthia (1983), *Brothers: male dominance and technological change* (London, Pluto Press).

Cockburn, Cynthia (1985), *Machinery of Dominance* (London, Pluto Press).

Cockburn, Cynthia (1988), 'The Gendering of Jobs' in Walby (ed.) *Gender Segregation at Work* (Milton Keynes, Open University Press), pp.29-42.

Cockburn, Cynthia (1991), *In the Way of Women: men's resistance to sex equality in organizations* (Basingstoke, Macmillan).

Cockburn, Cynthia and Ruza Furst Dilic (eds.) (1994), *Bringing Technology Home: gender and technology in a changing Europe* (Buckingham, Open University Press).

Cockburn, Cynthia and Susan Ormrod (1993), *Gender and Technology in the Making* (London, Sage Publications).

Collinson, David L. (1992), *Managing the Shopfloor: subjectivity, masculinity and workplace culture* (Berlin and New York, Walter de Gruyter).

Collinson, David and Jeff Hearn (1994), 'Naming Men as Men: implications for work, organization and management' in *Gender, Work and Organization*, Vol.1, No.1, pp.2-22.

Collinson, David and David Knights (1986), '"Men Only": theories and practices of job segregation in insurance' in *Gender and the Labour Process* (Aldershot, Gower), pp.140-177.

Collinson, David, David Knights and Margaret Collinson (1990), *Managing To Discriminate* (London and New York, Routledge).

Connell, R.W. (1983), *Which Way is Up?* (Sydney, George Allen and Unwin).

Connell, R.W. (1985), 'Theorising Gender', *Sociology*, Vol.19, No.2, pp.260-272.

Connell, R.W. (1987), *Gender and Power* (Oxford, Polity Press).

Connell, R.W (1991), 'Live Fast Die Young – The Construction of Masculinity among Young Working Class Men on the Margin in *Australia-New Zealand Journal of Sociology*, Vol. 27, No.2, pp.141-171.

Connell, R.W. (1995), *Masculinities* (Oxford, Polity Press).

Coontz, Stephanie and Peta Henderson (eds.) (1986), *Women's Work, Men's Property: The origins of Gender and Class* (London, Verso).

Coote Anna and Beatrix Campbell (1982), *Sweet Freedom: the struggle for women's libertion* (London, Picador).

Corea, Gena (1985), *The Mother Machine* (London, Women's Press).

Corea, Gena, Renate Duelli Klein, Jalna Hanmer, Helen B. Holmes, Betty Hoskins, Madhu Kishwar, Janice Raymond, Robyn Rowland and Roberta Steinbacher (1985), *Man-Made Women: how new reproductive technologies affect women* (London, Hutchinson).

Coulson, M., Magas, B and Hilary Wainwright (1975) 'The housewife and her labour under capitalism – a critique' in *New Left Review*, No.89, pp.59-71.

Coward, Rosalind (1983), *Patriarchal Precedents* (London, Boston and Henley, RKP).

Coyle, Angela (1984), *Redundant Women* (London, Women's Press).

Coyle, Angela and Jane Skinner (eds.) (1988), *Woman and Work: positive action for change* (Basingstoke, Macmillan).

Craig, C., E. Garnsey and Jill Rubery (1984), *Payment Structures and Smaller Firms: Women's employment in Segmented Labour Markets*, Research Paper 48 (London, Department of Employment).

Crompton, Rosemary and Gareth Jones (1984) *White Collar Proletariat; Deskilling and gender in clerical work* (London, Macmillan).

Crompton, Rosemary and Michael Mann (eds) (1986), *Gender and Stratification* (Cambridge, Polity Press).

Crompton, Rosemary and Kay Sanderson (1990), *Gender Jobs and Social Change* (London,Unwin Hyman).

Crosby, Faye J. and Karen J. Jaskar (1993), 'Woman and Men at Home and at Work: Realities and Illusions' in Oskamp and Costanzo (eds.) *Gender Issues in Contemporary Society* (Newbury Park, Sage Publications), pp.143-171.

Cunnison, Sheila and Jane Stageman (1993), *Feminizing the Unions* (Aldershot, Avebury).

Davidson, Marilyn J. and Cary L. Cooper (eds.) (1987), *Women and Information Technology* (Chichester, John Wiley and Sons).

Davis, Kathy, Monique Leijenaar and Jantine Oldersma (eds.) (1991), *The Gender of Power* (Newbury Park, Sage Publications).

Deal, Terrence and Allen Kennedy (1982), *Corporate Cultures: the rites and rituals of corporate life* (Harmondsworth, Penguin Books).

Deakin, Rose (1984), *Women and Computing: the golden opportunity* (Basingstoke, Macmillan).

Deere, Carmen (1979), 'Rural women's subsistence production in the capitalist periphery' in Cohen, Gutkind and Brazior (eds.) *Peasants and Proletarians* (London, Hutchinson), pp.127-149.

De Lauretis, Teresa (1987), *Technologies of Gender: essays on theory, film, and fiction* (Basingstoke, Macmillan).

Delphy, Christine (1977), *The Main Enemy: A Materialist Analysis of Women's Oppression* (London, WRRC Publications).

Delphy, Christine (1984), *Close to Home* (London, Hutchinson).

Delphy, Christine (1992), 'Mother's union?' in *Trouble and Strife*, No.24, pp.12-19.

Delphy, Christine (1993), 'Rethinking Sex and Gender', in *Women's Studies International Forum*, Vol.16, No.1, pp.1-9.

Denzin, Norman K. and Yvonna S. Lincoln (eds.) (1994), *Handbook of Qualitative Research* (Newbury Park, Sage Publications).

Dex, Shirley (1985), *The Sexual Division of Work: Conceptual revolutions in the social sciences* (Hemel Hempstead, Harvester Wheatsheaf).

Dex, Shirley (1989), 'Gender and the Labour Market' in Gallie (ed.) *Employment in Britain* (Oxford, Basil Blackwell), pp.281-310.

Doeringer, Peter B. and Michael J. Priore (1971), *Internal Labor Markets and Manpower Adjustments* (Lexington Mass, D.C. Heath).

Easlea, Brian (1983), *Fathering the Unthinkable: masculinity, scientists and the nuclear arms race* (London, Pluto Books).

Easton, Loyd D. and Kurt. H. Guddat (1967), *Writings on the young Marx on Philosophy and Society* (New York, Doubleday Anchor Books).

Edholm, Felicity, Olivia Harris and Kate Young (1977), 'Conceptualizing Women' in *Critique of Anthropology*, Women's Issue 9 and 10, Vol.3, pp.101-130.

Edwards, Paul N. (1990), 'The Army and the Microworld: computers and the politics of gender identity' in *Signs*, Vol.16, No.1, pp.102-127.

Eisenstein, Hester (1984), *Contemporary Feminist Thought* (London, Allen and Unwin).

Eisenstein, Zillan R. (ed.) (1979), *Capitalist Patriarchy and the Case for Socialist Feminism* (New York, Monthly Review Press).

Engels, Frederich (1948), *The Origins of the Family, Private Property and the State* (Moscow, Foreign Languages Publishing House).

Engels, Frederich (1972), *The Origins of the Family, Private Property and the State* (London, Lawrence and Wishart).

Evans, Mary (1990), 'The Problem of Gender for Women's Studies' in *Women's Studies International Forum*, Vol.13, No.5, pp.457-463.

Faulkner, Wendy and E. Arnold (eds.) (1985), *Smothered by Invention: Technology in Women's Lives* (London, Pluto Press).

Fee, Elizabeth (1986), 'Critiques of Modern Science: Relationship of Feminism to Other radical epistemologies' in Ruth Bleier (ed.) *Feminist Approaches to Science* (New York, Pergamon Press), pp.42-56.

Feldberg, R. and E.N. Glenn (1984), 'Male and Female: Jobs and Gender Models in the Sociology of Work' in Siltanen and Stanworth (eds.) *Women in the Public Sphere* (London, Hutchinson), pp.11-41.

Firestone, Shulamith (1970), *The Dialectic of Sex* (London, Women's Press) (1979 edition).

Fisher, Susan (1994), 'Librarians and Networks: Breaking the Boundaries that bind us' in Adam, Green, Emms and Owen *Women, Work and Computerization: breaking old boundaries - building new forms* (Amsterdam, Elsevier), pp.393-407.

Fitzsimons, Annette (1987), 'Politics of Antonio Gramsci' in *Critical Social Research*, Vol.2, No.2, pp.1-95.

Fitzsimons, Annette (1994), 'Gender, Technology, Power' in Lennon and Whitford (eds.) *Knowing the Difference: Feminist Perspectives on Epistemology and Knowledge* (London, Routledge), pp.122-132.

Fonow, Mary M. and Judith A. Cook (eds.) (1991), *Beyond Methodology: Feminist Scholarship as Lived Research* (Bloomington, Indiana University Press).

Foreman, Ann (1978), *Femininity as Alienation* (London, Pluto Press).

Foucault, Michel (1972), *The Archaeology of Knowledge* (London, Tavistock Publications).

Foucault, Michel (1979), *Michel Foucault: Power, Truth, Strategy* (Sydney: Feral Publications).

Foucault, Michel (1985), *The Use of Pleasure: The History of Sexuality*, Vol.2 (London, Penguin Books).

Foucault, Michel (1986), *The Care of the Self: The History of Sexuality*, Vol.3 (London, Penguin Books).

Foucault, Michel (1990), *The History of Sexuality, Vol.1: an introduction* (Harmondsworth, Penguin).

Fraser, Nancy (1989), *Unruly Practices: Power, Discourse and Gender in Contemporary Social Theory* (Oxford, Polity Press).

Friedman, Alan (1989), *Computer Systems Development: history organization and implementation* (Chichester, Wiley).

Game, Ann and Rosemary Pringle (1984), *Gender at Work* (London, Pluto Press).

Gardiner, Jean (1975), 'Women's domestic labour' in *New Left Review*, No.89, pp.47-58.

Geertz, Clifford (1975), *The Interpretation of Cultures: selected essays* (New York, Basic Books).

Giddens, Anthony (1987), *Social Theory and Modern Sociology* (Cambridge, Polity Press).

Giddens, Anthony (1995), *Sociology* (Oxford, Polity Press).

Gill, Rosalind and Keith Grint (1995), 'The Gender-Technology Relation: contemporary theory and research' in Grint and Gill (eds.) *The Gender-Technology Relation: contemporary theory and research* (London, Taylor and Francis), pp.1-28.

Gluckmann, Miriam (1990), *Women Assemble: Women Workers and the New industries in Inter-War Britain* (London, Routledge).

Goldthorpe, John H. (1980), *Social Mobility and Class Structure in Modern Britain* (Oxford, Clarendon Press).

Gomez, M. Carme (1994), 'Bodies, machines, and male power' in Cockburn and Dilic (eds.) (1994), *Bringing Technology Home: gender and technology in a changing Europe* (Buckingham, Open University Press), pp.129-146.

Gorz, Andre (1982), *Farewell to the Working Class* (London, Pluto).

Gouldner, Alvin. (1954), *Patterns of Industrial Bureaucracy* (London, Routledge and Kegan Paul).

Graham, Hilary (1984), *Women, Health and the Family* (Brighton, Wheatsheaf).

Gray, Ann (1987), 'Behind Closed Doors: video recorders in the house' in Baehr and Dyer (eds.) *Boxed in: women and television* (London and New York, Routledge), pp.38-54.

Green, Eileen, Jenny Owen, and Den Pain (eds.) (1993), *Gendered By Design? information technology and office systems* (London, Taylor and Francis).

Grieco, Margaret and Richard Whipp (1986), 'Women and the Workplace: gender and control in the labour process' in Collinson and Knights (eds.) *Gender and the Labour Process* (Aldershot, Gower), pp.117-139.

Griffiths, Dot (1985), 'The exclusion of women from technology' in Faulkner and Arnold (eds.) *Smothered by Invention* (London and Sydney, Pluto Press), pp.51-71.

Grint, Keith and Rosalind Gill (eds.) (1995), *The Gender-Technology Relation: contemporary theory and research* (London, Taylor and Francis).

Grosz, Elizabeth (1990), 'Contemporary Theories of Power and Subjectivity' in Gunew (ed.) *Feminist Knowledge* (London and New York, Routledge), pp.59-120.

Grosz, Elizabeth (1994), *Volatile Bodies: Toward a Corporeal Feminism* (Bloomington and Indianapolis, Indiana University Press).

Hakim, Catherine (1979), *Occupational Segregation*, Department of Employment Research Paper 9 (London, HMSO).

Hakim, Catherine (1981), 'Job segregation: trends in the 1970s', *Employment Gazette*, Vol.89, No.12, pp.521-529.

Halberstam, Judith (1994), 'F2M: The Making of Female Masculinity' in Doan, (ed.) *The Lesbian Postmodern* (New York, Columbia University Press), pp.210-228.

Hall, Catherine (1982a), 'The butcher, the baker, the candlestickmaker: the shop and the family in the Industrial Revolution' in Whitelegg et al. (eds.) *The Changing Experience of Women* (Oxford, Martin Robertson), pp.2-16.

Hall, Catherine (1982b), 'The home turned upside down? The working-class family in cotton textiles 1780-1850' in Whitelegg et al. (eds.) *The Changing Experience of Women* (Oxford, Martin Robertson), pp.17-29.

Hamilton, Roberta (1978), *The Liberation of Women* (London, Allen and Unwin).

Hamilton, Roberta and Michèle Barrett (1986), *The Politics of Diversity* (London, Verso).

Hammersley, Martyn (ed.) (1993), *Social Research: Philosophy, Politics and Practice* (Newbury Park, Sage Publications).

Hammersley, Martyn (1995), *The Politics of Social Research* (Newbury Park, Sage Publications).

Hammersley, Martyn and Paul Atkinson (1983), *Ethnography: Principles in Practice* (London, Tavistock).

Hanmer, Jalna (1983), 'Reproductive Technology: The Future for Women' in Rothschild (ed.) *Machina Ex Dea: Feminist Perspectives on Technology* (New York, Pergamon Press), pp.183-197.

Haralambos, Mike and Mike Holborn (1990), *Sociology: themes and perspectives* (London, Unwin Hyman).

Harding, Sandra (1986), *The Science Question in Feminism* (Milton Keynes, Open University Press).

Harding, Sandra (ed.) (1987), *Feminism and Methodology* (Milton Keynes, Open University Press).

Harding, Sandra (1991), *Whose Science? Whose Knowledge?* (Milton Keynes, Open University Press).

Haraway, Donna J. (1988), 'Situated knowledges', *Feminist Studies*, Vol.14, pp.575-599.

Haraway, Donna J. (1991), *Simians, Cyborgs, and Women: the reinvention of nature* (London, Free Association Books).

Hartmann, Heidi (1981), 'The Unhappy Marriage of Marxism and Feminism' in Sargent (ed.) *Women and Revolution* (London, Pluto Press), pp.1-41.

Hartmann, Heidi (1982), 'Capitalism, Patriarchy and Job Segregation by Sex' in Giddens and Held (eds.) *Classes, Power and Conflict* (Basingstoke, Macmillan), pp.446-469.

Hartsock, Nancy (1990), 'Foucault on Power: A Theory for Women' in Nicholson (ed.) *Feminism/Postmodernism* (New York and London, Routledge), pp.157-175.

Hearn, Jeff (1985), 'Men's sexuality at work' in Metcalf and Humphries (eds.) *The Sexuality of Men* (London, Pluto Press), pp.110-123.

Hearn, Jeff (1987), *The Gender of Oppression: Men, Masculinity and the Critique of Marxism* (Brighton, Wheatsheaf).

Hearn, Jeff and David Morgan (1990), *Men, Masculinities and Social Theory* (London, Unwin Hyman).

Hearn, Jeff and Wendy Parkin (1984), *'Sex' at 'Work': The power and paradox of organisation sexuality* (Brighton, Wheatsheaf).

Hearn, Jeff, Deborah L. Sheppard, Peta Tancred-Sheriff, and Gibson Burrell (1989), *The Sexuality of Organisation* (London, Sage Publications).

Hekman, Susan J. (1990), *Gender and Knowledge: Elements of a Postmodern Feminism* (Oxford, Polity Press).

Henriques, Julian, Wendy Hollway, Cathy Urwin, Couze Venn and Valerie Walkerdine (1984), *Changing the Subject, Psychology, Social Regulation and Subjectivity* (London and New York, Methuen).

Henwood, Flis (1993), 'Establishing Gender Perspectives on Information Technology: Problems, Issues and Opportunities' in Green, Owen and Pain (eds.) *Gendered by Design?* (London, Taylor and Francis), pp.31-49.

Hollway, Wendy (1989), *Subjectivity and Method in Psychology: Gender, Meaning and Science* (Newbury Park, Sage Publications).

Hollway, Wendy (1984), 'Gender difference and the production of subjectivity' in Henriques, Hollway, Urwin, Venn, Walkerdine (eds.), *Changing the Subject: Psychology, social regulation and subjectivity* (London and New York, Methuen), pp.227-264.

Jackson, Stevi (1992), 'The Amazing Deconstructing Women' in *Trouble and Strife*, Vol.25, Winter.

Jacobs, Jerry A. (ed.) (1995), *Gender Inequality at Work* (Newbury Park, Sage Publications).

Jacobus, Mary, Evelyn Fox Keller and Sally Shuttleworth (eds.) (1990), *Body/Politics: women and the discourses of science* (New York and London, Routledge).

Jaggar, Alison M. (1980), *Feminist Politics and Human Nature* (Sussex, Harvester Press).

Jordanova, Ludmilla (1987), 'Gender, Science and Creativity', in McNeil (ed.) *Gender and Expertise* (London, Free Association Books), pp.152-157.

Jowell, Roger, Sharon Witherspoon, and Lindsay Brook (eds.) (1988), *British Social Attitudes the 5th Report* (Aldershot, Gower).

Kahn, Joel S. and Josef R. Llobera (1981), *Anthropology of Pre-Capitalist Societies* (Basingstoke, Macmillan).

Kaluzynska, Eva (1980), 'Wiping the Floor with Theory – A survey of Writings on Housework' in *Feminist Review*, No.6, pp.27-54.

Kanter, Rosemary (1977), *Men and Women of the Corporation* (New York, Basic Books).

Kaplan, Ann E. (1979), 'Is the Gaze Male?' in Snitow, Stansell and Thompson (eds.) *Powers of Desires: The politics of sexuality* (London, Virago Press), pp.309-327.

Keller, Laurie Smith (1992), 'Discovering and Doing: Science and Technology, an introduction' in Kirkup and Keller (eds.) *Inventing Women: Science Technology and Gender* (Oxford, Polity Press with Open University Press), pp.12-32.

Kelly, Joan (1979), 'The Doubled Vision of Feminist Theory' in *Feminist Studies* No.5, pp.216-227.

Kidder, Tracey (1981), *The Soul of the New Machine* (New York, Avion Books).

Kidder, Tracey (1982), *The Soul of the New Machine* (Harmondsworth, Penguin Books).

Kirkup, Gill and Laurie Smith Keller (eds.) (1992), *Inventing Women: Science Technology and Gender* (Oxford, Polity Press with Open University Press).

Knight, Chris (1991), *Blood Relations: Menstruation and the Origins of Culture* (New Haven and London, Yale University Press).

Kondo, Dorinne, K. (1990), *Crafting Selves: Power, Gender and Discourses of Identity in a Japanese Workplace* (Chicago and London, University of Chicago Press).

Kraft, Philip (1977), *Programmers and Managers: The Routinisation of Computer Programming in the United States* (New York, Springer Verlag).

Kraft, Philip (1979), 'The Industrialization of Computer Programming: From Programming to Software Production' in Zimbalist (ed.) *Case Studies in the Labor Process* (New York, Monthly Review Press).

Kraft, Philip and Steve Dubnoff (1984), 'Women in software' in *Computing*, Feb, p.21.

Kuhn, Annette and Ann Maire Wolpe (eds.) (1978), *Feminism and Materialism* (London, Boston, Henley, RKP).

Landry, Donna and Gerald MacLean (1993), *Materialist Feminisms* (Oxford, Blackwell Publishers).

Laws, Sophie (1990), *Issues of Blood: the Politics of Menstruation* (Basingstoke, Macmillan).

Lennon, Kathleen (1995), 'Gender and Knowledge' in *Journal of Gender Studies*, Vol.4, No.2, July, pp.133-143.

Lennon, Kathleen and Margaret Whitford (1994), *Knowing the Difference: Feminist Perspective in Epistemology* (London, Routledge).

Lewis, Jane (1984), *Women in England 1970-1950: sexual divisions and social change* (Brighton, Whetsheaf).

Lloyd, Anne and Liz Newell (1985), 'Women and computers' in Faulkner and Arnold (eds.) *Smothered by Invention* (London and Sydney, Pluto Press), pp. 238-251.

Long, J and J. Dowell (1989), 'Concepts of the discipline of HCI: craft, applied science and engineering', in Sutcliffe and Macaulay (eds.) *People and Computer V – HCI '89* (Cambridge, Cambridge University Press), pp.9-32.

Lukes, Steven (1974), *Power: A Radical View* (Basingstoke, Macmillan).

MacKenzie, Donald and Judy Wajcman (eds.) (1985), *The Social Shaping of Technology* (Milton Keynes, Open University Press).

MacKinnon, Catherine (1979), *Sexual Harassment of Working Women* (New Haven and London, Yale University Press).

Mackintosh, Maureen (1977), 'Reproduction and Patriarchy: A Critique of Meillassoux, "Femmes, Greniers et Capitaux"' in *Capital and Class*, Vol.2, pp.119-127.

Mackintosh, Maureen (1981), 'The Sexual Division of Labour and the Subordination of Women' in Young, Wolkowitz and McCullagh (eds.) *Of Marriage and the Market: Women's Subordination in International Perspective* (London, CSE Books), pp.1-15.

Mandel, Ernest (1972), *Late Capitalism* (London, New Left Books).

Martin, Jean and Ceridwen Roberts (1984), *Women and Employment: A Lifetime Perspective*, OPCS, Dept. of Employment (London, HMSO).

Martin, Roderick and Judith Wallace (1984), *Working Women in Recession* (Oxford, Oxford University Press).

Mason, Jennifer (1996), *Qualitative Researching* (Newbury Park, Sage Publications).

Maynard, Mary (1990), 'The re-shaping of sociology? trends in the study of gender', *Sociology*, Vol.24, No.2, pp.269-290.

Maynard, Mary (1994), 'Methods, Practice and Epistemology: the Debate about Feminism and Research' in Maynard and Purvis (eds.), *Researching Women's Lives from a Feminist Perspective* (London, Taylor and Francis), pp.10-27.

McDonough, Roisin and Rachel Harrison (1978), 'Patriarchy and Relations of Production' in Kuhn and Wolpe (eds.) *Feminism and Materialism* (London, Boston, Henley, RKP).

McNay, Lois (1992), *Foucault and Feminism* (Cambridge, Polity Press).

McNeil, Maureen (ed.) (1987), *Gender and Expertise* (London, Free Assoc. Books).

Mead, Margaret (1935), *Sex and Temperament in Three Primitive Societies* (Gloucester, Peter Smith).

Meillassoux, Claude (1975), *Maidens, Meal and Money: Capitalism and the Domestic Community* (Paris, Malpeso).

Metcalf, Andy and Martin Humphries (1985), *The Sexuality of Men* (London, Pluto Press).

Middleton Chris (1983), 'Patriarchal Exploitation and the Rise of English Capitalism' in Gamarnikow, Morgan, Purvis and Taylorson (eds.) *Gender, Class and Work* (London, Heinemann), pp.11-27.

Millett, Kate (1970), *Sexual Politics* (London, Rupert Hart-Davis).

Mills, Albert J. and Peta Tancred (1992), *Gendering Organizational Analysis* (Newbury Park, Sage Publications).

Mills, Sara (1992), 'Negotiating Discourses of Femininity' in *Journal of Gender Studies*, Vol.1, No.2, pp.271-285.

Mitchell, Juliet (1971), *Women's Estate* (Harmondsworth, Penguin Books).

Mitchell, Juliet (1974), *Psychoanalysis and Women* (Harmondsworth, Penguin Books).

Morgan, David (1992), *Discovering Men; Sociology and Masculinites* (London, Routledge).

Morgan, Gareth (1986), *Images of Organizations* (Beverley Hills, Sage).

Morris, Judith (1989), *Women in Computing* (Surrey, Computer Weekly).

Morris, Meaghan and Paul Patton (eds.) (1979), *Michel Foucault: power, truth, strategy* (Sydney, Feral Publications).

Morse, Janice M. (ed.) (1994), *Critical Issues in Qualitative Research Methods* (Newbury Park, Sage Publications).

Mundorf, N., S. Meyer, E. Schulze and P. Zoche (1995), 'Families, Information Technologies, and the Quality of Life: German research approaches' in *Research Institute for Telecommunications and Information Marketing*, Internet, August 1995.

Murray, Fergus (1993), 'A Separate Reality: Science, Technology and Masculinity' in Green, Owen and Pain (eds.) *Gendered by Design?* (London, Taylor and Francis), pp.64-81.

Myrdal, Alva and Viola Klein (1968), *Women's Two Roles: Home and Work* (London, Routledge).

Nichols, Theo and Huw Beynon (1977), *Living With Capitalism: class relations and the modern factory* (London, Routledge and Kegan Paul).

Nicholson, Linda J. (1990), *Feminism/Postmodernism* (New York and London, Routledge).

Oakley, Ann (1972), *Sex Gender and Society* (London, Temple Smith).

Oakley, Ann (1974), *The Sociology of Housework* (London, Martin Robertson).

Oakley, Ann (1981), 'Interviewing women: a contradiction in terms', in Roberts, H. (ed.), *Doing Feminist Research* (London, Routledge and Kegan Paul), pp.30-61.

Oakley, Ann (1985), *Housewife* (Harmondsworth, Penguin).

O'Brien, Mary (1981), *The Politics of Reproduction* (London, Henley, Boston, RKP).

Oppenheimer, Valerie K. (1970), *The Female Labor Force in the United States: Demographic and Economic Factors Governing its Growth and Changing Composition* (Cal., University of California Press).

Ortner, Sherry B. (1974), 'Is Female to Male as Nature is to Culure' in Rosaldo and Lamphere (eds.), *Woman Culture and Society* (Stanford, Stanford University Press), pp.67-87.

Papers on Patriarchy (1976), *Patriarchy Conference London 1976* (London, Women's Publishing Collective).

Perry, Ruth and Lisa Greber (1990), 'Women and Computers: an introduction' in *Signs,* Vol.16, No.1, pp.74-101.

Peters, Thomas J. and Robert H. Waterman jr. (1981), *In Search of Excellence* (New York, Harper and Row).

Phillips, Anne (1981), 'Marxism and Feminism' in Feminist Anthology Collective *No Turning Back* (London, Womens Press), pp.90-98.

Phillips, Anne and Barbara Taylor (1980), 'Sex and Skill' in *Feminist Review*, No.6, pp.79-83.

Pollert, Anna (1981), *Girls, Wives, Factory Lives* (London, Macmillan).

Pons, Valdo (1988*), Introduction to Social Research: a text prepared for students* (University of Hull).

Poovey, Mary (1989), *Uneven Developments: the ideological work of gender in mid-Victorian England* (London, Virago Press).

Potter, Jonathan and Margaret Wetherell (1987), *Discourse and Social Psychology: Beyond Attitudes and Behaviour* (Newbury Park, Sage Publications).

Pringle, Rosemary (1988), *Secretaries Talk: sexuality, power and work* (London, Verso).

Purcell, Kate (1989), 'Gender and the Experience of Employment' in Duncan Gallie (ed.) *Employment in Britain*, (Oxford, Basil Blackwell), pp.157-186.

Purvis, Tony and Alan Hunt (1993), 'Discourse, ideology, discourse, ideology, discourse, ideology' in *British Journal of Sociology*, Vol.44, No.3, pp.473-499.

Ramazanoglu, Caroline (1989a), *Feminism and the Contradictions of Oppression* (London, Routledge).

Ramazanoglu, Caroline (1989b), 'Improving on Sociology' in *Sociology*, Vol.23, No.3, August, pp.427-442.

Reinharz, Shulamit (1992), *Feminist Methods in Social Research* (Oxford, Oxford University Press).

Reiter, Rayna R. (1975), *Toward an Anthropology of Women* (New York and London, Monthly Review Press).

Reiter, Rayna R. (1977), 'The Search for Origins' in *Critique of Anthropology*, *Women's Issue*, No.9/10, Vol.3, pp.5-24.

Reskin, Barbara F. and Heidi I. Hartmann (eds.) (1985), *Women's Work, Men's Work: Sex Segregation on the Job* (Washington, D.C., National Academy Press).

Rich, Adrienne (1984), 'Compulsory heterosexuality and lesbian existence' in Snitow, Stansell and Thompson (eds.) *Desire: the politics of sexuality* (London, Virago), pp.212-242.

Roberts, Helen (ed.) (1981), *Doing Feminist Research* (London, Routledge and Kegan Paul).

Rosaldo, Michelle Zimbalist (1974), 'Woman Culture and Society: A Theoretical Overview' in Rosaldo and Lamphere (eds.), *Woman Culture and Society* (Stanford University Press), pp. 18-42.

Rose, Hilary (1986), 'Beyond Masculinist Realities: A Feminist Epistemology for the Sciences' in Bleier (ed.) *Feminist Approaches to Science* (New York, Pergamon Press), pp.57-76.

Rothschild Joan (ed.) (1983), *Machina Ex Dea: Feminist Perspectives on Technology* (New York, Pergamon Press).

Rowbotham, Sheila (1973), *Hidden from History* (London, Pluto Press).

Rowbotham, Sheila (1982), 'The Trouble with Patriarchy' reprinted in Evans (ed.) *The Woman Question: Readings on the Subordination of Women* (London, Fontana), pp.73-79.

Rubery, Jill (1978), 'Structured labour markets, worker organisation and low pay' *Cambridge Journal of Economics*, Vol.2, pp.17-36.

Rubery, Jill, Colette Fagan and Jane Humphries (1992), *Occupational Segregation in the UK* (UMIST, Manchester School of Management).

Rubery, Jill and Colette Fagan (1993), *Occupational Segregation of women and men in the European Community*, Supplement 3/93. Report for the Commission of the European Communities.

Rubery, Jill and Frank Wilkinson (eds.) (1994), *Employer Strategy and the Labour Market* (Oxford, Oxford University Press).

Rubin, Gayle (1975), 'The Traffic in Women: Notes on the Political Economy of Sex' in Reiter (ed.), *Toward an Anthropology of Women* (New York and London, Monthly Review Press), pp.157-210.

Rutherford, Jonathan (ed.) (1990), *Identity: Community, Culture, Difference* (London, Lawrence and Wishart).

Rutherford, Jonathan (1992), *Men's Silences: predicaments in masculinity* (London and New York, Routledge).

Saffioti, Heleieth, I.B. (1978), *Women in Class Society* (New York and London, Monthly Review Press).

Sanday, Peggy Reeves (1981), *Female Power and Male Dominance: On the Origins of Sexual Inequality* (Cambridge, Cambridge University Press).

Sargent, Lydia (ed.) (1981), *Women and Revolution* (London, Pluto Press).

Savage, Mike and Anne Witz, (eds.) (1992), *Gender and Bureaucracy* (Oxford, Blackwell).

Sawicki, Jana (1991), *Disciplining Foucault* (New York and London).

Scutt, Jocelynne (ed.) (1990), *The Baby Machine: Reproductive Technology and the Commercialisation of Motherhood* (London, Green Print).

Seccombe, Wally (1974), 'The Housewife and her Labour Under Capitalism' in *New Left Review*, No.83, pp.3-24.

Sedley, Ann and Melissa Benn (1982), *Sexual Harassment at Work* (London, National Council for Civil Liberties).

Segal, Lynn (1990), *Slow Motion: changing masculinities, changing men* (London, Virago).

Seidler, Victor J. (1989), *Rediscovering Masculinity: reason, language and sexuality* (London and New York, Routledge).

Shapiro, Gillian (1994), 'Informal Processes and Women's Careers in Information Technology' in Adam, Green, Emms and Owen (eds.) (1994), *Women, Work and Computerization: breaking old boundaries – building new forms* (Amsterdam, Elsevier), pp.423-438.

Siltanen, Janet (1994), *Locating Gender: occupational segregation, wages and domestic responsibilities* (London, UCL Press).

Siltanen, Janet, Jennifer Jarman and Robert M. Blackburn (1995), *Gender Inequality in the Labour Market: occupational concentration and segregation* (Geneva: International Labour Office).

Smith, Dorothy E (1988), *The Everyday World as Problematic: A Feminist Sociology* (Milton Keynes, Open University Press).

Smith, Dorothy E. (1990), *Texts, Facts, and Femininity: exploring the relations of ruling* (New York and London, Routledge).

Smith, Paul (1978), 'Domestic Labour and Marx's Theory of Value' in Kuhn and Wolpe (eds.) *Feminism and Materialism* (London, Boston, Henley, RKP) pp.198-219.

Snow, Jon (1995), 'All the news that fits on screen' in *The Guardian*, Tuesday, September 19th, 1995, p.15.

Social Trends (1995), Vol.25, London, HMSO.

Soper, Kate (1991), 'Postmodernism, subjectivity and the question of value, in *New Left Review*, Vol.186, pp.120-128.

Stacey, Margaret (1981), 'The division of labour revisited or overcoming the two Adams' in Abrams, Deem, Finch and Rock (eds.), *Practice and Progress: British Sociology 1950-1980* (London, George Allen and Unwin), pp.172-190.

Stanley, Autumn (1983), 'Women Hold Up Two-Thirds of the Sky: Notes for a Revised History of Technology' in Rothschild (ed.) *Machina Ex Dea: Feminist Perspectives on Technology* (New York, Pergamon Press), pp.5-22.

Stanley, Liz and Sue Wise (1983), *Breaking Out: Feminist Consciousness and Feminist Research* (London, Routledge and Kegan Paul).

Stanley, Liz and Sue Wise (1993), *Breaking Out Again: Feminist Ontology and Epistemology* (London, Routledge).

Stanworth, Michelle (ed.) (1987), *Reproductive Technologies* (Oxford, Polity Press).

Strober, M. H. and C.L. Arnold, (1987), 'Integrated Circuits/Segregated Labour: Women in Computer-Related Occupations and High-Tech Industries' in National Research Council (ed.) *Computer Chips and Paper Clips: Technology and Women's Employment* (Washington, National Academy Press).

Thompson, E.P. (1978), *The Poverty of Theory and other essays* (London, Merlin Press.)

Thompson, Paul (1978), *The Voice of the Past: Oral history* (London, Oxford Press).

Thompson, Paul and Eddie Bannon (1985), *Working the System: the shop floor and new technology* (London and Sydney, Pluto Books).

Tillon, Germaine (1983), *The Republic of Cousins: Women's Oppression in Mediterranean Countries* (London, Al Saqi Books, Zed Press).

Tolson, Andrew (1977), *The Limits of Masculinity* (London, Tavistock).

Tong, Rosemary (1989), *Feminist Thought: a comprehensive introduction* (London, Unwin Hyman).

Trescott, Martha Moore (1983), 'Lillian Moller Gilbreth and the Founding of Modern Industrial Engineering' in Rothschild (ed.) *Machina Ex Dea: Feminist Perspectives on Technology* (New York, Pergamon Press), pp.23-37.

Tuana, Nancy (ed.) (1989), *Feminism and Science* (Bloomington, University of Indiana Press).

Turkle, Sherry (1984), 'Women and Computer Programming' in *Technology Review*, Nov/Dec, pp.49-50.

Turkle, Sherry and Seymour Papert (1990), 'Epistemological Pluralism: styles and voices within the computer culture' in *Signs*, Vol.16, No.1, pp.128-157.

Vogel, Lisa (1981), 'Marxism and Feminism: unhappy marriage, trial separation or something else?' in Sargent (ed.), *Women and Revolution* (London, Pluto Press), pp.195-217.

Vogel, Lisa (1984), *Marxism and the Oppression of Women* (London, Pluto Press).

Wajcman, Judy (1983), *Women in Control* (Milton Keynes, Open University Press).

Wajcman, Judy (1991), *Feminism Confronts Technology* (Oxford, Polity Press).

Walby, Sylvia (1986), *Patriarchy at Work* (Cambridge, Polity Press).

Walby, Sylvia (ed.) (1988a), *Gender Segregation at Work* (Milton Keynes, Open University Press).

Walby, Sylvia (1988b), 'Segregation in employment in social and economic theory' in Sylvia Walby (ed.), *Gender Segregation at Work* (Milton Keynes, Open University Press), pp.14-28.

Walby, Sylvia (1989), 'Theorising patriarchy' in *Sociology*, Vol.23, No.2, pp.213-244.

Walczak, Yvette (1988), *He and She: men in the eighties* (London and New York, Routledge).

Weber, Max (1930), *The Protestant Ethic and the Spirit of Capitalism* (London, Unwin University Books) (tenth impression 1970).

Webster, Juliet (1994), 'Gender and Technology at Work: 15 years on' in Adam, Green, Emms and Owen (eds.) (1994), *Women, Work and Computerization: breaking old boundaries – building new forms* (Amsterdam, Elsevier), pp.311-324.

Weedon, Chris (1987), *Feminist Practice and Poststructuralist Theory* (Oxford, Basil Blackwell).

Weeks, Jeffrey (1981), *Sex, Politics and Society: the regulation of sexuality since 1800* (London and New York, Longman).

Weeks, Jeffrey (1985), *Sexuality and its Discontents: meanings, myths and modern sexualities* (London and New York, Routledge).

West, Candice and Don Zimmerman (1987), 'Doing Gender' in Lorber and Farrell (eds.) *The Social Construction of Gender* (Newbury Park, Sage Publications), pp.13-38.

West, Jackie (ed.) (1982), *Work, Women and the Labour Market* (London, Routledge and Kegan Paul).

Westwood Sallie (1984), *All Day Every Day* (London, Pluto).

Wetherell, Margaret and Jonathan Potter (1992), *Mapping the Language of Racism: Discourse and the Legitimation of Exploitation* (Hemel Hempstead, Harvester Wheatsheaf).

Whisker, Brenda, Jacky Bishop, Lillian Mowin and Trish Longdon (1983), *Breaching the Peace: a Collection of Radical Feminist Papers* (London, Onlywoman Press).

Whitelegg, Elizabeth, Madeleine Arnot, Else Bartels, Veronica Beechey, Lynda Birke, Susan Himmelweit, Diana Leonard, Sonja Ruehl and Mary Anne Speakman (eds.) (1982), *The Changing Experience of Women* (Oxford, Martin Robertson in association with The Open University).

Whyte, William Foote (1955), *Street corner society: the social structure of an Italian slum* (Chicago, University of Chicago Press).

Williams, Raymond (1979), *Marxism and Literature* (Oxford, Oxford University Press).

Willis, Paul (1977), *Learning to Labour: how working class kids get working class jobs* (Farnborough, Saxon House).

Wilkinson, Sue and Celia Kitzinger (eds.) (1996), *Representing the Other: A Feminism and Psychology Reader* (Newbury Park, Sage Publications).

Wise, Sue and Liz Stanley (1987), *Georgie Porgie: Sexual Harassment in Everyday Life* (London, Pandora Press).

Witz, Anne (1992), *Professions and Patriarchy* (New York and London, Routledge).

Wolpe, Harold (1979), 'Introduction to the articulation of mode of production' in *Economy and Society*, Vol. 4, pp.445-448.

Women's Studies Group CCCS (1978), *Women Take Issue* (London, Hutchinson).

Wright, Rosemary and Jerry A. Jacobs (1995), 'Male Flight From Computer Work: A new Look at Occupational Resegregation and Ghettoization' in Jacobs (ed.) *Gender Inequality at Work* (Newbury Park, Sage Publications), pp.334-379.

Yeandle, Susan (1984), *Women's Working Lives: patterns and strategies* (London, Tavistock).

Young, Iris (1981), 'Beyond the Unhappy Marriage: A Critique of Dual Systems Theory' in Sargent (ed.), *Women and Revolution* (London, Pluto Press), pp.43-69.

Zimmerman, Jan (1986), *Once Upon the Future: A Woman's Guide To Tomorrow's Technology* (New York and London, Pandora Press).

Index

working class women *see* factory
    work studies
working conditions, factories
    30-1, 32, 36, 43

Young, I. 16, 17